In Spirit and in Truth

In Spirit and in Truth

The Music of

African American Worship

Melva Wilson Costen

Westminster John Knox Press

LOUISVILLE • LONDON

Scripture quotations from the New Revised Standard Version of the Bible are copyright © 1989 by the Division of Christian Education of the National Council of the Churches of Christ in the U.S.A. and are used by permission.

Scripture quotations marked NIV are from *The Holy Bible, New International Version.* Copyright © 1973, 1978, 1984 International Bible Society. Used by permission of Zondervan Bible Publishers.

The chart in appendix B is adapted from *African American Christian Worship* by Melva Costen. © 1993 by Abingdon Press. This book can be purchased at cokesbury.com.

Book design by Sharon Adams
Cover design by Jennifer K. Cox
Cover illustration: Dale Kennington/SuperStock

First edition
Published by Westminster John Knox Press
Louisville, Kentucky

This book is printed on acid-free paper that meets the American National Standards Institute Z39.48 standard. ♾

PRINTED IN THE UNITED STATES OF AMERICA

04 05 06 07 08 09 10 11 12 13 — 10 9 8 7 6 5 4 3 2 1

Library of Congress Cataloging-in-Publication Data

Costen, Melva Wilson, 1933–
    In spirit and in truth : the music of African American worship / Melva Wilson Costen.
        p. cm.
    Includes bibliographical references.
    ISBN 0-664-22864-X (alk. paper)
    1. Church music—United States. 2. African Americans—Music—History and criticism.
I. Title.

ML2911.C67 2004
781.71'0089'96073—dc22   2004050888

This book is dedicated
to the memory of my husband

JAMES HUTTEN COSTEN
October 5, 1931–April 11, 2003

*T*his dedication is a tribute to fifty-three years of loving and growing together with James Hutten Costen. Basic to Jim's life was his love and commitment to Jesus the Christ, whose life and ministry served as a model for his own life. His desire to become an ordained servant of God began with his sense of call to the priesthood of the Roman Catholic Church, into which he was baptized at the age of seven. Born in Omaha, Nebraska, to Baptist parents, Jim spent most of his time at the Catholic Church, first as a student in the Catholic elementary and junior high school, and later as a regular participant in the worship life of the church. His dying father, who was impressed with the discipline that his sons were receiving in the Catholic parochial elementary school, encouraged his baptism into the Roman Catholic Church.

At the age of sixteen, Jim was inspired by the work and ministry of a Presbyterian minister, the Reverend Charles Tyler, whose congregation was temporarily relocated to a building across the street from Jim's house. Jim subsequently joined the church, affirming his call to ministry, but then as a Presbyterian minister. With the aid of Rev. Tyler, the former Omaha Presbytery agreed to help finance Jim's education so that he could attend Johnson C. Smith University and Johnson C. Smith Theological Seminary in Charlotte, North Carolina. His enrollment at Johnson C. Smith (a year before my arrival) included a brief sojourn as a member of the football team, during which time he was given the name "Omaha" by a classmate who, like others on the campus, had no idea that there were black folks in Nebraska! The name was so embedded in his persona that I was shocked to be asked by the minister who presided at our wedding, Dr. Arthur H. George, "Do you take James H. Costen to be your wedded husband?" My response was, "Do you mean 'Omaha'?" which evoked a moment of laughter during the ceremony.

We talked a lot during our early years of marriage about the size of our family. "After I finish seminary," Jim said, "our contribution to the population should be at least six children, preferably six boys!" He was concerned about the longevity of the Costen name. However, he was willing to be content with a "human trinity," two boys and a girl, who helped stretch his contribution beyond the recommended six, into seven grandchildren and, at present, two great-grandchildren.

It was Jim's encouragement and support that allowed me to pursue with diligence a master's degree in music in order to enhance the use of my education degree from Johnson C. Smith University. This encouragement was couched in a challenge from Jim that I should pursue this degree at a place where I might be denied entrance and respect for my musical gifts. Therefore, I enrolled as one of a few blacks in the master's degree program in music at the University of North Carolina in Chapel Hill.

This challenge was predicated on Jim's concern for the prevailing systemic racism and segregated education systems, which hindered quality education for African Americans. He was denied admittance to one graduate program of theological education at one institution, but persevered until he was accepted at another. He was able to rally numerous communities to participate in peaceful support of efforts that broke down barriers, including voter registration. Our children, like their mom, walked with their heads held high as Jim led us into courtrooms and ultimately into integrated schools, hotels, restaurants, neighborhoods, and churches. Jim ran for mayor of the city of Rocky Mount, North Carolina, and his narrow loss only energized his enthusiasm to search for sources of communal pain and then work vigorously to provide solutions. These efforts brought us into close contact with Martin Luther King, Jr., and finally to Atlanta, Georgia, where Jim was called by the United Presbyterian Church to establish an interracial congregation in a neighborhood that was just experiencing white flight. This was an attempt by our denomination to model integration and inclusivity.

Years later, in 1969, Jim accepted a call to serve as dean of Johnson C. Smith Theological Seminary when the institution was moved by the denomination from Charlotte, North Carolina, to its current location at Interdenominational Theological Center (ITC) in Atlanta, Georgia.

When I accepted an appointment in the music and worship department at ITC, I complained of the inadequate documentation of African American liturgical and musical histories. Jim suggested that I fill these gaps. This led to my research on various aspects of the African origins of African American liturgy and music. Together we experienced the sources, sounds, and smells of baptismal waters plummeting down steep falls into huge bodies of water described most adequately by Africans as a gift from God. The melodies, harmonies, rhythms, bodily movements, and additional expressions of praise that we were allowed to explore together are truly gifts from God! With cameras and tape recorders, we covered thousands of miles of terrain, immersed in human histories that soon reconnected in the bloodstream of Africans in America.

During a three-month sabbatical initiated by Jim while he was president of Interdenominational Theological Center (ITC), we visited ten countries on the continent of Africa, where ITC graduates from a variety of denominations were then located. The excitement of seeing "his students" combine their natural leadership abilities with their theological education brought Jim to a new level of awareness of the ways God uses persons and institutions to carry forth God's will. The ecumenical ethos of ITC solidified our understanding of the importance of denominational cooperation and unity.

Jim listened with keen interest to chapters of this book as they unfolded, and expressed approval with applause, smiles, and a barrage of supporting words. He grunted and mumbled in an uncanny way when he was not pleased. The look he gave me when he asked, "How is the book coming?" suggested a sense of urgency on his part to see the finished product soon. I recalled this same look on numerous occasions as I pursued a Ph.D. degree. His encouragement and support during my time in the program was overwhelming! Jim's sense of my need for affirmation and prayer on the morning of a four-day series of comprehensive exams helped to calm me. He took considerable time out of his schedule for conversation and prayer with me. He was with me when I defended my dissertation. As we awaited the verdict from the committee, he expressed his fear and concern that I had said more than was necessary. Fear turned into joy as we received news of a job well done!

During his last days on earth, while lying on his bed in the hospital, Jim sang from his vast repertoire of sacred songs, hymns, and spirituals that expressed the essence of his faith. Singing in the family occurs regularly, most often around the piano and when we are traveling, so we were a bit surprised when Jim burst into song while in the intensive care unit, and shortly after awakening from a deep sleep. We know now that the songs that he chose deliberately softened for us the shock of his passing. It is my belief as well that this was his way of communicating with me through a medium that he knew I would understand. From "Wade in the Water," a reminder of his approaching full baptism into the death and resurrection of Jesus the Christ, to the words of his final song, the Prayer of St. Francis of Assisi, "Lord Make Me an Instrument of Thy Peace," Jim affirmed his hope for life eternal.

Contents

Preface

> *God is spirit, and those who worship God must worship in spirit and*
> *truth.*
>   John 4:24 in *An Inclusive Language Lectionary: Readings for Year A*

*T*hese familiar words set the theological context, the motive, and the highest
aspiration of the body of Christ gathered to worship and scattered as disciples
to serve. "God is spirit, and those who worship God must worship in
spirit. . . ." As spirit, God is not localized, restricted, or confined to places or
things. As spirit, God is free, beyond human control, and thus attempts at
manipulation are to be avoided. As spirit, God remains open to receive the
spiritual gifts we humans can offer: love, obedience, faithfulness, and truth.

And yet there is more: Those who worship God must worship in *truth*. True
worship occurs when the gift of music is returned to the divine Originator as
an extension and expression of love, praise, obedience, faithfulness, and truth.

This book explores the development of music that emanates from African
American people, who freely yielded to the spirit in order to be channels for
the creation of a variety of musical forms and styles. As a religious people,
African Americans would also use music as a special means of worshiping God.

The various forms and styles of music created and utilized by African Americans continue to provide the shape and substance of the total life of a musically gifted, inventive, and improvisatory people. The plethora of scholarly
research on the origin and evolution of African American music attests to the
depth and richness of the African religious and musical heritage and the importance of the folk-oral tradition as a basic and necessary means of communication. The continuity of the African heritage is facilitated and enhanced by the
African primal belief system grounded in an understanding that the Supreme
Being sets all things in motion. One's identity is never conceptualized nor
enacted in isolation from the heartbeat of the total community, the rhythm of

nature, and the divine harmony established at creation. These concepts remain active in the bloodstream of Africans in the Diaspora wherever communal life takes root. Through ritual practices—singing, dancing, storytelling, drama, and other aesthetic expressions—African people demonstrate similarities in cultural behavior. There are some who refer to this phenomenon as "cultural memory," a subjective term that denotes thoughts and practices that are understood and communicated unconsciously or indirectly. This connective capacity of Africans in the North American Diaspora as "soul" or "soul force" is a gift from God that has allowed African people to survive the horrors of enslavement.

Music is clearly a theological thread in the fabric of African American existence that connects sacred and secular aspects of life and assists in personal and communal quests to find meaning amid ongoing racial injustices. In a strange and alien land, African people continued to weave a tapestry upon which numerous African American works of art would emerge. The first and foremost artistic design, the spiritual, became the foundation for other African American musical forms and styles. Like other African-related tapestries, the religious and artistic threads of musical expression cannot be separated into "sacred" and "secular" compartments but are integral to the whole tapestry. A closer look at this tapestry reveals the first authentic "nationalistic music" part of the New World later named the United States of America. How often can we find this displayed in annals of American history? Among the most heated disputes in the nineteenth century occurred in 1893 when Antonin Dvorak, Czech composer and musical director of the National Conservatory of Music in New York City, suggested, in response to the possibility of founding a national school of composition, "I am now satisfied that the future of music of this country must be founded upon what are called Negro melodies. This must be the real foundation of any serious and original school of composition to be developed in the United States."[1]

Although a discussion of this matter is not continued in this book, it is referenced here as a reminder of the gift of African American music to the American tapestry in particular, and ultimately to the world. It is also a reminder of the significant influence that music and other African American artistic forms and styles have made and continue to make as expressions of God's grace and ongoing creation. A detailed discussion of musical expressions in worship perceived through the eyes of faith and through liturgical lenses of African American people at worship is the basic focus of this book.

Previously published histories of African American music often affirm the interrelationship of music for worship and so-called secular music, and some of this history will be reiterated throughout this book. However, too often the sociopolitical history overshadows or neglects an explanation of theological and philosophical foundations of music in the context of worship. This is not to deny the tremendously important role that music played in facilitating social change in America through the twentieth century, for this is an example of God's divine spirit at work through the people! This book will examine the role of music in the hands, mouths, bodies, and souls of African Americans as they ascribe all praise, honor, power, and glory to God in Jesus the Christ! The general question raised throughout is, What's going on when certain musical expressions take place in worship? For example, What is really going on when the organist/keyboardist accompanies the preacher near the end of her/his sermon? In some coastal sections of Georgia and South Carolina there is a tendency for the leaders to form a circle before or after altar prayer. Does this have anything to do with the "ring shout"? How has this ritual continued over the centuries? There is no way that this can be done without recalling aspects of social history that are totally intertwined with African and African American spirituality.

The initial history of communities of Africans in the North American Diaspora is centered around slave communities, which will be the pivotal points for this discussion. As this history evolves, attention will be given to blacks who were legally free from enslavement but not free from societal bondage. We know, for example, that the first African immigrants were considered indentured servants and not slaves. Some came directly from England, where Africans had lived since the middle of the sixteenth century. Others of African blood came from Spain, Portugal, and the West Indies, where they might have received a Christian baptism in their homelands or at sea. Some completed their terms of indenture and accumulated property, purchased slaves, established communities, and were able to get their names into official records.

One such person was Anthony Johnson, who arrived from England in 1621, finished his term as an indentured servant, and lived as a free black American. One can only speculate what happened to William, the infant son of African parents, Isabella and Antonio, born in America, and baptized by the Church of England (ca. 1624–1625). William, like his parents, is listed without a surname. What happened to runaway slaves whose history might not have been recorded? Were they able to find solace or freedom to worship with African Americans who had otherwise been granted freedom? These and many other historical gaps increase the desire to know and incorporate the worship and music experiences of nameless and faceless African Americans whose stories may not have been told.

It is quite clear that common historical origins and practices did not produce identical patterns of worship among African Americans. Diversity is understood also in relation to membership in the body of Christ: "For just as the body is one and has many members, and all the members of the body, though many, are one body, so it is with Christ. For in the one Spirit we were all baptized into one body. . . and we were all made to drink of one Spirit" (1 Cor. 12:12–13). Different situations and differences in human needs dictate an inevitable diversity. In addition to these factors, each denomination has determined its own theology and polity, which are foundational to worship practices. There are also many common features that often distinguish and define a unique African American worship ethos according to geographical locations rather than by denominational differences. My own generation grew accustomed to common worship and music practices across denominational lines. I grew up in a small rural South Carolina community, with an ecumenical representation of Baptist, Presbyterian, Pentecostal, and African Methodist Episcopal churches. As in many southern communities, there were frequent opportunities to hold joint services and exchange pastors and choirs, especially during baptisms, funerals, and summer revivals. Since there were farming families in each of the churches, schedules in school and church centered around farm schedules. Local pastors and members carefully respected the individual schedules of churches by avoiding conflicts and by participating as if each special event for one church was an extended family occasion for the community. We did not call these shared worship times "ecumenical," because they were basic to life and intricately related to the survival and ongoing security of the community. Furthermore, the word *ecumenical* was not a part of the shared vocabulary of the community.

Too often a focus on the distinction and uniqueness of worship in historically black denominations neglects or negates similarities between historically black churches and many black congregations that are part of Euro-American denominations. The freedom of separate worship spaces is a "license" to worship and sing freely. Furthermore, there is a trend among black Baptist congregations to connect with traditionally Euro-American Baptists,[2] and a growing movement toward interracial nondenominational worship.

The African American ethos incorporates feelings of kinship, togetherness, and belonging with spiritual dynamics in musical elements and in the flow of worship, reflecting the uniqueness of African American worldviews and cultural practices. These features provide the reason for African Americans to "sing in the Spirit"!

One other concern prompts the need for this book. African American congregations are falling into a trap in which worship has become a mode of entertainment rather than a means of spiritual empowerment. This could be happening because of a lack of knowledge of the history and evolution of the African American religious and musical heritage. This could also be a cultural trap deliberately contrived by individuals who have tried to demean the African American experience by halting the forward thrust of a rich heritage that has now reached global proportions. On the other hand, persons who simply want to identify with the soul of a marginalized people without calling it African American could have "innocently" maneuvered the trap. Admittedly, during the latter quarter of the twentieth century, African American and Euro-American worship and resulting music forms and styles have undergone similar trends. Church musicians, clergy, liturgical leaders, and scholars are inundated with reminders of musical problems in the context of worship. Local and national music and worship conferences and workshops are held frequently in an effort to mobilize leaders to help solve problems related to music for worship in local congregations. Books flood the market with biblical and cultural reminders of the naturalness, inevitability, and importance of change accompanied by human adjustment to that which appears to be new.

Some of the terms used to express the existing tensions between the various styles of Euro-American worship—such as "worship wars,"[3] "cultural wars,"[4] "dumbing down,"[5] and "blended worship"[6]—are not relative to the soulful evolution of African American worship. Rather than fight worship wars, African Americans have used the gift of silence and retreated to clandestine places in order to establish separate worship spaces and sanctuaries. Rather than "dumb down," our action has included reaching outward with hospitality to ensure a place in worship for others who had (also) experienced rejection. The "blending" of worship elements and improvising what we borrow is an African practice that has helped create and maintain the African American ethos that extends beyond the sanctuary.

Congregations are likely to become trapped and misled by directions presented through the media and transmitted by those congregations that can afford to constantly update their liturgical technology (microphones, lighting, overhead displays) if their clerical and musical leadership has a limited understanding of African American religious and music heritage. There is sufficient evidence to support the fact that some congregations have fallen into liturgical traps and are unaware of the bait that lured them there. Without sufficient knowledge of the African and African American liturgical history, worshipers often miss opportunities to reclaim and affirm traditional African American spirituality.

> For every thing they took away, we came up with something new
> We sang some new songs, and danced us some new dances
> See, you can put a hurting on the body, but you can't touch the soul.[7]

The repetition of the word "new" in this observation by a former slave provides one of many examples of hope in the midst of suffering. In spite of human efforts to destroy the humanity or soul of Africans in the North American Diaspora, something *new* was created through divine intervention. Admittedly, the new songs and new dances for worship were not created *ex nihilo*. There is hope that the divinely created newness assures humankind that Almighty God is in complete control over all of creation and that God's power will be evidenced ultimately.

This book is designed to challenge the people of God to reclaim and affirm traditional African American spirituality and its presence in African American music experienced in worship. It will explore music for worship in African American congregations through biblical, historical, theological, and liturgical lenses. Consideration is given both to historically black denominations as well as to African American congregations in denominations established and governed predominantly by Euro-Americans. The role of music as a theological thread in the fabric of African American existence will be emphasized, connecting sacred and secular aspects of life with the celebration of God, so that worship of the Lord Almighty can occur in spirit and in truth.

Chapter 1

African Foundations
of African American Liturgical Music

African American sacred music traditions are rooted in the primal world-views of African traditional religions. The plural reference to *religions* is a reminder that the continent of Africa is not only huge but also represents more than a thousand different cultural societies, each with its own religious systems. Religion is the strongest element in ancient cultural traditions and probably exerted the greatest influence upon the thinking and living of African peoples.[1] Traditional religions pervade all aspects of life, thereby eliminating a formal distinction between the sacred and the secular. Since this holistic religious worldview and other aspects of African belief systems are shared among the various societies, there is also a fundamental way of knowing, symbolizing, and conceptualizing that transcends societal differences.

According to biblical accounts and ongoing research, Africa is the cradle of civilization and thus can be considered the origin of many music traditions of the world. The reason, perhaps, that Africa is overlooked in many of the narrated and published "civilization stories" is due to the color symbolism of blackness as a negative concept. Rather than perceiving that the darkness and warmth of the soil provides the necessary nutrients for life in all of its radiance, much of the literature and perception is centered on blackness and the absence of light and therefore reflective of a state of ignorance and despair. Howard Thurman gave serious consideration to this matter in his observation, "The identification of blackness with evil, with the ominous, the destructive, the terrifying, is all through the language both sacred and profane. Black magic is evil; so is black crime, but a white lie is acceptable."[2]

Even on the heels of a new era of acceptance that "black is beautiful" and that the Afrocentric view is firmly rooted in most African American worship settings, many African Americans are still uncertain about the depth of meaning inherent in these phrases. Despite the efforts to "discover and recover the African roots of music in African American liturgy," there is a tendency among

1

some pastors and worship leaders to function with a "surface" Afrocentric mindset.[3] This happens most often when there is insufficient research to become rooted in the knowledge of the plethora of African cultures on the continent and in the African Diaspora. Research must continue in local settings so that changes can be incorporated at the grassroots level.[4] The concept of Afrocentricity stresses the understanding of the black experience as an extension of African history and culture. Molefi Asante is the major proponent of this term, which has roots in the writings of early twentieth-century African and African American scholars. Afrocentricity, as defined and employed by Asante, literally is "a mode of thought and action in which the centrality of African interests, values, and perspectives predominate. In regards to theory, it is the placing of African people in the center of any analysis of African phenomena."[5] The outcome of this form of critical thinking, research, and writing is helpful, mainly for the self-identity of black people and people of other cultures around the world whose identity has been shaped and critiqued by people who are currently in power and dominating the culture.

This concept is not at all new to African Americans in religious institutions where the dominance of power is nonblack. Although the term was not used, the idea existed far back into the period of slavery, when the "Invisible Institution"—clandestine worshiping communities—was forced to emerge. The emergence of black caucuses in religious organizations where blacks are in the minority (Roman Catholic and Protestant) began before the Civil War and has continued in some form, openly or in secret. Bibles that highlight black contributions to the religious heritage provide a current enhancement of black self-identity. African American hymnals were created deliberately for use by African Americans during the nineteenth century, and are obviously needed in this century, along with other liturgical documents that ensure a continuance of pride and dignity for the whole church, regardless of denominations. Separate black denominations and separate worship spaces in Euro-American traditions exist as symbols of freedom of choice and as a sign of the need to ensure a continuance of self-granted human dignity. Perhaps Afrocentric approaches will also help in a universal critique of what went wrong and what continues to undermine Christian evangelism based on Eurocentric hegemony.

African Traditional Religions: The Anchor for Music in African American Liturgy

With the impetus of intensive research led by African scholars, there are sufficient data to support a continuum of concepts and practices from African traditional religions in the global African Diaspora. Africa is the anchor that holds music as the theological thread that runs through the fabric of African American existence. A brief review of a ritual scene will help secure the anchor.

The musical anchor begins in rites and rituals of the community. In many diverse ways, the voice, the entire body, and human-designed instruments have ritual and symbolic value. As the "officiating member" of the ritual leadership team, the *musician* is responsible for certain unique functions in order to ensure that music serves the purpose of the ritual. The voice, for instance, conforms to a precise pitch and timbre, and it is used with a special technique determined not by the musician but by the particular ritual and the logical placement of the music in the ritual. Sometimes the musician is required to give greater importance to vocal production than to the words. The circumstances and other actions of the ritual also determine the choice of musical instrument. Where the *shaman* (high priestess/priest, witch doctor, medicine man, or obeah doctor) is involved, he or she informs the gathered community of the arrival of the spirit by a pronounced change in the rhythm of the drum. Similarly, certain wind instruments with slow, low-pitched tones may symbolize or incarnate one kind of spirit, and the lively, shrill, piping tones of flutes evoke reminders of another kind of spirit. In some societies (e.g., in Gabon), the light, high-pitched notes of the harp indicate that a spirit is beginning to take possession of the harp. In other societies, the musical sound indicating the beginning of the possession process is often a shared secret among the shamans.

In traditional African cultures, music and dance play an active role in religious and healing rites, and in rites of passage in the "rhythm of life" of individual members of the community. Both the voice and instruments depict whatever is needed during rituals, and these sounds vary within local societies. There is an awareness of the spiritual and magical power of music; thus, music is used according to certain perceived needs. Physical responses and activities following certain kinds of music are also interpreted in light of the perceived power and energy that emanates.

The healing musician makes use of a large range of vocal sounds and technical human sound productions. The important role of the healing power of the rhythms of the drum continues into the twenty-first century.[6] Much of what happens in the healing process is a secret kept by drummers who are divinely "called" to the task and have spent years of apprenticeship to perfect the healing art. One of the most important factors is that the drummer does not have a "repertoire of rhythms" available for certain symptoms. The secret is in knowing the technique for finding the proper sound combinations that will help restore the ill person to health.[7] In explaining the use of drums in rituals, Yaya Diallo notes:

> In the context of secret societies, there are no messages that come from the invisible world to the visible one without passing through someone in a trance, or someone who is considered mad. Initiations within the societies can qualify people to go into a trance as well as to prepare the musicians for their role in inducing trances and bringing people back to normalcy.[8]

In the healing process, simple and complex melodic and rhythmical procedures for incantations are used, such as cries, hollers, chants, shouts, the shaking of rattles, murmuring, and whistled sounds. The links with the tonal language of the local community and the "religious" chants are very strong. Long chromatic phrases and the use of rare vocal and instrumental timbres are frequent, and cacophonies are used to repel or personify the evil spirit. One author gives an example from parts of Europe of a continuation of this practice, known as the "Noise of Darkness," which accompanies portions of the Holy Week rituals in the Roman Catholic Church.[9]

Prior to their prolonged enforced importation, largely from West Africa to the New World, African peoples understood religion, music, and movement as integral to all of life. African theologians contend that all African traditional religions are essentially monotheistic in the sense that there is acknowledgment and belief in one "high" God who created a perfect universe,[10] with inhabitants in human and nonhuman form. This "high" creative God is, therefore, the ultimate source of order and final decisions. When evil is present and can be detected in human diseases, misfortunes, and disasters, it is believed that the cosmos has been thrown into disorder. During such times, a *diviner* is needed to discover what needs to be done to correct the situation. Diviners also intervene on behalf of the community to determine the source or author of the misfortune, the proper punishment necessary, and the appropriate rite, ritual, and music to be used to eradicate the evil. Some missionaries in sub-Saharan Africa still ponder the value of traditional African religions in present-day Christianity.[11]

Each African society has religious beliefs and belief systems that determine ritual practices, ceremonies, forms, and styles of music for invoking and appeasing the "high" God. Many African religions are polytheistic in that large numbers of lesser gods, spirits, ancestors, and other divinities stand between God and humankind. In spite of the diversity of African traditions represented by so many societies and language differences, there are fundamental concepts about God that transcend societal and tribal differences. This has been determined by comparing concepts as they are expressed in proverbs, songs, prayers, names, stories, myths, and religious ceremonies.[12] According to these oral documents, many concepts about God are identical to those of Christianity. Africans in general worship one God, called by different names but understood and translated as High God, Creator, Provider, Judge, Ruler, Father, and Mother (in both matriarchal and some patriarchal societies).

Thus, in addition to being heirs of Clement, Origen, Tertullian, Cyprian, Athanasius, Augustine, and Africans who participated in the early shaping of Christianity, African American Christians have inherited a legacy in African traditional belief systems. This heritage has helped to shape and clarify the beliefs of African Americans and to provide a foundation for worship and their understanding of music for worship as part of a holistic liturgical act.

African Spirituality and Primal Worldviews

The term *primal* means "basic" or "fundamental" rather than "primitive" or "undeveloped" as previously understood by most people.[13] This is not to suggest that primal worldviews are more fundamental or more authentic than other religious systems, but rather that in historical fact they have been widely used across all continents and have preceded and contributed to all other known religious systems of humankind. As John Taylor suggests, primal worldviews continue to reveal many of the basic or primary features of religion.[14] This is especially true as the historical foundations of African American Christianity and liturgical actions are determined.

Sufficient scholarly energy has been spent researching and discussing the acculturation and the survival of Africanisms in American life and culture, so this subject will not be addressed here.[15] What is absolutely clear is that African cultural influences have affected African American culture, especially through various religious belief systems and spiritual practices. The most significant feature in the diversity of African spirituality that has continually shaped and reshaped liturgical actions in African American worship is the primal understanding of cosmology in which the Almighty God, the Divine Spirit, or nature is the absolute and supreme primordial reality that systematically orders the universe. As expressed in an African proverb, "God is the first and last word of all our affairs." *Nature* for African people refers to the material forms of reality and creation. *Spirit* is that dynamic, cosmic force that exists in all creation providing movement, energy, and vitality. Nature and spirit are, therefore, the highest realms of existence and are made visible or manifest through God's creativity in the universe. The African *universe* is understood as a unified spiritual totality in which all things and all beings are holistically related and, therefore, organically interdependent. Both spiritual and material beings are necessary for order and for a meaningful reality to exist. Spiritual being or existence gives force and energy to matter; material being or existence gives form to the spiritual.

As with other forms of diversity among African peoples, there is no one universal understanding of cosmology or the sacred cosmos. Nevertheless, there is a shared fundamental outlook about the Divine and basic similarities that are paralleled by shared aspects of language and means of communicating. Although there is diversity within and between African communities and cultures regarding beliefs and expressions, a firm cosmology informs the African ritual practices that shape the music and other liturgical offerings. This cosmology transcends the complex nuances of various religious beliefs and practices and can be considered the unifying thread that binds African and African American spiritual belief systems. It continually links African American worshipers and musicians within and across denominations and religious belief systems.

A significant characteristic of African and African American spirituality is the concept of freedom: the freedom of God to have God's "own way" and the freedom of the people as the community of faith to respond to God's divine freedom. From African roots of spirituality, Africans in America honed and flamed African American culture and consciousness, which has as its catalyst the constant quest for human freedom. The freedom to exist without humanly designed encumbrances evokes and feeds the creative desire to make a way when there is no way, to make a new way out of existing matter, and to rely upon the immediacy of the environment and divine intervention. With careful scrutiny, one will recognize the importance of koinonia, or communality, in each of these processes. One person might initiate an idea, but the community must claim the idea and help facilitate its development in order for the idea to work. In African traditions this is an acknowledgment that no individual exists in isolation from others—"I am because we are; because we are, therefore I am." Herein is the soulforce that is synonymous with African culture, which continues in African American worship. It involves the *celebration* of the acts of God in history; the *interpretation* of the biblical actions into particular times and places, including the "now"; the *affirmation* of God's existence today and in the future; and the *transformation* of human life for the service of God. Out of these come elements or primal expressions of worship that are unique to African people in the Diaspora: praise, prayer, healing, shouting, dancing, singing, and playing instruments.

John S. Mbiti reminds us that the word *worship* does not exist in many traditional African languages. Furthermore, the term *worship*, used previously by anthropologists who were not theologians but who collected and transcribed much of the information, was used loosely and without careful attention to its meaning.[16] In using the term broadly to mean "human acts of turning to God," Mbiti indicates that such acts might be formal, informal, regular, extempore, communal or individual, ritual or nonceremonial, through word or deed.[17] Mbiti draws a distinction between sacrifices and offerings, and the importance of various forms and postures of prayers and other appeals to God is understood. Among prayer forms are invocations, appeals to God, blessings, and prayers of thanksgiving. Evidence suggests that Africans in the North American Diaspora were familiar with the concept of intermediaries and other specialists who approached God on behalf of individuals or communities. There were priests, diviners, medicine men, prophets, seers, mediums, oracles who acted as mouthpieces for particular deities, rainmakers, elders, and other special people (both men and women) who served as mediators. The functions of mediators were determined by particular societies, based on local cosmologies and worldviews. The time and place for worship were determined by community needs, with evidence that communities did not approach or appeal to God when things were going well.

African Primal Worldviews: Cosmology and Music in Worship

There is a plethora of evidence among various societies of the use of shrines, temples, altars, certain sacred rocks, and underneath certain sacred trees as places of worship. However, there is little written information on African religions concerning the place and use of music, singing, and dancing in worship. According to written records and transcriptions from oral traditions, there is natural integration of music and dance with all aspects of African life, especially to mark or celebrate transitions in life, from birth to death. Mbiti acknowledges the absence or brevity of details, and then cites a few examples, thus providing evidence of the importance of these integrative artistic activities in understanding and invoking the Divine:

> The *Bavenda* are said to worship God with singing and dancing. . . . When the *Ila* invoke [God] to send them rain, they do so with singing and presumably dancing. . . . [A]t their annual sacrifices and prayers, the *Jie* affirm with singing that God will give them rain and cause the crops to grow. They dance and rejoice as well. . . . At their big religious assemblies, the *Shona* used to use cymbals and trumpets, with much clapping of hands and singing. . . . The *Tonga* ceremony of praying for rain is accompanied with communal singing and dancing. . . . Among the *Warjawa*, when there

is public need, whole communities assemble to sacrifice, dance and call upon God for [God's] aid. . . . The *Ga* have different songs and styles of dancing for each of their divinities. . . . The *Fajulu* narrate that before heaven and earth were severed, the inhabitants of both worlds used to invite each other to festivities at which there were dances. They picture dancing and music as dating from the primeval days of human existence.[18]

Olaudah Equiano (or Gustavus Vassa), who is acknowledged as one of the first Africans to write a book in the English language, provided the following observation in his eighteenth-century autobiography: "We are almost a nation of dancers, musicians, and poets. Thus every great event . . . is celebrated in public dances which are accompanied with songs and music suited to the occasion."[19]

In traditional African cultures, life is not compartmentalized or segmented into sacred or religious realms. Life is viewed and lived holistically, with music functioning in a variety of ways. Religious beliefs and practices are expressed and transmitted orally through actions that govern daily existence in various societies.

Amid the diversity of religious beliefs, languages, symbols, and musical styles, there are fundamental concepts that are common throughout the continent. This is especially true of sub-Saharan Africa, the homeland of the largest number of Africans enslaved and transported to the Americas from the seventeenth to the nineteenth centuries. The common manifestations of musical expressions are historically grounded in black African roots that form a network of distinctive yet interrelated traditions that overlap in style. This can be attributed to similarities in worldviews and social contexts, as well as to the nomadic tendencies of some African people. One should not hastily assume, however, that such similarities make all African music practices the same. Perhaps because of the complex grouping of African peoples into tribes, ranging from as few as two thousand to as many as fifteen million, diversity can be expected. Just as there is diversity in language and linguistic systems, there is diversity in the music of Africa, causing it to be, according to a leading ethnomusicologist, "ethnic bound."[20] That is to say, each society practices its own variant of language so that there is a linguistic style that is unique to the Yoruba, or Hausa, or Akan, or Ewe; there is also a Yoruba variety of African music, or an Akan variety, and so forth.[21]

This point is equally relevant in reference to Africans in the Diaspora. Although there are similarities in the manner of production or in the use of tonal material, one should not assume that all black music is alike, or that all African Americans will or should like the same forms and styles of black music. Africans in America claim and reclaim the heritage that allows for uniqueness in musical gifts and preferences because of the overlap in aspects of style and the improvisatory gift of making a new way out of existing materials.

The distinct relationship between African and African American music making is based upon the continuation of an African conceptual approach to music in the African American context. First and foremost is the continuous belief in the affective or transforming power of vocal music. Individuals participate in singing to help ease the pain of work, not only for themselves but also for those within the sound of the song. In addition to transforming the environment, the community is unified as people join in, either as singers or as listeners.

Other characteristics of African music are: the communal process of creating songs and recreating or reworking old songs with new materials, the integration of thoughts and actions in songs, a natural holistic sense of rhythm, and the use of a wide variety of percussion and stringed instruments. Music making throughout the continent is most often communal and intergenerational, and is not intended merely for the ear but for all the senses and faculties of the body. African musicologist Francis Bebey is insightful in his observation that music "reflects Africa's vision of the world on earth and the world beyond, a world of change and movement, a world in permanent search of betterment and perfection."[22]

The process of music making involves one or several leaders and the gathered community in improvisatory, call-and-response activities. This not only engages the community in corporate activities; it creates a cyclical quality characteristic of much of African music and life. It is also symbolic of continuity and wholeness as well as of the openness to the possibility of newness and renewal. This functional and inclusive dimension of music continues in the creative bloodstream of African peoples in the Diaspora.

Vocal Music

The major aim of African peoples in the creation of any sound is to express life in all of its aspects. Combinations of sounds are not predicated on that which might be pleasing to the ear, but rather on that which helps translate and express common, everyday life experiences and feelings into meaningful sounds. In many African environments, a portion of daily life experiences is one's capacity for the expression of the supernatural. As in other cultures, the human voice is the most natural, artistic, and spontaneous means of musical expression. Consequently, singing is the most common form of musical expression in African cultures. The beauty of singing is determined by the function that it serves rather than by a norm imposed by other cultures. Francis Bebey notes quite discerningly:

> The utilization of the voice by musicians in black Africa—its timbres and the different nuances obtained by means of artifices unknown to the rest of the world (stopping the ears, pinching the nose, vibrating the tongue in the mouth, producing echoes by directing the voice into a receptacle, etc.)—largely accounts for the confusion, or rather the incomprehension that almost inevitably confronts the non-African listener when he first hears black African music.[23]

Non-Africans who understand and have adapted interpretations within the African context have discovered that variances in vocal tonalities communicate different meanings that only the local community understands. For instance, in some African societies, a mellow, fully matured tone communicates tenderness and thoughtfulness; "teasing" tones are used to reflect satire or sarcasm; and husky tones by males or females communicate indiscreet or clandestine adventure.

Songs emanate from the intonations, rhythms, accents, and inflections of the speech patterns and spoken words of particular African societies, especially in Bantu languages.[24] Each of the characteristics cited provides a particular meaning to a word. Therefore, to alter either creates confusion in communication.[25] Singing provides a confirmation of one's individual incorporation into the community, and anyone can and is expected to sing. Each society acknowledges specialists, or *griots*, who are encouraged to study as apprentices under the guidance of teachers in the community. One of the requirements of the *griot* is to document and communicate the history of the community. A person may also be called a *griot* if his or her task is simply to function as a soloist, leader, or conductor of a group, or if he or she knows the broad outlines of the community's vocal repertoire but may not have a specialty as a singer.

Melodies and harmonies range from simplistic to highly complicated, and are sung with emphatic gusto or slowly and contemplatively. Many songs are antiphonal, with varying call-and-response techniques that lend themselves to interlocking and overlapping phrases. They are syncopated and highly rhythmical, evoking intricate physical and instrumental accompaniment, or hymnic with slow harmonic progressions. Songs are guttural and strident in vocal quality, with ululation or high, shrill vocal sounds or wails and other improvisatory sounds. African songs also utilize soft melodic lines with emotion-filled contrapuntal harmonic weavings of voices that symbolize the presence of the Holy Spirit speaking to the community. Performances of each of these forms and styles can move listeners and participants to powerful emotional crescendos!

The relationship between the intonation of music and language is so intimate that it is possible to tune an instrument so that the music it produces is linguistically compatible. The integration of speech and song is natural, and both are incorporated in the creation and singing of songs (more or less *sprechstimme,* or recitative, in style*).* This can be observed when a *griot* tells a story in which the musicality of the *griot*'s language becomes the foundation of a song. I observed this process in East Africa, which led to the creation of a folk song. As the *griot* engaged the community in a story, listeners participated in a dialogical response that slowly developed into a unison melody, with harmonic parts added as the story unfolded. A few days later, a simple recall of this same melody triggered the memory of this particular story by those who had participated in its development. This was the process used in the shaping of many African American spirituals.

Songs are used also as a means of evaluating and criticizing life, as well as creating and expressing meaning in life. Thus, the texts of songs often have double entendres or dual meanings, with some of the ideas masked or stated symbolically in an effort to conceal criticism of established ways of life, politics, or of leaders in the community.

Textual and musical improvisations are also common features of African songs. A communal song introduced by a leader might undergo numerous changes before it is "finished" by the community or transported orally to other places. Singers are unusually adept at embellishing portions of the melody or text, adding or omitting several measures each time. Harmonic elements may be introduced in unison songs as the leader or the community adds intervals of a third, fourth, or fifth below the basic melodic line. Some songs give equal or greater weight to the words than to the music, while in others, greater attention is given to the structure and form of the music. However, it is the music, more than the words, that usually gives unity and coherence to songs. The poetic expression of song texts provides the foundation for changes in thought and mood, but the melody and harmonic and rhythmical structure define the character of the performance of certain categories of songs. Thus, the category of songs or function (whether for religious or civic occasions, work, or for entertainment) and the manner of expression is maintained, even when the words are simply nonsense syllables, meaningless phrases, or unfamiliar words.

One can conclude that the songs of African people provide a record of the history, beliefs, and values that a community holds in its collective memory, to be used as needed as a means of its survival. This African process continued in the Americas and in other places of the African Diaspora. Many of the forms and styles of African communal singing continue among Africans in the Diaspora, making it possible to identify unique and characteristically African musical features. In African American spirituals there is a natural propensity to incorporate a sense of awareness of the Creator, the universe, religion, and life into all new musical creations. The involvement of one's whole self along with the entire community epitomizes the African adage on human relatedness: "I am because you are; because you are, therefore I am." The poetic and musical uses of masks and symbols are a part of the African continuum of song, expressed with enthusiasm and a sense of hope. Masks and symbols are primal forms that represent artistic ways of getting at the root of life.

One of the most distinguishing aspects of African vocal music is the way in which music and speech are inseparable. J. H. Kwabena Nketia observes that African traditions deliberately treat songs as though they were speech utterances. Common practices include choral recitations; heightened speech in musical contexts; overlapping elements of speech, music, and rhythm; the use of rapid delivery of texts; explosive interjections; vocal grunts; and whispering.[26] My own exposure to performances on the West Coast includes evidence of spoken call-and-response segments, which evolve naturally into singing. There is also evidence of specific procedures that govern the manner in which speech, song, dance, drama, and instruments are to be used. Whereas some societies are rigid in structure, some *griots* encourage interruptions so that the audience can participate more fully.

The common stylistic elements that unite all sub-Saharan African vocal music are repetition, cohesiveness, and overlapping phrases with several meanings. Song styles function as symbols and reinforcement for social norms. It is also significant to note that vocal music is foundational for African rhythms, since the prime motive of the instruments is to reconstitute spoken language.[27]

Instrumental Music

Without a doubt, sub-Saharan Africans in the Diaspora on any alien soil carry the rhythmic pulse of a wide range of instruments that characterize their ancestral continent. This was equally true of seventeenth-century Africans enslaved and transported to the Americas. The sound and rhythm of instruments personify the pulse of the African soul and symbolically express the life and vitality of African people. The unfathomable variety of musical instruments throughout the continent is indicative of the creative gifts of individuals and societies to provide resources that are unique to local communities and yet usable in places far beyond their origin. The natural environmental materials available and the artisan skills of individual craftspersons largely determine instrumental variety, including the size and quality of tone. Instruments are transported from place to place through trade and other activities that bring members of different musical and religious cultures into contact with one another.

One significant factor in the making of musical instruments is the important practice of the individual handcrafting of each instrument, with the added feature of personal carvings and trademarks of local musical artists. Although the latter half of the twentieth century began to see the mass production of instruments, this is a new phenomenon predicated on commercial endeavors precipitated by travelers outside of African cultures. Well into the 1970s, there were few if any professional craftspersons who specialized in making instruments. According to Bebey, musicians make their own instruments to suit their own tastes. Musicians also teach the instrument the language it will speak in the musician's own tongue. Thus, two zithers (or *mvets)* that are made by musicians from two different African societies will not "speak" the same language. The xylophone made by a musician from Guinea does not have the same scale or language pattern as a xylophone made by a Bantu musician.[28]

The significance of the language of a people and its close relationship to a carefully constructed instrument and its player is predicated on the meaningful relationship between intonation and rhythmic nuances of speech. In the Bantu language, intonations provide meaning not only for words but also for phrases, so that any melodic contradiction between the way a word is spoken and the way it is sung is inconceivable. For instance, the Duala term *moto,* which means "humanity" or "man," is said or sung on the same tone or pitch with identical stresses on both syllables. If the two syllables are said or sung on different pitches or tones, the word loses its meaning. The term *muto* (woman) is said or sung using two different pitches, with the first tone being an interval of a third higher than the second tone (e.g., from F to A). Obviously, it is easy to move from speech into song—from instrumental intonations into song, and to reproduce the language on instruments. Musicians who work diligently to craft an instrument so that it "speaks" a particular language insist that linguistic factors are understood and adhered to. This is the major reason that a musician who makes an instrument for a particular community will not arbitrarily give it away or sell it to a person who has no knowledge of the language of the people for whose language the instrument was made.

The intonations of African languages, particularly the very musical Bantu languages, depict more than the tonic syllabic accents in European languages.

It is melodic intervals often prolonged with tied notes that give words their meaning. Therefore, the human voice and musical instruments are much more closely aligned than in Western thinking. This matter is stressed here in order to clarify much of what happened in early African American worship as the unique interrelationship between musical, linguistic, and instrumental styles was carried over to create specific liturgical styles. Many nuances of this three-way relationship continue in some worshiping communities as congregations interact and dialog in call-and-response fashion with the preacher, as the preacher employs musical tones to add meaning to the "preaching moment," and as instrumentalists (organ, piano, keyboard, drums, etc.) assist in shaping the experiential dimensions of worship.

The use of instruments in Africa is not restricted to musical functions. Some instruments are used as appropriate communication signals for attracting attention, assembling the community for various functions, and creating an atmosphere during communal rites and ceremonies. They are also used for transmitting verbal messages or for reinforcing verbal communication, and for specifying the movements of individuals such as priests, dancers, and members of the society undergoing sacred initiations.

Although the totality of African instrumental resources and functions throughout Africa is enormous, there are common factors that allow them to be categorized into four main groups, with a fifth designation to accommodate a particular instrument. These differ from the Western classification (strings, wind, brass, and percussion). African scholars and ethnomusicologists concur in this classification:[29]

1. *Idiophones*, literally "self-sounding instruments" or any source that requires only the source itself to produce the sound. This is the most common of all of the categories, ranging from the human body, to shakers (beaded gourds), the *sistrum* (an important instrument used in Ethiopian worship), cymbals of all descriptions and sizes, stamping sticks, thumb or hand pianos such as the *mbira* or *sansa*, earthenware, tin, lightweight oil drums, solid and hollow logs, and tuned instruments such as the xylophone. Some xylophones are intricately designed with gourds under a single key or a group of keys in order to add resonance to the sound that is produced. Another keyboard instrument, the *kalimba,* is known in the United States as a "thumb piano" and was popularized by the African American soul-rock group Earth, Wind, and Fire. This instrument is found all over the continent of Africa. The African students at Interdenominational Theological Center have identified the many names by which this instrument is known in local societies: *sanza, sanzi,* and *sanzo, likembe,* and *gibinji* (from Congo), *timbili* or *babute* (from Cameroon), and the *deza sanza.*

2. *Aerophones*, or instruments in which the sound is produced by the use of air, which includes simple reed pipes and flutes all the way to intricately designed wood and brass horns. A number of aerophones are made of animal's horns. Trumpets, on the other hand, are made from whole lengths of gourd, and with bamboo alone. Trumpets are used for signals and verbal messages as well as for playing music.

3. *Chordophones*, which include all varieties of stringed instruments, such as those designed simply with one string and those that are precursors of the harp, with ten to thirty strings. They are made by hand by exquisitely skilled artisans. Strings of chordophones can be plucked, pounded, or bowed, or the sound may be produced by blowing across the strings. Although the tuning system, usage, shapes, and names of instruments vary from one society to another, several kinds of lutes, zithers, and harps are found throughout the continent.

4. *Membranophones*, or instruments in which the sound is produced by vibrating stretched skin such as a drumhead that has been attached to hollow logs, earthenware vessels, large gourds (or calabash), hard fruit, or seashells. Drums are made in a variety of sizes and shapes: conical, cylindrical or semi-cylindrical, bottle-shaped, round, or square. Some are small and light enough to be carried, or so large that several persons may be needed to move a single one from one place to another. Some are single headed, and some are double headed. Drums may be played singularly or in pairs. Most drums are struck with a mallet or with the hand, but another effective means of playing is by friction. In order to play a drum by friction the drummer moistens the head (skin) of the drum and produces sound by rubbing rather than beating the drum.

5. *Lithophones,* or groups of basalt stones that are struck to produce sounds that can be incorporated into a piece of music. This is a very particular type of instrument limited to certain parts of sub-Saharan Africa, specifically northern Togo, northern Nigeria, and Cameroon. Such locations make it possible that some Africans transported from that region to the Americas during the slave trade might have been familiar with lithophones. This instrument is identified as a melodic instrument and is played by young boys in three Kabre regions of northern Togo during the farming cycle. For example, during the first days of mid-November, the lithophone is played to mark the end of the rainy season. In December, the lithophone announces the feast of the millet harvest but is not played after marking the feast. Huge lithophones are found in their natural formation in northern Nigeria in the regions of Kano and Jos. "The music they produce is still used in some villages for initiation and circumcision rites as well as for certain religious ceremonies. Stones are struck

with two-stone mallets or strikers. While one hand, usually the right, plays a melody, the left hand taps the rhythm on the largest stone."[30]

Many instruments of Africa are designed with symbolic meanings and specific performance practices in mind. They reflect the structure and laws of the society, by which the God Creator (*Mwari*) taught the first men who played the *deza sansa*. For the Lemba, God is synonymous with life.[31] The following story is repeated here in detail because of what it communicates about women, the birthing process, and about the entire community. It is also an excellent example of the depth of understanding of the Creator's connection with humankind through musical instruments that some slaves carried in their memories:

> The *Deza Sanza,* with its 22 keys, contained in a hemispherical calabash resonator, which represents the whole of creation and [humankind] that is seated in the python's belly. The striking of the notes to produce sound is an act of creation—the birth of a child who cries; the wooden frame represents the women who have come to assist at the birth. Every single component part of the *Deza* is symbolic: the calabash resonator is the womb; the sound . . . is the child that is born; the string that is tied around the calabash represents the python skin that encircles the village; the keys are the people who are seated inside the python—8 men (the high notes), 7 old women represented by copper keys (copper being the metal of the womenfolk—the Lemba people consider red to be the feminine color); the hole in the rectangular sound-box is the deflowered maiden, and so on.[32]

Rhythm

Rhythmic movement (dance), singing, and poetic expression in African cultures are interrelated as a composite of one aesthetic phenomenon. What is most obvious in this phenomenon is the natural sense of rhythm that characterizes African music. Rhythm, the ordered recurring alternatives of strong and weak elements in the flow of movement, reflects the African sensitivity to the rhythm of the cosmos received and translated into kinetic energy. This ability to transform impulses into physical expression is often centered on a "metronomic sensibility," wherein a steady recurring beat can be easily located. This is especially apparent when a number of drums or other percussion instruments are involved and accents occur at different places in the music, creating a mixture of strong pulses and syncopation. A person with keen sensitivity will be able to recognize a central pulse that helps provide and promote unity in the performance. The nature of the cosmos and the nature of life is such that underneath the steady, recurring rhythm there can be shifting rhythms and accents, and life can happen in unaccented places! This is the African understanding of the "rhythm of life."

African people are attuned to the rhythm of life in the universe, which explodes into dancing and singing, not by simply one person but by the community. This happens in most all gatherings, including worship and other times of communal ritual expression. Rhythm is foundational for ritual action among African people. In traditional cultures the community is called together for any number of reasons. The signal for most of these regularly occurring rituals is the sound of music. For distant gatherings the drums or loud sounding aerophones are used to reach the people. The rhythm of instruments also communicates particular events, which members of the community will understand. In many societies, when a child is born, there is a special rhythmical drum call signaling the event as well as the baby's sex to everyone in the village. This rhythmical phenomenon continues today for other African daily life events, including rites of passages and special occasions such as marriages, deaths, times for worship, and the arrival of visitors. Special rhythms are also used in healing rituals and are often discreetly combined with regular communal dancing and singing.

Rhythm is reflective of the creation account in the first chapter of Genesis, which suggests that the Almighty God ordered life by way of a rhythmical creation process or movement in time. Thus, the rhythm of life, in addition to the rhythm of the cosmos, is of divine origin and serves to facilitate human functions such as the heartbeat, breathing (inhalation/exhalation), blood pressure (systolic/diastolic), and body temperature. Each of these is attuned to musical sound and will respond to variables in volume, rate, and pitch. Studies have also revealed that musical sound, pitch, and rhythm can regulate stress-related hormones, boost the immune system, alter perceptions of time and space, increase endorphins, affect memory and the ability to learn, boost productivity, stimulate digestion, and affect endurance. This is why instrumental and vocal rhythms can contribute to healing and health and, conversely, sickness and pain.

With the understanding that vocal sounds and structures preceded instrumental sounds, scholars have emphasized the importance of words in establishing rhythms and in their aural transmission of them. Some of the most direct influences of Africa have been found in the difficult rhythms of spirituals, blues, and other vocal forms. The tonal fluidity of languages is inherent within much of the vocal music. The performance of music and dance as well as Africans at work demonstrate the interrelationships among the senses; it is in everyday activities that rhythm is clearly understood as basic to life. One example is when several women stand around a large mortar or vessel carved out of a portion of a tree trunk and pound grain into cereal. Their alternate pounding of pestles, rising and falling like pistons, creates a rhythmical work cadence. If one person loses the beat, it interrupts the rhythm and disrupts the work. This example underscores the belief that music was created as much for its meaning as for the ear. Without meaning, music and all the elements involved lose their raison d'être.

In traditional African cultures, there is more uniformity in the choice and use of rhythms and rhythmic structures than in the choice and use of pitch and tonal systems. This is demonstrated in Africans' preference for idiophones and membranophones and the emphasis on percussive textures. Nketia notes that: "the music of an instrument with a range of only two or three tones can be effective or aesthetically satisfying to its performers and their audience if it has sufficient rhythmic interest."[33]

Instrumental rhythms are structured in both linear and multilinear forms, and are based on the syllables of songs or as abstract rhythm patterns. Rhythms can be in strict time, giving the feeling of a regularized beat, or they may be metrically free. Strict metrical patterns are controlled by a fixed time span and divided into pulse structures of twos or threes, which might alternate within the same composition. Part of the genius of African drumming is the ability of some performers to keep the basic pulse while adding or deleting rhythms and phrases without altering the overall rhythmical pattern. Since this is difficult, African traditions facilitate this process by allowing the basic pulse to be externalized or actualized. This is done by having an idiophone, a membranophone, or handclapping to maintain a steady pulse.

Scholars tend to agree that African ritual music exists as a way of translating the experiences of life and the spiritual world into sound. African vocal and instrumental techniques express a desire to tell the truth. Each tone and bodily expression that is offered is a reflection of life itself. Thus, the technique used is adapted from the particular aspect of life being depicted. This continues to a large extent in ritual music of African Americans in the twenty-first century. The musical creativity and artistry of traditional Africans supported their understanding of ritual in a deeply mysterious universe in which African peoples sought union with the one supreme invisible God, lesser gods, spirits, and the living dead. Dominique Zahan contends that this was a universe in which the use of euphemism, symbol, allegory, and secrets were normal for the oral expression of society.[34]

The idea of this traditional African universe with elements of African life, myth, ritual, song, rhythms, and movement provided the foundation for African American sacred rituals and music. Many of these elements are present in African American worship and music even today.

The Coptic and Ethiopian Churches

And the LORD God planted a garden in Eden . . . and there he put the man whom he had formed. . . . A river flows out of Eden to water the garden, and from there it divides and becomes four branches. The name of the first is Pishon; it is the one that flows around the whole land of Havilah, where there is gold; and the gold of that land is good; bdellium and onyx stone are there. The name of the second river is Gihon; it is the one that flows around the whole land of Cush [Ethiopia]. The name of the third river is Tigris, which flows east of Assyria. And the fourth river is the Euphrates. (Gen. 2:8–14)

Then an angel of the Lord said to Philip, "Get up and go toward the south to the road that goes down from Jerusalem to Gaza." . . . Now there was an Ethiopian eunuch, a court official of the Candace, queen of the Ethiopians. . . . He had come to Jerusalem to worship and was returning home; seated in his chariot, he was reading the prophet Isaiah. . . . And as [Philip and the eunuch] were going along the road, they came to some water; and the eunuch said, "Look, here is water! What is to prevent me from being baptized?" . . . Philip and the eunuch went down into the water, and Philip baptized him. (Acts 8:26–38)

These two biblical reminders are significant in a discussion of the biblical heritage of African and African American Christianity. First, the Genesis account establishes the location of the Garden of Eden on the continent of Africa, and second, the account of the baptism of the Ethiopian eunuch cites the importance of Africa and African people in the heritage of the Christian faith. These are also reminders of the involvement of North Africans in ancient liturgies long before the period of slavery. With these biblical reminders, the roots of the Ethiopian and Coptic churches are established.

The Coptic Church

The people of the land now called Egypt or Copt, from the term *kermit,* meaning "black," originated in the interior of Africa in the geographical area around the Nile River and the Rift Valley. *Copt* also refers to the language spoken in Egypt before Arabic became the common language. Coptic Christians trace their ancestry to the flight of the Holy Family into Egypt shortly after the birth of Jesus, and to the days of Mark the apostle, who established the Coptic church in the first century, as early as 43 C.E. Ancient Coptic churches were built to commemorate the various resting places of the Holy Family. Egypt also became the great center of monastic life from the fourth century forward.

By the fifteenth century there were as many as 300 monasteries and nunneries in Egypt. There are more than seven million Coptic Christians in Egypt today, where Muslim and Christian families have lived in mutual understanding and cooperation for centuries.

The Coptic and Ethiopian Churches belong to a third group of Eastern Orthodox churches that broke away from the Orthodox Church over doctrinal issues.[35] Features of Coptic worship are as follows:

- The worship space is dark, with little light from their narrow windows, reflective of the earliest churches;
- Lamps are dimly lit, giving prominence to exquisite carvings;
- The Divine Liturgy is central, and is usually that of St. Basil the Great; liturgies of St, Gregory and St. Mark are reserved for special occasions;
- The service is shaped so that everyone present can be involved;
- The pace of the liturgy is slow and the congregation is emotionally and vocally involved in the refrains of the litanies.

Music is an inseparable part of the liturgy, and the entire service is sung. The effect is that the music, including the intoning of the priest, is indeed worship itself! A *schola,* or choir, is available to lead the singing in large gatherings. Choir members are often theological students, who are required to know the music since it is inseparable from the liturgy. Chants are performed in unison, and the percussion instruments usually keep time with a fast-paced and intricately syncopated beat. The Sanctus (Holy, Holy, Holy) is a highly emotional time in the Divine Liturgy, which is enhanced by the percussion accompaniment. Some chants are accompanied with finger cymbals and triangles, a practice introduced during the Middle Ages. According to oral traditions, Coptic and Ethiopian Christians utilized their whole body in worship from the beginning. This is not at all surprising for African Christian people, because traditional African religious practices were not far removed from their religious life, and they would not have been discontinued even as the liturgy was in its nascent stages. While handclapping and bodily movements were not considered "normal" for other Orthodox traditions, it is hardly expected that black people would have been "unmoved" as they experienced the awesome power of God in worship.

Coptics and other Christians attend worship as often as three times a week. The music and flow of the liturgy are learned rapidly and remain familiar. The liturgy is also highly valued by the Coptic Church, and thus far, music of the liturgy has not taken on aspects of the twentieth and twenty-first centuries' popular culture. Popular music uses much from Western and African American music including electronic organs, guitars, synthesizers, violins, flutes, and so forth. The trend currently is to incorporate some elements of popular music into Sunday school classes, but so far never in the Divine Liturgy!

The Ethiopian Orthodox Church

Ethiopia is one of the most ancient nations in the world. It is a country of beautiful people, a lively culture, and deep spirituality. The Ethiopian Orthodox Church is an indigenous and integral church of Africa, and is one of the oldest churches in the world. Before the introduction of Christianity, belief in and use of the Hebrew Bible (Old Testament) had been accepted in Ethiopia. The monotheistic belief in the one true God of the Israelites had its origin in the history of the reign of the Queen of Sheba (1 Kings 10). Her son, Menelik, who was fathered by King Solomon (and whose name means "son of a king"), journeyed to Jerusalem to meet the king. Solomon instructed Menelik in the law of Moses and allowed him to remain in Jerusalem. When he returned home three years later, he took the ark of the covenant with him to Axum, the ancient capital of Ethiopia. Upon his arrival with the ark, the Queen of Sheba gave up her throne to Menelik, who ruled Ethiopia for twenty-five years. Thus began a line of monarchs who ruled Ethiopia in an unbroken dynasty for nearly 3,000 years through the reign of Haile Selassie, the 237th emperor of Ethiopia.

The roots of Judaism in Ethiopia can be traced through Menelik I and his bringing the ark of the covenant from Jerusalem. The ark has elevated interest in Axum and the Church of Sion Mariam (St. Mary of Sion), which is the mother church of the more than 22,000 Ethiopian Orthodox churches. Judaism was practiced in Ethiopia from this time until Christianity was accepted in 328 C.E.[36] The form of Judaism professed is pre-Talmudic, and includes worshipers making pilgrimages to the Holy Land. It was in this tradition that the Ethiopian eunuch came to Jerusalem.

Christianity was adopted in Ethiopia following the arrival of two Coptic Christians, Frumentius and Aedesius, after a shipwreck landed them on Ethiopian shores in 328. This marked the beginning of the relationship between the Egyptian Coptic Church and Ethiopian Church. Frumentius was consecrated and appointed as the first bishop by Patriarch Athanasius. The Ethiopian Church also developed a desert monastic tradition from the fifth century forward. Many of the monks were highly educated and translated the Bible from Syrian, Coptic, and Greek into Ge'ez, a language that is quite different from the locally spoken Amharic language. Although Ethiopia has had contact with the Jesuits and more recently with Protestants, it has not had much contact with the West.[37]

Lalibela

The monastic settlement known as Lalibela is located in a mountainous region north of Addis Ababa. This small village, previously called Roha, was renamed after King Lalibela, who reigned there in the twelfth century. Much attention is drawn to this settlement because eleven churches were excavated—literally hand carved—from a rock-hewn mountain. According to legend, men worked during the day and angels worked during the night until the churches were completed. The most famous of the churches of Lalibela is *Bet Giyoris* (St. George), also known as the Church of the Cross because it is in the shape of a cross. The tops of the churches are level with the ground, so one has to enter by climbing down into the space. The tallest structure is three stories in height. It took twenty-four years to complete all of the churches, which are now registered by the United Nations' Education, Scientific, and Cultural Organization (UNESCO) as a world heritage site. Over 500 monks and priests of the Orthodox Church live there.

Music in the Liturgy of the Ethiopian Orthodox Church

The music in the *kedessa* (liturgy) of the Ethiopian Orthodox Church has remained rather constant over the years. A key factor is perhaps the unique form of notation used for the liturgy. Although much of the music is memorized for the services, having a form of notation facilitates a process whereby the sacred music practices can be continued into the future. All priests, deacons, monks, and *dabtaras* (musicians) are required to know the music in the liturgy. The *dabtaras*, however, are given the responsibility of preserving the artistic tradition of the church. To prepare for this task requires intense training in traditional music (called *zema*), sacred dance (*aquaquam*), and how to accompany. In addition, they study the poetry (*qene*) of the church, theology, and church history. Like the Coptics, Ethiopians treasure their faith and the traditional liturgical expressions, especially the music. The ecclesiastical poetry must be a perfect "fit" to one of the traditional chants, for it will be heard as a commentary on Scripture. The poetry must also be written in the ancient church language of Ge'ez and conform to the strict rules of grammar.

In 1627 Jerome Lobo, a Jesuit priest, described the music in the Ethiopian rite. His words are summarized here for convenience:

- The instruments of music are little drums that they hang about their necks and beat with both of their hands; these are carried even by the Chief Men, and by the gravest of their Ecclesiastics.
- They have sticks likewise with which they strike the ground, accompanying the blow with the motion of their whole bodies.

- They begin their Consort [music making] by stamping their feet on the ground, and playing gently on their instruments.
- When they have heated themselves by degrees, they leave off drumming and fall to leaping, dancing, and clapping their hands, at the same time straining their voices to the utmost pitch, till at length they have no regard whether to the tune or the pauses. They seem rather a riotous rather than a religious assembly.
- For this manner of worship they cite the psalm of David "O clap your hands, all ye nations."[38]

Ethiopian Orthodox Christians believe that Yared, a sixth-century saint, created all their sacred chants. According to the legend, the chants were divinely given and recorded in a fourteenth-century *Synaxarium* (lives of the saints) called *Senkessar.*

At this time, there were no rules for the famous zema, or liturgical chant. The offices were recited in a low voice. But when the Saviour wanted to establish sacred chant, he thought of Yared and sent three birds to him from the Garden of Eden, which spoke to him with the language of men, and carried him away to the heavenly Jerusalem, and there he learnt their chant from twenty-four heavenly priests.

And when the king and queen heard the sound of his voice they were moved with emotion and they spent the day in listening to him, as did the archbishop, the priests and the nobility of the kingdom. And he appointed the chants for each period of the year . . . for the Sundays and the festivals of the angels, prophets, martyrs and the just. He did this in three styles: in *ge'ez, 'ezl* and *araray*, and he put into these three nothing far removed from the language of men and the songs of the birds and animals.[39]

There are some who believe that this music is much older than the time of Yared, and possibly that it has direct links to Hebrew music. In addition to similarities with Jewish temples in the names and the theology of sacred space, the dances link directly with descriptions in the Hebrew Bible. Michael Powne provides the following commentary:

The veneration accorded to the *tabot* in Abyssinia (Ethiopia) up to the present day, its carriage in solemn procession accompanied by singing, dancing, beating of staffs or prayer sticks, rattling of *sistra* and sounding of other musical instruments remind one most forcefully of the scene in 2 Samuel 6:5, 15, and 16. [40]

Most of the traditional texts have their music attached to them. The melodies have to be learned by the *dabtara* (singer), and once that is done there is no need for the Western symbols of the staff and notes. Additionally, there are *meleket* signs, which show the singer precisely how the melodies should be sung. Signs at the beginning of each chant indicate to which of the three distinct styles of chanting (*zema*) it belongs.

African Traditions in African American Worship

This brief review of African traditional religious practices and church structures created and governed by Africans is designed to whet the appetite of readers to delve more deeply into the subject. In addition to the information cited, there are numerous sources available that document the musical practices in general. The information from Wilson-Dickson's *The Story of Christian Music* (chaps. 33–38) has made a significant contribution to church music history. This is the first document of Christian music that extends from the Gregorian chant to black gospel. One additional resource that is related to Christian worship and music is *The Complete Library of Christian Worship*, which is available in seven volumes.[41] Fortunately, there are a few African ethnomusicologists who are gathering and publishing data, thus supplementing and authenticating music and liturgical practices on the African continent.

Some suggestions for incorporating African traditions in African American worship are outlined here:

- Africans currently in America from a variety of traditional cultures are available in large numbers and are anxious to assist congregations with adapting from African traditional religious cultures. Please incorporate the gifts, especially of theological seminarians, who could provide the appropriate rationale for utilizing rituals, music, symbols, and symbolism.
- Remember that cultural traditions in other places of the African Diaspora can be considered, but again solicit the theological help of persons from the tradition(s) and examine their usage in light of the theology of your particular denomination.
- Afrocentricity does not grant a "license" for worshipers to be indiscriminate in their choices of rituals or music for worship.
- Afrocentricity is not confined to wearing attire that connects one with a culture. Seek a depth of understanding that will help the congregation and choir understand the extent of looking Afrocentric with being Afrocentric and affirming with hospitality the need to extend the love of the idea with the love of the people.

Concerns over "surface" Afrocentric behavior were brought to my attention in music and worship classes at ITC. According to African seminarians in the United States from "modern" West Africa, there is concern that the interpretation of African liturgical actions and sacred musical performances often denotes a limited amount of knowledge, experience, and exposure to Africans and the interest of Africa. Molefi K. Asante's initial intent in 1980 was to clarify Afrocentric behavior.[42] The adaptation of African attire and sacred fabrics as vestments is indeed noble and impressive. However, some African sisters and brothers have advocated for an in-depth study of the use of certain fabrics that are sacred to particular societies and cultures that would be helpful to those who desire to use them appropriately. This need for study extends to adapted rites, rituals, and music performance practices in Africa and in the early African American Diaspora. This is particularly a concern as music for worship is *taken from* the congregation and granted full authority as performance music for choirs. As this has happened, congregations are entertained, or are drawn into participation because the music—rather than the Holy Spirit—pulls them in.

Recognizing that all borrowed practices are subject to metamorphosis when taken outside their original culture,[43] Africans and some African Americans in twenty-first-century America are concerned that some religious leaders are "running with a message" without hearing the good news. Research in the varied and diverse African American traditions further attests to broader boundaries than those often demonstrated by some who claim to function from an Afrocentric worldview. Some have become so intent on reclaiming the African and early African American heritage that they do not find that it is equally important to reclaim the people who made the traditional culture possible in Africa. This is an exciting and important time for African Americans to model the concepts of Asante by utilizing "the insight that comes from being born black in the U.S."[44] This realization grants us not only the desire but also the ability to create a new world. It also grants us an opportunity to liberate those who are trapped and sinking in the quicksand of looking Afrocentric without being or becoming people who understand that Afrocentricity is not merely a surface idea.

Chapter 2

Africans in America

*T*he seeds of African American songs were planted and nurtured in the womb of mother Africa and her descendants. The gift of song was tucked into the body, soul, and bloodstream of Africans who were brought to fertile grounds in northeastern Florida in 1565 to help protect the Spanish holdings in the New World. This small black colony continued its Roman Catholic tradition of worship, unaware that this inchoate settlement would become in less than 200 years a refuge for fugitive slaves from their own African continent. Nor did they anticipate that this small black Catholic township would be recognized as the oldest black town in what would later be called the United States of America. There is no record to attest to the singing ability of these Africans on a military outpost, nor to any form of liturgical chants that they might have sung during worship. Nevertheless, we can imagine that the gift of song embedded in their total beings must have burst forth as they worked, worshiped, or played.

But there were other Africans who were forced to journey to this strange environment on seafaring vessels. Their creative and improvisatory gifts, planted long before they were born, burst forth in songs even when conditions were not conducive to any vocal or physical expression. Their status as bonded servants and slaves hindered their freedom, their personhood, identity, and humanity. They missed the opportunity to form a ring in the open part of the village where each person could demonstrate his or her musical gifts with motions, gesticulations, and agility. These were not merely "show and tell moments"; they were moments of affirmation and assurance that their gifts of song, sound, and soul would not be "shut up in their bones," unexpressed, and unused as if to accommodate death. These were moments to affirm their oneness, their unity as a community. The seeds had been planted and nurtured to burst forth as needed, even in the midst of harsh slavery, to create community in the light of existential situations. These African souls arrived in physical pain and with mental anguish because of the circumstances leading to their capture and their mode of transportation to the New World. They arrived with the gift of a notoriously religious nature and with the seeds of songs and other musical forms that would help them to survive. There were indeed major disadvantages in their current status in that they were often situated away from people of their particular society. But perhaps the gift of a religious nature led them to shape community despite their environment.

During an earlier period of history, Africans and Europeans shared a common acceptance of slavery. There was also a common agreement over some aspects of economics, commerce, and revenue, for human enslavement has existed almost from the beginning of human history in practically every place on earth. Lerone Bennett, in his classic work, *Before the Mayflower,* provides a cumulative chronology of ancient slavery from the time before the birth of Moses to the "new" chapter of slavery, which began in the fifteenth century. He notes the following:

> Slavery is not a disgrace peculiar to blacks but a universal phenomenon that has been practiced in almost all centuries. Slavery was old when Moses was young. In Plato's Athens and Caesar's Rome, men—white, black and brown—were bought and sold. Slavery existed in the Middle Ages in Christian Europe and in Africa. In the ancient world almost everyone might become a slave.[1]

Bennett concluded with the observation that ancient slavery had little or nothing to do with race, but was justified principally by rules of war. Then, of course, there is the reality of the development of slavery in Africa, which was linked with the intricacies of the social caste system and the uncontrollable forces of nature. There is no one moment in history that can be identified as the starting point. In a tribal system, the weaker societies yield to stronger ones, and like tumbling dominoes, the status of societal groups shifts. Just as in other cultures, many African societies had rules that dictated how slaves were to be treated. In short, a slave owner never had the power of life and death over a slave. They were neither condemned by their color nor chained forever to a horrid fate as Africans were in seventeenth-century America. Twentieth-century scholars affirm that

> they lived lives similar to many western Europeans. They were tied to the fruits of the land and tended to consider themselves only temporarily enslaved. In other words they were still human, still capably in charge of their own destinies, still with their self-esteem and ability to dream intact.[2]

Prince Henry, born in Portugal in 1394, is historically significant because of his participation in early Portuguese explorations in Africa. At the age of twenty-five, Henry was governor of the southern coasts of Portugal and master (leader) of the Order of Christ. The combination of Henry's yearnings as an explorer, his ambition which rivaled that of a politician, and his zeal for mission led him to recruit sea captains who shared his visions. Thus, the explorations and plundering in Africa began. By 1444, the Portuguese explorers reached the Arguin Island, located off the West African coast, which later became the first processing area for the country's slave trading. After Pope Nicholas V defended "the enslavement of Persons," Portugal took advantage of its open opportunity to operate slaving stations all along the West Coast of Africa. Henry died in 1460, and new names appeared in the annals as proponents of slave trading. By 1469 the West African coast had been given such names as Ivory Coast, Gold Coast, and Slave Coast. Africans were transported to Hispaniola in 1505, and eventually the Antilles sugar plantations were farmed by African slaves. By the mid-sixteenth century, Africans were providing slave labor in the island colonies of Madeira and the Canaries.

In 1563, an adventurer from Plymouth, England, named John Hawkins, entered what is now Sierra Leone. His reputation for plundering was so great that Queen Elizabeth knighted him. His coat of arms was an African in chains. Hawkins's entry marked the beginning of the transportation of African slaves to America. This provoked the Spaniards, who were now participating in the exploration pursuit along with the Portuguese, and in 1568 his ship and cargo were confiscated, although he was able to escape. After this venture, England kept out of the slave trading business for nearly one hundred years.[3]

Roman Catholics in Sub-Saharan Africa

Among the important but often overlooked historical events of earlier centuries is the Roman Catholic missionary connections with sub-Saharan West Africa in the seventeenth century. This relationship was precipitated by Portuguese explorations in places now known as Angola at the end of the fifteenth century. Afonso, the eldest son of King Nzinga of the Congo, had accepted the Roman Catholic faith. With help from the Portuguese, Afonso won a fight for the throne as king of the Congo and ruled from 1506 to 1543. According to correspondence preserved in the "Archives of Simancas" in Portugal, Afonso hoped to convert his people to Catholicism and to utilize the technological knowledge of the Europeans to help his African community.[4] In a heated fray with the Portuguese over slavery, Afonso (known as Afonso the Good), was disappointed with the actions of the Portuguese clergy, who not only began to "live in concubinage with the women of the country" but also began to traffic in slaves.[5] After similar experiences with non-church workers from Portugal (stonemasons, shoemakers, etc.), Afonso discovered that slave trading was whetting the Portuguese appetite to be in Angola and other places on the African continent.

In an effort to stop the trafficking of slaves, Afonso attempted to establish Catholicism in Angola, which would be an institution separate from Portuguese politics. He sent his son, Henrique, to Portugal to study for the priesthood, a common practice among noble Congolese children. An education for Africans outside of African societies was also a way in which Western culture would be transported to African countries. Henry was ordained a priest sometime before 1518, and in 1521 he was made a bishop by Leo X.[6] As Cyprian Davis notes, with the death of Bishop Henrique in 1531 died the hope of a Congolese Catholic Church with direct access to Rome. King Afonso, who was dedicated to the gospel message and to the Roman Church, died in 1543, possibly aware of the impact of the Protestant Reformation and deeply aware of what the slave trade had done to the African continent.[7]

African Catholics in America

Black explorers accompanied Spanish and Portuguese explorers on their expeditions. They were with Pizarro in Peru, Cortes in Mexico, and Menendez in Florida. Thirty blacks were with Balboa when he "discovered" the Pacific Ocean. Some led expeditions, most notably Esteban (or Estevanico, the Spanish form of Stephen), who opened up New Mexico and Arizona for the Spaniards. This led to the emergence of the Roman Catholic Church in the United States.

Esteban was among the explorers in the 1536 Mexican territory exploration. He was a Spanish-speaking slave and a native of Azamor. Davis marks the arrival of Esteban with a dual reminder: "The first black man to traverse what is now the territory of the United States was Spanish-speaking and a Catholic. With his three companions, he is at the beginning of the story of Catholicism in the United States."[8] Esteban was at the forefront of other expeditions on behalf of the Catholic Church and was imprisoned and subsequently killed by Native Americans who did not believe that a black person could be a messenger for a white man. The 1565 settlement was particularly significant because it would later become part of Northern Florida, with St. Augustine as the center of the colony. By the 1700s, black slaves from Georgia and the Carolinas were welcomed to the Spanish settlement, granted refuge, and ultimately allowed to receive their freedom—provided they convert to the Roman Catholic faith.[9] Escaped slaves, now newly Roman Catholic, found a home in a free black settlement located northwest of St. Augustine and its Spanish fort, the Castillo de San Marcos.

Thus, the oldest town in what is now the United States was inhabited by a significant number of black Catholics. According to documents from this period cited by Cyprian Davis:

> Even before its establishment in 1738, a significant number of escaped slaves had arrived from the English settlements. The name given to the settlement was *Gracia Real de Santa Teresa de Moses.* In 1740 General Oglethorpe, the English governor of Georgia, led a military attack on the Florida colony. Oglethorpe's men took Fort Mose, and the women and children found refuge in the Castillo de San Marcos. The blacks formed part of the fighting force that defended St. Augustine and eventually drove the British away from Fort Mose and the Florida coast.[10]

St. Augustine included enslaved and free blacks as well as a military force of black soldiers from Cuba during the eighteenth and nineteenth centuries. Fortunately, the Catholics kept ecclesiastical records from 1565 to 1763 that still exist, with mention of blacks throughout.[11]

Just as slavery in Protestant colonies was at its peak in 1763, the Seven Years' War ended and the colony of Florida was ceded to the British. All Spaniards and persons with Spanish connections were moved from Florida to Cuba. This of course included blacks, slave and free. From 1763 to 1784, Great Britain controlled Florida, and Roman Catholicism, according to Davis, practically disappeared.[12]

Roman Catholicism began to rise again in the St. Augustine and Pensacola areas from 1784 to 1821, when Florida became part of the territory of the United States. The segregated records, the historic set of separate files on blacks and whites, provide a numerical listing of black membership. According to the records, a large number of blacks were baptized, both slave and free, with St. Augustine and Pensacola continuing as centers for black Catholics. In 1788, Cyril of Barcelona, the auxiliary bishop of Havana, insisted that slaveholders should baptize their slaves. There is insufficient evidence for how and when blacks were catechized, whether worshipers were segregated, and what the exact numbers of slave and free blacks were. Also unavailable is what music was used during the liturgy and to what extent blacks participated in singing. Evidence suggests that the Spanish or European parish leaders transported the music, and that the black community of Catholics was not sufficiently together to have created a unique black Catholic genre of songs. This far removed from Vatican II and its urging of black Catholics to reclaim the African heritage, it must be assumed that the African element of "black music" in worship did not exist.

By 1634, Catholicism had been accepted in Maryland, where the second Lord Baltimore, Cecil Calvert, had founded a colony and granted freedom of religion for all Christians. Black slaves were rapidly imported into this colony from the first quarter of the eighteenth century. Like other families in the colony, Catholics were slaveholders and religious corporations owned slaves to facilitate the work on their plantation estates. Davis notes quite adequately that the Catholic Church prior to the Civil War was a community that was itself an image of slavery—the Catholic Church in chains![13] Since black Africans who happened to be Catholics felt the pain of colonies in chains, there was indeed a mutual feeling of powerlessness as blacks connected with conditional Christianity.

Africans in American Protestant Communities

With increasing demands for slave labor, a vigorous slave trade from 1619 to 1860 created communities of slaves in the West Indies and on the American continent. Africans in the West Indies were able to continue many of their religious and musical practices. Living and working conditions in the West Indies were conducive to the preservation of West African cultural patterns because of the many instances of absentee European landlords and their lack of interest in the cultural activities of their African workers.

When slaves were transported to the mainland, geographical locations and the level of severity of the slave system prevented some African practices from being continued. Africans in America were discouraged from continuing, overtly at least, the holistic manner of living with which they were familiar. With new arrivals from the West Indies or directly from Africa, African musical and religious traditions persisted, quite often in secrecy. Expressions of dance and song and the playing of African instruments burst forth during work, worship, and the infrequent times allowed for leisure.

Conditional Christianity, in which whites baptized Africans in order to legalize their importation, was of course not new to some Africans in America. As early as 1664, laws relegated slaves of African descent to perpetual bondage. The colony of Virginia was the first to enact a law that stated in essence that the conferring of baptism would not alter the conditions of the person as to her or his bondage or freedom. By 1706, six colonies had legislated that baptism was not a threat to a slaveholder's legal rights.[14] When slaveholders on Protestant plantations reluctantly allowed slaves to be evangelized, the special vows prepared for slaves placed limits on the gospel message. Many slaves "subjected" themselves to baptism in order to receive some semblance of freedom. The baptismal agreement was as follows:

You declare in the presence of God and before this congregation that you do not ask for this holy baptism out of any design to free yourself from the duty and obedience that you owe to your Master while you live, but merely for the good of your soul and to partake of the graces and blessings promised to the members of the church of Jesus Christ.[15]

From 1619 until near the end of the nineteenth century, Africans arrived, and communities were established in the West Indies and on the North American continent. Gifts of the African culture that survived the African slave trade, and ultimately shaped the spirituals, included such styles as

- call-and-response dialogical participation,
- extemporaneous singing,
- storytelling in song or storytelling linked with song,
- communal involvement in the shaping of songs,
- improvisation of texts and melodies,
- embellishing of melodies and rhythms,
- highly intensive singing with special vocal effects such as falsetto, ululation, groans, shouts, and guttural tones.

The melodic scales were predominantly pentatonic and modal, with embellishments ranging from simple grace notes, vocal turns built around a single note, and bending of tones to highly florid, melismatic musical phrases. Other African characteristics are

- rhythmic complexities in the music and in the manner of delivery,
- extended repetition of short melodic phrases,
- handclapping and other bodily percussion rhythms.

African American spirituals are defined as religious folk songs created, shaped, and transmitted orally by communities of African people enslaved in America. In keeping with the African folk song tradition, spirituals are spontaneous testimonials and documentation of existential experiences, theological beliefs, and attitudes. There is most often some evidence of continuity that links current situations with past experiences. As an orally transmitted music form, folk songs undergo changes and variations, reflecting particular times and situations of the singing communities. Henry E. Krehbiel observes in this connection that "folksongs are echoes of the heartbeat of the vast folk, and in them are preserved feelings, belief and habits of vast antiquity . . . not only in the words . . . but also in music."[16]

The process by which the spirituals were honed allowed for individual and communal expression of the heartbeat of an enslaved people seeking freedom and justice. The process was a means of perpetuating significant elements of holistic African primal worldviews, continuing the understanding that there is no separation between the secular and the sacred. Earlier scholars who questioned the absence of religious phraseology in some of the spirituals did not take into consideration the African worldview that all of life is essentially religious. It is religious in a broad sense that every human being regardless of culture must have something to believe in and live by. John Lovell encapsulates this in his observation that

> they [spirituals] were not religious songs in the sense of a compartment of life, nor religious in the sense of the theology of the camp meeting, nor religious because they often use Biblical symbols. . . . They were religious and spiritual because they tried, with inspired artistry, to pose the root question of life, of before life and beyond life, and to react to these questions as the aroused human being and the bestirred folk have done since the rosy dawn of literature.[17]

Africans enslaved and transported to North America from 1619 forward came from various societies and tribes with different languages; thus, there were no common linguistic utterances for many years.[18] The first songs were no doubt African chants individually offered in the workplaces, not as solos but as a primary means of establishing some form of communication. With large numbers of newly captured Africans enslaved subsequently by law, developing a common linguistic tongue was indeed a slow process. Nevertheless, communal songs emerged through a process for which their African heritage prepared them. By trial and error Africans in America transformed the Euro-American language into a singing language whose intonations resembled their own ancestral tongues. By shifting accents, eliding certain syllables, restructuring the pronunciation of words, and emptying themselves into the music and text, enslaved Africans created a soulful song form that has spawned many additional forms and styles.

Syncretisms: From African Beliefs and Euro-American Christianity to African American Christianity

Sufficient data suggests that Africans were possibly exposed to the Christian faith along the Gulf of Guinea and in the West Indies during the Middle Passage, prior to their enslavement as African Americans. There is also the possibility that some slaves may have made a partial transition from their native religions to Christianity prior to mainline evangelization. Slaves brought to the West Indies as early as 1517 had been educated as Catholics, and by 1540 there was a black man in Quivira, Mexico, who had taken holy orders.[19]

In 1619, a year before the Pilgrims landed in Massachusetts on the *Mayflower,* the first permanent African settlers arrived in Jamestown, Virginia, and were put to work as indentured servants. Portuguese sailors had stolen this group of persons from a Spanish vessel bound for the West Indies. Among the group of twenty-one African passengers were Isabella and Antoney, who later married. Their son, William, was born in approximately 1623 and was baptized in the Church of England.[20] It is not certain whether Isabella or Antoney were baptized before they left Africa or when they arrived in the New World. Unfortunately, there are no records detailing other aspects of their lives. As indentured servants they were eventually freed to live among landowners, some of whom became successful businesspersons along the Pungoteague Creek on the Eastern Shore of Virginia.

According to the first detailed census in 1624–1625, persons of African descent constituted nearly 2 percent of the total population of 1,227 persons, all of whom lived in three settlements in Virginia.[21] This period marked the beginning of African families in the New World, for they were individuals whose rite of passage to slave ships might have been a hasty baptism in order to legalize their slave status.

During this period, slaveholders were reluctant to engage in any form of systematic evangelization of slaves. Their initial hesitancy was due to their concerns that Africans were incapable of learning and thus unfit to seek conversion into the Christian faith. There is documentation in the Dutch Reformed Church, New Amsterdam, as early as 1638 of the desire for a teacher to train Dutch and African children in the knowledge of Christ. The baptism and reception of a "Negro" woman into the church in Dorchester, Massachusetts, in 1641 is evidence that some time was given to providing Christian instruction for the edification of individual Africans in America, albeit outside of the sanctuary.[22]

The first organized efforts to convert Africans to Christianity occurred in 1701 with the establishment of the Society for the Propagation of the Gospel in Foreign Parts (SPG) by the Church of England. Of great significance was the introduction and continued use of psalm singing in the religious instruction of African Americans. Eileen Southern cites numerous instances from primary sources, including the following from 1726 that describes how the rector and vestry of a certain congregation observed that

> upwards of a hundred English and Negro servants attended the catechism on Sundays and sang psalms at the close of the instruction. In the same church the Reverend Richard Charlton reported to his superior in 1741 that forty-three Negroes were studying psalmody with the church organist. . . .

I can scarce express the satisfaction I have in seeing 200 Negroes and White persons with heart and voice glorifying their Maker.[23]

Numerous primary sources affirm the importance of singing as a preferred activity of the religious experience for Africans enslaved in America. Their musical gifts and preference for psalmody is referred to in an often cited quote from a letter written by Presbyterian missionary Samuel Davies to supporters in London: "The Negroes above all the Human Species that I ever knew, have an Ear for Musick, and a kind of [ecstatic] Delight in *Psalmody* and there are no Books they learn so soon or take so much pleasure in, as those used in the heavenly part of divine Worship."[24]

The psalms and hymns of Isaac Watts, noted English preacher and hymnist, were well loved by the slaves who were able to receive religious instruction. Some of Watts's settings were published in colonial editions as early as 1729. The missionaries recognized the slaves' preference for Watts, and so they requested Watts's hymnals along with Bibles in their orders sent to London. Since the persons in bondage had not been given an opportunity to be educated, their capacity for remembering facilitated their creative gifts. The spoken and sung words that slaves remembered would be reshaped into new melodies and harmonies by a small group of workers and recreated in songs that later became known as spirituals. These "creators" may never have attended a worship service, nor were they concerned about doctrines of a faith of a people that they did not understand. Their chief concern might have been the joy of singing and creating with a folk community with whom they were of equal status. Songs with biblical terms would be familiar to plantation owners and overseers, and thus could be easily created and performed by slaves with the intent of communicating a dual message. Many biblical terms were used as codes to communicate messages within the slave community, especially escape routes to freedom and clandestine meetings for worship, and to announce the locations of Underground Railroad stations. Exposure to the English language and concepts of the Christian faith, along with thoroughly ingrained African worldviews, were combined into an early shaping of a theology lived out and expressed in songs.

The earliest songs are identified as African chants, work songs, and field cries for freedom. The chart at the end of this chapter provides a visual clue of the evolutionary process and the overlapping of traditions. New songs in a "strange and alien land" allowed Africans in America to preserve their feelings and beliefs in the midst of their bondage.

The structural pattern of these new songs reflects the African song tradition, which allows the individual to be in continual dialogue with the community. Spirituals, like other music of the slaves, allowed a potential outlet for communal binding and expression characteristic of African peoples. Lawrence Levine notes that "slave music confronts us with evidence which indicates that, however seriously the slave system may have diminished the central community that had bound African societies together, it was never able to destroy it totally or to leave the individual atomized and psychically defenseless."[25]

Though the term *spiritual song* was in use long before the African American spiritual emerged, the religious roots of spirituals as a genre are in the folk song tradition of African peoples. Africans sang in North America as they had sung on the African continent, on slave ships, and in the Middle Passage. During the transition from Africa to the Americas and from their native languages to newly acquired languages, musically creative African peoples continued, naturally, what they had been accustomed to doing. With strict laws supporting the slave system, musical expressions developed among enslaved communities of African Americans as a means of survival, as well as a means of communication.

The exact date of origin of spirituals as a musical genre cannot be established, nor is it known exactly when the term *spiritual* (or "sperichil") was first used to identify this African American musical genre. It is clear, however, that spirituals emerged prior to the reluctant, half-hearted, and sporadic Christian evangelization of slaves in the Americas. In an environment where Christian slave owners doubted the mental abilities of their "human cargo" and their capacity for understanding the tenets of the faith, African slaves found comfort in their own religious traditions. Their human plight led them to continue their own African chants and create new songs that transcended linguistic barriers. They moaned, hummed, and sang as they worked, creating new song forms that would be foundational to the spirituals. African chants, field hollers, work songs, and personal and communal cries of liberation are the musical precursors for the content, forms, and styles of spirituals.

Before examining and classifying the texts of some of the spirituals as "liturgical music," it must be made clear from the outset that words alone are insufficient as an approach to classifying African American songs as "religious" or "nonreligious." For people who do not dichotomize "sacred" and "secular," any song shaped in response to the actions of the Creator at work in the universe can be considered sacred or religious. Therefore, one must consider the text and melody, the social context, and the manner of performance. In view of the fact that this folk song genre evolved as a communal process over a period of time, the original intent and usage was obviously determined by the communities participating in the process.

Numerous scholars have approached the study of spirituals from a sociological perspective, emphasizing their origin from needed changes in society, protest, and resistance to slavery.[26] This documentation affirms the possibility that all spirituals were not shaped by Christian believers, since some African American slaves remained skeptical about converting to the religion of their oppressors. Certain metaphors, key words, phrases, and biblical names served dual purposes in the spirituals, providing "freedom traveling" directions to thousands of slaves.

The Invisible Institution

Although some of the slaves were allowed to worship with the planters in designated areas, much of the shaping of African American worship forms took place in secret, out of the sight and hearing range of Euro-American planters. In such clandestine places as "brush harbors" in the woods, in swamps and slave cabins, slaves transformed the Americanized version of Christianity into forms with which they could identify. The practice of worshiping in these secret places later became identified as the "Invisible Institution." This label affirms the clandestine or "invisible" nature of separate worship spaces, where the slaves officially constituted mutual relationships, worldviews, religious behavioral patterns, and political actions.[27] Regular Sunday worship in local churches (when permitted) was paralleled by secret services whenever slaves were able to "steal away." According to testimonies from slaves, slaves forbidden to attend church or to even pray risked floggings to attend secret gatherings to worship. They prayed and poured out their sufferings and needs of the day.[28] In song, Africans in America were lifted closer to God and to each other as they struggled to bear the conditions of their forced existential situation. Singing provided the divine channel through which God spoke and believers responded, and this remains true today.

Camp Meetings

Camp meetings were a special feature of Euro-American frontier life. Large revivals in Kentucky and Tennessee spawned the camp meeting tradition, which served as an emotional release for families of planters and slaveholders who sought an escape from daily "boredom." In 1798, three congregations in Logan County, Kentucky, founded this religious movement under the leadership of a Presbyterian minister who was later joined by Methodists and Baptists. Few African American slaves were allowed to attend the initial services, and those who did attend might have been free blacks. As slaves were granted opportunities to attend, they contributed mightily to the physical and emotional fervor of the evening religious experience.

The evangelical fervor of the Great Awakening appealed to the slaves' natural propensity to sing and for holistic physical involvement in worship. They attended camp meetings in large numbers and worshiped and sang with Euro-Americans. In this environment, many slaves were converted. Some African Americans found in the camp meeting not only their first extensive exposure to Christianity but also a religious atmosphere better suited to their spiritual and emotional needs. Camp meetings also accelerated the growth and spread of African American spirituals. After the regular services, African Americans would continue the momentum in separate quarters with a preacher whom the community had designated and a bottomless reservoir of biblical stories, faith expressions, and personal testimonies waiting to be shaped into spirituals. Their uninhibited enthusiasm for singing punctuated each element of worship and stirred the souls of a people who knew that they would face the reality of their human bondage at dawn after the benediction was pronounced.[29]

Another religious practice that utilized spirituals for Africans in the North American Diaspora was the "ring shout." This practice originated in the Southeast and can best be described as a ritualized group activity clearly of African origin, lasting up to five hours.[30] The ring shout was an example of the fusion of the sacred and secular, music, and dance. After a detailed description of this dance in *African American Christian Worship*, the author notes:

> Since regular dancing for the converted was prohibited by the evangelizers, care was taken to distinguish between their Spirit-filled inspiration and cathartic longings from mere worldly dancing. One way to do this was to refrain from lifting the feet from the floor or crossing one foot over the other as would happen in regular dancing.[31]

Power in black music, according to Samuel Floyd, centers in his interpretation of the "ring shout" of African origin. He argues that

> from the ring [shout] emerged the shuffling, angular, off-beat additive, intensive, unflagging rhythms of shout and jubilee spirituals, Rag time, R&B [rhythm and blues]; . . . the less vigorous but equally insistent and characteristic rhythms of "sorrow songs" and blues; and all the musical genres derived from these and other early forms.[32]

Early Published Collections of Spirituals

With the incorporation of spirituals in many current denominational and ecumenical hymnals, a larger number of worshiping communities can experience the variety of forms and styles from this vast repertoire of songs. Equally significant in these collections is some evidence about the longevity of spirituals as liturgical offerings. One cannot express with certainty that musicians, even African Americans whose heritage of song is founded upon this tradition, will keep the spirituals alive with even a portion of the fervor and sincerity that the thousands of black creators invested.

One of the most definitive scholarly documentations of the spirituals is the work of John Lovell, Jr., whose research in the 1970s revealed that there were approximately six thousand independently cataloged spirituals in five hundred original collections published before 1940.[33] While this number is astounding, there is no doubt that this number represents hardly more than a mere fraction of songs that were lost from disuse or buried in the memory of those who were "carried home" before the songs could be recorded. Since this time, the number of songbooks that include spirituals for liturgical use has increased dramatically. In addition to the plethora of new arrangements of the six thousand extant spirituals identified, new, unpublished spirituals continue to emerge from congregational repertoires, especially in the "low country" of South Carolina and Georgia. This is an affirmation of the strength and ongoing process of the oral tradition. It is my contention that spirituals are constantly in the process of "becoming" as they are adapted to address spiritual needs in new contexts.

The first published collection of spirituals, *Slave Songs of the United States*, was published in 1867.[34] The melodic settings are based on what the editors heard, combined with their interpretation of rhythms and bending of phrases. Without the availability of recording equipment, transcribers are required to listen several times to the same phrase, which is often rendered differently each time. Despite possible inaccuracies, this collection opened the door to the reality of a repertoire of songs that continue to live almost a century and a half later.

The "Directions for Singing," which follow the table of contents, are concerned primarily with the manner in which the songs were performed.[35] Immediately noticeable is documentation of the different ways slaves were treated in the states represented and the specific matters affecting their religious development. Charles P. Ware gathered the largest collection of spirituals on St. Helena Island, off the coast of Georgia. The geographical location of this isolated island lends itself to a continuation of African and West Indian traditions, and to the establishment of a common language. Songs are included from the Sea Islands and the following slave states: Delaware, Maryland, Virginia, North Carolina, South Carolina, Georgia, Tennessee, Arkansas, and Mississippi.

Other collections of spirituals were published after the emergence of black colleges and universities in the late nineteenth century. Two significant early collections are *The Story of the Jubilee Singers with Their Songs*[36] and *Religious*

Folk Songs of the Negro as Sung at Hampton Institute.[37] Compilations by Nicholas Ballanta, James Weldon Johnson and J. Rosamond Johnson, and Fisk University professor John W. Work set the momentum for the numerous collections that followed.[38]

As could be expected, some early commentary on spirituals negated their authenticity as unique songs of an enslaved people. The most prevalent arguments against their authenticity have been adequately refuted and are recalled here for information. There is neither sufficient space nor is it this author's intent to recall the names of authors, either for or against the arguments.[39] Some claimed that the spirituals

- were borrowed from so-called Euro-American spirituals and other songs of slaveholders,
- contained no evidence of an African heritage and that Africa was too far removed from the creators of the spirituals,
- were strictly otherworldly in nature, with slaves wishing only for a physical death to escape, and
- related strictly to a desire to return to Africa.

Characteristics of the Spirituals

Spirituals provide a historical record of a people who, in their oppressed status, discovered the values and the order needed to survive in an alien land. They did this by creating an internal universe with which they were familiar as African people. Initially, it was illegal to permit a slave to read, write, and assemble in a group of more than five or six persons. By 1700, American slavery had been declared legal, and the laws restricting the social gathering of slaves had begun to be enforced. There is some evidence that if family connections among slaves were encouraged or permitted, the slave family existed primarily for the utilitarian purpose of the slave economy.[40]

The historical roots of the African past were not destroyed under the laws of slavery. The heritage of the "oral tradition" was maintained, especially through music, song, and dance. Matters of concern that the slaves were not able to express in public places were expressed in songs through words and symbols that the slave owners could not interpret. Songs and musical expressions that led to the shaping of spirituals include such genres as African chants, cries for deliverance, moans, and "field hollers." These allowed the slaves to maintain a sense of humanity and identity among themselves, but also kept hope alive. They marked the beginning of religious music, some of which was shaped and flamed in worship settings.

An outline of key characteristics of the spirituals follows:

- similarity to African songs in form, intervallic structure, harmony, and rhythm;
- sequence of usage of modes (major, pentatonic, mixed, or vague);
- melodic intervals that do not regularly employ many large skips but are vocally diatonic, reflecting the rise and fall of vocal inflections;
- repetitive melodies that lend themselves to ornamentation and other forms of improvisation;
- a characteristic style governed by the emotional state, with sliding on and off the note;
- improvised texts that reflect sensitivity and quick responses to the whole range of human emotions;
- texts from the Bible (King James Version), daily life experiences, the world of nature, and personal experiences of religion;
- texts often filled with symbols and masks, unique imageries, with allusions and hidden double-coded meanings;
- the speed of songs and ending rhythmic cadences governed by the character and the spirit of the text;
- the use of antiphonal, "call-and-response" mode, which is effective for communal participation;
- the use of various rhythms, from slow and plaintive to pulsating and energetic;
- the use of texts that most often include personal "I" and "me," generally in order to allow each person to feel as if she or he were in the midst of the story or action or in total agreement and identity with the idea;
- recurring themes of hope and confidence in the Almighty/Most High.

In order to understand the spiritual, it is necessary to identify themes and meanings in accordance to the needs and desires for expression and communication among the people as a folk community. The melodies, harmonies, and rhythms created to carry forth the texts are examples of folk creations from a wide range of subjects. Some are considered "sorrow songs," which stress the hope and underlie the sorrow that the community is experiencing at the moment.[41] Some are cries and pleas to unite the community for common goals of physical freedom and for freedom of the human spirit.

No matter how spirituals are phrased, they communicate essentially the faith expression of an oppressed people. Many are exuberant expressions of the joy that members of a community internalize when hope in Jesus the Christ gives them reason to live. Few songs surpass their truthfulness, spontaneity, and uninhibited expressions of life.

African American Music Timeline

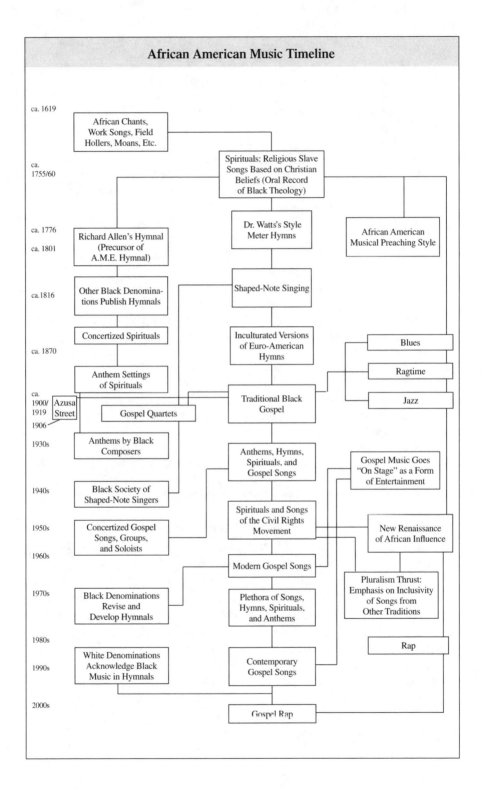

Chapter 3

African American Hymnody

The hymn is one of the genres of music that African Americans adapted for use early in their worship experiences. The word comes from the Greek *hymnos,* which is "a song of praise to a god or hero." This definition implies a free poetic form set to music rather than poetry that rhymes and is organized so that each stanza is sung to the same music. This latter form of composition is strophic. The opposite of strophic is through composed, in which new music is used for each stanza.

Examples of songs of praise to the Divine can be traced to non-Western traditions before and during the Christian era (C.E.). A few examples are the Vedic hymnals of East India from as early as 1500 B.C.E., the Egyptian "Hymn to Aton," dating from 1300 B.C.E., and Chinese hymns dating from the T'sang dynasty (618–907 C.E.). Significant among these hymns is the "Hymn to Aton," which was found in a tomb at Tell el-Amara, Egypt, the capital of the so-called reforming pharaoh, Akh-en-Aton (Amenhotep IV, 1380–1362 B.C.E.). This hymn expresses the universal beneficence and recreating power of the sun disc (Aton) with reminders that each new day is a new creation. Because of similarities in both content and form, scholars over the centuries have concurred that the writer(s) of Psalm 104 borrowed from this Egyptian hymn.[1]

The earliest Christocentric definition of the term *hymn* is provided by Augustine of Hippo (354–430) in his commentary on Psalm 148:

> Hymns are songs containing the praise of God. If there be praise, and it is not of God, it is not a hymn; if there be praise, and praise of God, and it is not sung, it is not a hymn. If it is to be a hymn, therefore, it must have three things: praise, and that of God, and song.[2]

This definition might not have been familiar to Africans in America during the seventeenth and eighteenth centuries when they were exposed to the Protestant Psalter and the hymns of Isaac Watts. Nevertheless, evidence abounds to the existence of African bonded servants who enthusiastically sang hymns. This further attests to the natural musical gifts of African people. In 1707, Watts, an English minister, published the first of many hymns that would eventually change the course of Protestant hymnody in general and initiate a lineage of African American liturgical music. Watts's concept of hymnody and congregational praise incorporated his concern that Christian songs should go beyond the words of Scripture to include original expressions of praise, thanksgiving, devotion, and yearnings for spiritual renewal. Watts was able to demonstrate his ability to express this in his "hymns of human composure," which encourage outward expressions of inner feelings and deep emotions. He also demonstrated in his hymnic outpourings that Hebrew psalms could be interpreted and made useful for Christian worship by giving them Christian content, applicable to contemporary contexts. A few examples that continue in the African American worship experience include:

- Psalm 23—"My Shepherd Will Supply My Need"
- Psalm 72—"Jesus Shall Reign"
- Psalm 90—"O God, Our Help in Ages Past"
- Psalm 117—"From All That Dwell Below the Skies"

With hymns such as these, Watts provided an impetus and vision for other hymn writers, including Charles Wesley. His model was also a strong factor in promoting and nourishing evangelical revivals. The hymns of Isaac Watts and the growth of hymnody influenced African American music and the liturgical musical style of the black church into the second millennium.

Some of the characteristics of Watts's hymns, which clearly appealed to African American slaves, include: (1) use of uncomplicated metrical systems, with a preference for common, long, and short meters; (2) simplicity of vocabulary and dominance of one-syllable words; and (3) frequent use of repetition.

During the Great Awakening in the 1730s, a new religious movement swept the colonies, bringing with it lively congregational hymn singing and emotional preaching. This form of worship freed black worshipers to become emotionally involved, in what was at that time a "foreign" religion but one they would soon shape in the light of their own existential situation and African worldviews. Again, numerous references exist regarding the ability of African worshipers to grasp the melody of the revival songs. In instances when the words were not clear, Africans improvised during the worship services, "doctoring" the texts and tunes in private quarters.

While some religious workers among the Africans enslaved in America highlighted evidence of spiritual and emotional growth, Rev. Samuel Davies (who became president of Nassau—later Princeton University in New Jersey) acknowledged progress in their intellectual capacities. In addition to books with texts of psalms and hymns, spelling books were among the gifts from England. Davies describes the eagerness with which Africans at worship helped each other find the lines of the texts that were being sung, and then break out in "a torrent of sacred harmony, enough to bear the whole congregations to heaven . . ."[3]

Metrical Patterns

The interchangeable expressions "meter hymns" and "meter music" are African American designations for an improvised style of Protestant lined-hymn singing in nonmetrical fashion. The term *meter*, which means "measure," refers to the systematic measurement of rhythmic accents in poetry and music. The terminology used and the manner of measuring the accents of the text of poetry and music were inherited from ancient Greece. The most prevalent poetic metrical unit is the iambic foot, which consists of an unaccented syllable followed by an accented syllable.[4] An example of a hymn utilizing the iambic foot is Isaac Watts's "When I Survey the Wondrous Cross," whose first stanza appears below with the accented syllables in uppercase letters:

When *I* sur*VEY* the *WON* drous *CROSS*	(8 syllables)
On *WHICH* the *PRINCE* of *GLO* ry *DIED*	(8 syllables)
My *RICH* est *GAIN* I *COUNT* but *LOSS*	(8 syllables)
And *POUR* con *TEMPT* on *ALL* my *PRIDE*	(8 syllables)

In a musical setting of poetry, the number of syllables in a single line rather than the kind and number of metrical feet is the determining factor of meter. A single line of poetry is called a *verse*. Thus, the line "When I survey the wondrous cross" is considered one verse. Four lines of poetry or four verses comprise a *stanza*. Thus, the four lines above are considered one stanza of the hymn. An occurrence of eight syllables in each line is identified as "long meter," and it is indicated either by numbers (8888; 8.8.8.8; or 88.88), or by the letters *LM*. Another example is this familiar setting of the "Doxology":

Praise God from whom all blessings flow;	(8 syllables)
Praise him all creatures here below;	(8 syllables)
Praise him above ye heavenly host;	(8 syllables)
Praise Father, Son, and Holy Ghost.	(8 syllables)

A hymn containing eight lines of poetry with the same number of syllables in each line is identified as a long meter doubled (LMD, or 8888 8888). A familiar hymn in this meter is "Sweet Hour of Prayer."

A stanza of four lines with eight syllables in the first and third lines and six syllables in the second and fourth lines is identified as "common meter," indicated either by numbers (8686; 8.6.8.6; or 86.86), or by the letters *CMA*. Doubling of the lines of each stanza is likewise indicated "common meter doubled" or *CMD*. An example of common meter is "Amazing Grace":

Amazing grace! How sweet the sound	(8 syllables)
That saved a wretch like me!	(6 syllables)
I once was lost but now am found	(8 syllables)
Was blind, but now I see.	(6 syllables)

An example of common meter doubled (CMD) is "It Came upon the Midnight Clear":

It came upon the midnight clear,	(8 syllables)
That glorious song of old,	(6 syllables)
From angels bending near the earth,	(8 syllables)
To touch their harps of gold;	(6 syllables)
"Peace on the earth, good will to all,	(8 syllables)
From heaven's all gracious King."	(6 syllables)
The world in solemn stillness lay	(8 syllables)
To hear the angels sing.	(6 syllables)

In like manner, short meter (SM; 6686; 6.6.8.6; or 66.68) indicates stanzas of four lines of poetry, with the first, second, and fourth lines consisting of six syllables each, and eight syllables in the third line. An example of short meter is "A Charge to Keep I Have":

A charge to keep I have,	(6 syllables)
A God to glorify,	(6 syllables)
A never dying soul to save,	(8 syllables)
And fit it for the sky.	(6 syllables)

Short meter doubled is indicated as *SMD* or 6.68.66.68.6. An example is "This Is My Father's World":

This is my Father's world,	(6 syllables)
And to my list'ning ears	(6 syllables)
All nature sings, and round me rings	(8 syllables)
The music of the spheres.	(6 syllables)

This is my Father's world;	(6 syllables)
I rest in me in the thought	(6 syllables)
Of rocks and trees, of skies and seas;	(8 syllables)
His hands the wonders wrought	(6 syllables)

Another variation applicable to this and other metrical settings is the addition of a refrain. An example of short meter with refrain is "Rejoice, Ye Pure in Heart":

Rejoice, ye pure in heart;	(6 syllables)
Rejoice, give thanks, and sing;	(6 syllables)
Your glorious banner wave on high,	(8 syllables)
The cross of Christ your King.	(6 syllables)
Rejoice, rejoice, rejoice give thanks and sing.	(Refrain)

Other songs for worship are identified by the number of syllables in each line of poetry or by the abbreviation *irr.* An example is "What a Mighty God We Serve!" (77667; 7.7.6.6.7; or *irr.*):

What a mighty God we serve;	(7 syllables)
What a mighty God we serve;	(7 syllables)
Angels bow before him,	(6 syllables)
Heav'n and earth adore him;	(6 syllables)
What a mighty God we serve.	(7 syllables)

Two additional meters no longer in use are the *hallelujah meter* (6.66.68.8) and *particular meter* (PM), apparently another designation for *irregular*. Neither of these designations is in current hymnals, but they were both used occasionally during the nineteenth century.

Meter Hymns

Terminology such as we have just seen was of no concern to seventeenth- and eighteenth-century African Americans in bondage. Their ability and desire to sing and their gift for improvising found a new arena in which to offer praise to Almighty God in spirit and in truth. Hymnbooks were not available for use by congregations, and like many Euro-American worshipers, African Americans would have found having the words in hand a hindrance, since many could not read. The early hymnals contained texts of songs most often with the alphabetical reference to the meter (e.g., LM, CM, SM), but did not include music. It was necessary for a song leader or precentor to chant or line out both the words and the melody, phrase by phrase or line by line, with the congregation repeating the leader. It was the responsibility of the precentor to establish an appropriate pitch and to project the sound loudly enough so that the congregation's interest could be maintained. This style of singing was established by Euro-American worshipers in the 1640s and was adapted from the Church of England.

This procedure was observed and practiced by African American worshipers who had no idea or concern that metrical terminology and accents of poetry had been adapted from the Greeks or that they were used in folk psalmody in England and Scotland because of the illiteracy among Europeans. Africans in the first colonial century joined in singing metrical versions of the psalms to a few tunes remembered by song leaders. They were, no doubt, a part of congregations that sang by rote from *The Bay Psalm Book* of 1640, the first book printed in America with an English imprint. Black faces no doubt wore mixed expressions of joy and pain as they sang tunes that were offered in newly improvised versions at worship, weddings, funerals, or wherever freedom was granted to sing. The 1698 edition of *The Bay Psalm Book*, which was published with music and is acknowledged as the oldest existing music of American imprint, might have been a familiar document for some African American "deacons," and the source of some lined psalms in clandestine gatherings.

The "lined hymn" style was also known as "surge singing" because of the way in which the congregation rushed into singing the song, often before the completion of a phrase by the precentor. The lined approach to singing was similar to the call-and-response process deeply embedded in their African heritage and continued in their work songs and in the shaping and transmitting of spirituals.

Psalm singing in the Euro-American styles and the African call-and-response style coexisted and ultimately became the foundation for black meter hymnody. The singing of psalms by African Americans in their own meetings might have served several purposes: as an expression of their enjoyment of psalmody, or as a means of creating "free" time and space simply to sing to the glory of God and to edify each other.[5] Indeed, one reason could have led to another, thus providing an opportunity for the shaping of the black lined-hymn tradition. In private spaces, African Americans borrowed the terms *common meter*, *long meter*, and *short meter*, added soul to the skeletal Euro-American form, and created an oral form and style that continues today as a uniquely African American liturgical form. Fortunately, many of the tunes have continued in the memory of congregations and individuals and have been transmitted through the centuries. Many of these melodies have been scored in skeletal form, and like songs in all folk traditions, they take on a new meaning and new life according to existential situations.

Unlike the metered psalms and Watts's hymns that reached full expression during the Great Awakening, African American-metered music had nothing to do with an accurate metrical reading or setting of the text. The rhythm was established by the designated song leader and identified either as long meter, short meter, or common meter. Particular styles of metered hymnody emerged in local communities, but such styles were defined by the community and were therefore not identical. The focus was on a description of the meter. "Long" meant that the phrases were long and that the song would be sung for a long time. "Short" meter meant that the phrases were shorter and would consume less time. The meaning of "common meter" was never quite clear. The words were lined out or actually "tuned" melodically by the song leader or "deacon," followed by the surging in of the congregation often before the leader finished. The congregation sang what they could remember of a melody, creating and overlaying newly improvised melodies that were not only appropriate for the text but evoked a deeply spiritual worshiping ethos.

This style of singing among Euro-Americans received negative comments and ultimately led to the introduction of the fundamentals of music, "singing schools," and the publication of practical instruction books on singing. Thomas Walter, an early-eighteenth-century clergyman and writer, describes the singing in Euro-American churches:

> The tunes are now miserably tortured and twisted and quavered in our churches, into a horrid medley of confused and disorderly voices. Our tunes are left to the mercy of every unskilled throat to chop and alter and to twist and change. I have myself paused twice in one note to take a breath. No two [men] in the congregation quaver alike or together. It sounds in the ears of a good judge like five hundred tunes roared out at the same time, with perpetual [interferings] with one another.[6]

By 1720, Euro-American congregations set about to improve the manner and quality of congregational singing by emphasizing exact pitches and strict tempos with no improvisations. Singing schools were organized so that people could be instructed in proper singing and sight reading. The use of organs was encouraged in churches as a way of accompanying instruments for congregational singing. Trained singers were organized into church choirs, and compilations of Psalters and hymns with music were made available for congregational singing. By 1838, music was established in the public schools of Boston, and singing schools later became foundational for public school music programs in numerous other urban settings.

Dr. Watts's Meter-Hymn Performance Style

In African American communities the practice of "lining out" and "raising hymns from the floor" continues as an example of the oral tradition of African Americans. In many places in the southeastern United States, especially among (but not limited to) African American congregations, this tradition continues. In small southern communities, lined hymn singing permeates worship across denominations in most if not all black congregations, including Presbyterian, African Methodist Episcopal (AME), African Methodist Episcopal Zion (AMEZ), Christian Methodist Episcopal (CME), Baptist, and, on rare occasions, Pentecostal. This tradition is confined to deeply emotional worship services, and is often referred to as "Dr. Watts's style," since its earlier usage related to an African American manner of singing hymns by Isaac Watts. Wyatt Tee Walker has observed, "The meter hymns in no way displaced the spiritual music. It simply represented an expanding religious consciousness and changed social context that was reflected in the growing musical repertoire of the ex-slaves."[7]

Metered hymns are performed without instrumental accompaniment in varying manners but with the following characteristics: The song leader (deacon or deaconess) "lines out" or presents the first line of the hymn melodically, in a type of voice production or vocal recitation that is partially sung and partially spoken (*sprechstimme,* in German). The congregation can surge in near the end of the line and establish and shape a melody. This line is spiritually massaged unhurriedly by the congregation as members identify with the thoughts expressed according to their spiritual needs. The second line is then offered, with all lines subsequently presented and sung. This is truly an oral tradition that varies from place to place and must be learned through experience. Efforts to accompany this form of congregational singing have been attempted throughout the centuries. The fact that this genre originated in an era when instruments were not available to worshipers is not the reason to avoid instruments. Lined metered hymns should be sung a cappella. There are occasions in current worship services when instrumentalists attempt to take over the leadership. By so doing the traditionally a cappella performance practice is negated. A skilled, aggressive song leader can alter this situation by "reclaiming" the intended a cappella practice for the congregation.

The Importance of Black Meter Music

Like other barometers of the social and religious status of a people, black meter music served in the past as a gauge for the worship and social life of African Americans. During the late seventeenth and early eighteenth centuries, musical forms and styles continually overlapped, with a gradual decline in congregational use of spirituals. Admittedly, there was no empirical research conducted in African American congregations during these critical years. Much that has been written is speculation. There were also apparent trends leading to the development of gospel music. In addition, historically black denominations and the number of black congregations in Euro-American denominations increased. Assuming that the emergence of meter as an oral art form occurred at the end of the eighteenth century with peak involvement occurring during the nineteenth century, this form also paralleled the antebellum, reconstruction, and postreconstruction eras. It also paralleled the development of life in the city and the church in the North, where some African American middle-class persons who could read and those who generally loved music could attend concerts held at African American churches. In addition, the emergence of black meter music coincided with the publication of newspapers such as *Freedom's Journal*, the first black newspaper in the United States (1827–1829), *The Rights of All* (1829), the *Weekly Advocate* (1837), the *Colored American* (1837–1842), and Frederick Douglass's paper, the *North Star.*

Meter hymns are an ongoing reminder of the stability of the sacred heritage. They are one form of sacred music that has not gone on stage to become a form of entertainment. This was attempted for a brief period, but this form quickly returned to the black sanctuary, where it survives and thrives and where the clergy and musicians understand its African American–centered status.

African American Hymnody

Christian hymnody is a collective term for the sacred song literature designed to express the attitude of believers about God and God's purposes in human life in and through Jesus the Christ. Ideas expressed in these texts should embody the lived experiences of the community and stretch singers and listeners to hear God speak beyond their own experiences as they affirm the wideness of the body of Christ. The musical support of the text should be simple enough to inspire and unite the gathered community as their feelings and emotions put them in touch with the power of the Holy Spirit. Together, both text and music should thrust the congregation into the depth of their being so that they can be nurtured, healed, and sent forth into God's world to be of service.

African American hymnody is the specific area of the collective body of songs that has emerged from black people. As suggested by Wendell Phillips Whalum, African American hymnody is "all serious music that is sacred to the Black experience . . . [and] all the serious music that falls within the boundaries of Christianity as it seized the Black experience as well as that serious music which was sacred to the experience, but not necessarily Christian in nature."[8]

While affirming this understanding of African American hymnody, this section will focus on the African American heritage of denominational and ecumenical strophic hymns as recorded in hymnbooks and other scholarly published sources. Fortunately, the information available in published hymnals and other resources supports my belief that African Americans, both in oral musical traditions and in published form, have always taken corporate theological witness seriously. An affirmation of the textual expression of hymns chosen for African American liturgical usage is a more recent scholarly pursuit that is presented more or less in summary here.[9] This includes the choices of hymn texts composed by nonblacks but adapted for use in African American worship across denominations and congregations. This ecumenical heritage ultimately led to the compilation and publication of the *African American Heritage Hymnal* during the early years of the twenty-first century.

A study of the texts of published hymnals reminds us of the importance of documenting the liturgical life of a people in the truest sense of the word, so that present and future generations can profit from lived experiences expressed in song.

The Evolution of Published Hymnals by African Americans

The African Methodist Episcopal Church

Although various Baptist congregations are often touted as the first separate African American congregations established, African American Methodists are noted for their adamant withdrawal, which subsequently led to the founding of other African American denominations.[10] Richard Allen, a self-educated former slave and ordained Methodist minister who led a significant withdrawal movement from Euro-American congregations to African American denominations, is also distinguished as the compiler and publisher of the first African American hymnal in 1801. His pocket-sized, words-only publication, reflective of hymn collections by Euro-Americans, initiated the longest, best-documented, and most instructive hymnal history of all African American denominations.

The first African American liturgical document, *A Collection of Spiritual Songs and Hymns Selected from Various Authors* by Richard Allen, contains fifty-four hymn texts without titles or tunes, drawn chiefly from the collections of Isaac Watts, the Wesleys, and other hymnists, including Allen himself.[11] Richard Allen, who clearly recognized the importance of music for African American worshipers, selected hymns that might have been popular at that time, then composed his own while keeping the theology familiar to worshipers across denominations. In keeping with the practice of that time, neither titles nor the names of composers were appended to hymns, and the size of the compilations was such that it could be slipped into a woman's purse or a man's pocket. Even the lengthy wording of the title of the book was part of the ongoing psalmody and hymnody traditions. A second enlarged edition of the hymnbook was published by Allen within the same year and printed by T. L. Plowman, with ten additional hymns and a change in the title: *A Collection of Hymns and Spiritual Songs from Various Authors.*

In terms of the availability of Allen's original collections, J. Roland Braithwaite notes that there are only two extant copies of the original hymnal. One copy of the first edition is in the Seabury-Western Theological Seminary in Evanston, Illinois, and one copy of the second edition is in the American Antiquarian Society in Worcester, Massachusetts. A title page of the second edition is in the Library of Congress in Washington, D.C. In a lengthy introduction to the facsimile edition of Richard Allen's 1801 hymnal, Braithwaite provides a comparison of Allen hymnals with other hymnals available from the early nineteenth century. Braithwaite notes, "The discussion of the place of the Allen books in the history of American hymnals indicates his awareness of the established repertory of the hymnals that would be used by the churches which attracted the common folk and his recognition of the growing body of camp meeting spiritual songs."[12] Among the sixty-four hymns in the second edition, thirteen were composed by Isaac Watts, affirming the popularity of Watts's hymns among African Americans. Five of the hymns were composed by Charles Wesley, three by John Newton, three by James Maxwell (an early Scottish Methodist), and six by recognized English writers. Other songs were from a body of evangelistic songs composed by local revival ministers and traveling preachers. Evidence of the Great Awakening and the Second Awakening can be found in this repertoire, for the songs satisfy the revival needs of ordinary folks among the Methodists, Baptists, and Presbyterians.[13] Eight of the hymns included are:[14]

"Am I a Soldier of the Cross?" (Watts)
"Awake My Heart" (Watts)

"And Are We Yet Alive?" (Charles Wesley)
"In Evil, Long I Took Delight" (John Newton)
"How Happy Every Child of Grace" (Charles Wesley)
"Lord, What a Wretched Land This Is" (Watts)
"When I Can Read My Title Clear" (Watts)
"Ye Virgin Soul Arise" (Augustus Toplady)

Richard Allen is also credited with the practice of adding a refrain, *any* refrain, to hymn texts composed by any author. This is a form of improvisation, which infuses a large amount of informality into the worship service. This "wandering refrain" or "wandering chorus" is attached at random to the end of a hymn or psalm. The only remaining published examples of the wandering refrain are in a hymnal published by a Native American minister, Samuel Occom, in 1774. Allen's additions, however, differ in that he attached one refrain from a particular song to any song that he chose to add it to, which was entirely unique.[15] Eileen Southern contends that this process was a foretaste or progenitor of the nineteenth-century camp meeting and (white) gospel hymn.[16]

Although it took 186 years for a reprint of the original hymnal and a thorough analysis of its content, Braithwaite has provided a valuable addition to hymnic history. A summary of some of Braithwaite's findings is listed here because of their value to the discussion of music in African American liturgy.[17]

- The hymns included provide guidance as to the repertoire of songs that African American worshipers in Philadelphia across denominational lines might have been familiar with.
- The hymns reflect prevailing theology among the "ordinary folk."
- No doubt Richard Allen and the song leaders among the earliest AME worshipers were aware of the tunes familiar to the congregation. Although tunes are not provided, an alert precentor would determine the meter and establish a tune that the congregation could follow or improvise upon. (Twenty-four of the hymns are in common meter, and two are in common meter doubled.)
- Although the suggested tunes are not available, one can assume that worshipers would employ the African American folk tunes that were in vogue.

Missing from both 1801 hymnals are African American spirituals. Eileen Southern, however, asserts that there are source materials that indicate that poetic timber might have shaped spirituals. Southern speculates that "Behold the Awful Trumpet Sounds" might be one such example. All six stanzas are listed below with motifs highlighted in italics:

No X

Behold the awful *trumpet sounds,*
The sleeping dead to raise,
And calls the nations underground;
O how the saints will praise!

Behold the Savior, how he comes
Descending from his throne,
To burst asunder all our tombs
And lead his children home.

But who can bear that dreadful day
To see the world in flames;
The burning mountains melt away
While rocks run down in streams.

The falling stars their orbits leave;
The sun in darkness hide;
The elements asunder cleave;
The moon turn'd into blood.

Behold the universal world
In consternation stand;
The wicked into Hell are turn'd;
The Saints at God's right hand.

O then the music will begin,
Their Savior God to praise.
They are all freed from every sin,
And thus they'll spend their days.

Among the spirituals anticipated in the hymn above are "My Lord, What a Morning," "Steal Away," "Rocks and Mountains," and "Don't Fall on Me." Another hymn in this first publication, "See How the Nations Rage Together," is, by inference, one of the songs attributed to Allen. With such a well-defined hymnic history, it is curious why AME chroniclers have not included the original 1801 hymnal in the denomination's list of official hymnals. Admittedly, the church was not officially organized until 1816. To disregard the inaugural hymnal, in which a second edition was available within the same year, followed by a new edition in 1808, is to deny an important part of the church's history. Over the years denominational records have referred to the hymnal of 1818 as the first denominational book of the church. In her definitive scholarly work, Southern acknowledges Allen's efforts to produce the first African American hymnal and his significant contribution to black religious history:

Although Allen was not a formally trained minister, he was extremely intelligent and highly articulate. . . . The importance of this first hymnal designed expressly for an all-black congregation cannot be overemphasized. Whereas Allen might have used the official Methodist hymnal, instead he consciously set about to collect hymns that would have a special appeal to the members of his congregation, hymns that undoubtedly were longtime favorites of black Americans.[18]

The first official hymnal of the newly constituted African Methodist Episcopal Church, *The African Methodist Pocket Hymn Book*, was published in 1818. Richard Allen served as chair of the committee, with Daniel Coker and James Champion assisting. This hymn book includes 314 hymns and songs, fifteen from Allen's previous hymnal, with all titles organized by theological themes according to the various states of Christian experience; it shares 244 concordances with the official Methodist Episcopal hymnal in current use. In the preface of the 1818 hymnal, Allen notes, "Having become a distinct and separate body of people, there is no collection of hymns we could with propriety adopt. . . . And we flatter ourselves, the present edition will not suffer by a comparison with any collection of equal magnitude."[19]

African Methodist Episcopal members in general claim the distinction of being "singing Methodists" and the adopted heirs of John and Charles Wesley. The African heritage of song and freedom in singing is also acknowledged and adhered to by some more than others. Like other denominations there is not, nor should there be, a unanimous opinion about which historical background should prevail. Liturgically, the denomination draws its ordering of worship, polity, and praxis from the tradition of John and Charles Wesley, but with a sufficient amount of infusion from Richard Allen, Daniel Payne, and other African Americans along the way. Thus, a unique liturgical form has been created, so that a unique AME ethos permeates worship and musical styles throughout the denomination. Throughout the ages, according to the published hymnody of the church, the leaders have listened and responded to God's divine intervention. Fortunately, there has been a balance between theologians and musicians. It is exciting to learn of the interaction between Richard Allen and Daniel Payne and to hear of the challenges they faced concerning certain kinds of music and worship styles. In the twenty-first century, we recognize similar concerns in a new language. In 1919 Charles Stewart, a minister with both musical and theological training, called for revisions in an obviously outdated hymnal that had been published by the church in 1898. All denominations can resonate with his words reminding the church during the first two decades of the twentieth century that "the world is ever changing"—and so must our hymnody:

While our hymnal at the time it was last received was a most worthy effort and a distinct credit to the church and race, it is not today in touch with the wonderful progress of the church and race since that time. We have grown very rapidly and with our growth the world of religion and music and people have also wonderfully changed, so therefore our hymnal, is in need of hands in touch with the spirit of the church and a musical knowledge sufficient to give us today another hymnal, based upon the present one and sufficient to meet the needs of our present church.[20]

The African Methodist Episcopal Zion Church

Published hymnody in the African Methodist Episcopal Zion Church was instituted in 1839 and continues into the present. Prior to the publication of its most recent hymnal in 1996, the AMEZ Church contributed to the creation and spread of folk music in the community, in homes, and in corporate worship services. Like other Africans in America who were led to Methodism, this community of faith was attracted to John Wesley's opposition to the whole system of slavery, his commitment to Jesus Christ, and the evangelical appeal to the suffering and oppressed. Bishop William J. Walls notes in his scholarly history of the AMEZ Church that black members were first listed in the yearly conference records of white Methodism in 1786, and that Zion Methodism was born in New York in 1796 in a house on Cross Street (formerly a stable), with the determination to follow the example of the humble beginnings of Christianity with the birth of Christ.[21]

The conditions of slavery and other forms of persecution inspired black leaders of the John Street Church in New York to establish a separate community of believers and worshipers. Among the founders were James Varick (first bishop), Abraham Thompson, and William Miller. The first name given by the founders at the incorporation in 1801 was "The African Methodist Episcopal Church in New York." The church was firmly established in 1820 when the leaders voted themselves out of the Methodist Episcopal Church and published their first *Discipline*.[22] Because of confusion caused by two church organizations with the same name, the General Conference voted in 1848 to make Zion a part of the denominational name.[23]

Activities led by the Zion Church in New York in 1807 provided William Hamilton, one of its founders, with an opportunity to compose a hymn. The specific occasion was an act by the British Parliament to abolish the slave trade of Africans in the United States one year before the U.S. law went into effect. In celebration of this act, people of African descent in New York held a celebration at Zion Church, the city's only black church at that time. Hamilton composed the hymns for the day.[24] Unfortunately, these hymns do not appear among extant documents. However, Hamilton's poetic skills are documented in a letter that he wrote to the governor of New York in 1796, challenging the contradictory ways of slaveholding Christians who urged freedom for black slaves. Hamilton punctuates the narrative portion of his letter with two stanzas of his own poetry:

> Is there as ye sometimes tell us
> Is there one who reigns on high
> Does he bid them buy and sell us
> Spreading from this throne the sky?
>
> Deem our nation brutes no longer
> Till some reason they can find
> Worthy of regard and stronger
> Than the color of our kind.[25]

On the occasion for which Hamilton wrote two hymns, James Varick preached the historic "Sermon of Thanksgiving on the Occasion of the Abolition of the African Slave Trade," the first recorded sermon in history preached by an African on behalf of African people.[26]

Music in AME Zion Liturgy

In 1820 the AMEZ Church established a list of rules for worship. They were adopted in order to establish uniformity in public worship, although their focus is on the general method of preaching.[27] While they only refer to music in relation to the elements of the evening service, it is clear that the focus is on simplicity, promptness, and appropriate use of Scripture. Later in the *Book of Discipline,* the following is outlined under the title "Of Spirit and Truth of Singing":

In order to guard against formality in singing:

1. Choose such hymns as are proper for the congregation; do not sing too much at once, seldom more than five or six verses.
2. Let the tunes be suited to the words; and let the preacher stop occasionally and ask the people: Now! Do you know what you said last? Did you speak no more than you felt?
3. Do not suffer the people to sing too slow: and in every large society let them learn to sing, and let them learn our tunes first.
4. Let the women constantly sing their parts alone; let the men be silent except those who understand the notes; and sing the bass as it is composed in the tune book.

5. If a preacher needs help in singing, let him call assistance to his side.
6. Exhort every person in the congregation to sing; and when the singers would teach a tune to the congregation, they must only sing the tenor.[28]

Keyboard instruments were probably not available to the early Zion worshipers, and hymns might then have been lined out by a song leader. There is sufficient evidence to suggest that some of the worshipers could read notes from the staff. This indicates exposure to singing schools, where the rudiments of music had been taught since the latter part of the eighteenth century. Also apparent in this important document is the need for the preacher to be able to sing. According to Walls, the practice of singing a hymn before the sermon was in vogue early in the liturgical life of the AMEZ Church (perhaps referred to as the sermonic hymn). The tradition then was to remain seated as the hymn was sung.[29]

One can only speculate that before the inaugural publication of the hymnal of 1839, the singing Zion Methodists used the hymnal of the Methodist Episcopal Church. This is based on the fact that it and the subsequently published hymnal of 1858 were abridged editions of the Methodist Episcopal Church hymn book of 1831.[30] Neither publication expresses much concern for social issues, since both focus on personal salvation. Jon Michael Spencer observes, "Although written by the superintendents rather than by the publishers . . . the preface to the 1858 AMEZ hymnal seems to reflect the provincialism of northern, second generation freedmen in the Zion Church, a stance that was unaccepting of worship styles characteristic of the southern, 'invisible institution.'"[31] The preface, which encourages worshipers to avoid irregularity in singing and to sing with understanding, is taken by Spencer to mean that the denomination's northern origin encouraged a more intellectual and ordered worship rather than the style reflective of southern worship. For Spencer this concept continued, for the 1872 and 1892 hymnal revisions continued to reflect a strong leaning toward Methodist hymnody, with the latter hymnal including some of the popular gospel hymns of that day (five by the editor) and a collection of hymns by AMEZ ministers. The theological thrust of the ministers is basically Wesleyan, focusing on topics of faith, endurance, sanctification, salvation, and the crucifixion and resurrection of Jesus.

The hymnal published in 1909 was a duplication of the 1892 Methodist Episcopal hymnal, but it was the first hymn book printed by the AMEZ Publishing House in Charlotte, North Carolina. The introductory material and "Formula of Service" were prepared by the AMEZ hymnal committee. In the same year, an original collection of hymns titled *Soul Echoes: A Collection of Songs for Religious Meetings* was published corporately by African American clergy, including the Reverend Charles Tindley of the Methodist Episcopal Church and Bishops Caldwell and Coppin of the AME Church. The publication contained fifty hymns, twenty-five of which were composed in a style similar to spirituals. Tindley's hymns captured the mood of the black urban population, and are considered the foundation for the black gospel song genre made famous by Thomas Dorsey. Although it sold rapidly in the AMEZ Church, this collection was not adopted by the denomination.

The revised edition of *Soul Echoes* included arrangements by F. A. Clark, William D. Smith, Daniel Payne, R. William Fickland, and L. J. Coppin, as well as a few contemporaries of Watts and Wesley. This publication stimulated interest in an ecumenical common hymnal for the AME, AMEZ, CME, and "colored" Methodist members of the Episcopal churches. Meetings were held into the 1940s. The CME Church withdrew from the project, but the AME and AMEZ churches continued the dialogue, and commissioners were established in both churches. By 1944 the report from the joint commission was that a manuscript was in process. The effort stalled when the AME Church published its own hymnal, with the title, *Allen Hymnal*. The AMEZ portion of the former joint commission eliminated songs that had specific AME connectional references and moved ahead with its publication of the 1957 *New A.M.E. Zion Hymnal*.[32]

The African Methodist Episcopal Zion Bicentennial Hymnal (1996) contains 734 musical entries, eighty pages of AMEZ ritual and lectionary Scriptures, and an alphabetically arranged index of twenty-four pages. Since there is no index of authors and composers, determining the content of the hymnal in general and the African American composers in particular is quite tedious. In addition to hymns by Wesley and Watts, the volume includes selections from composers such as Fred Pratt Green, Les Garrett, Bill Gaither, Joe Wise, Hal Hopson, as well as African American songs such as "Lift Every Voice."

The Christian Methodist Episcopal Church

The hymnal of the Christian Methodist Episcopal Church is almost an exact duplication of *The New National Baptist Hymnal* (see page 214). It is, however, encased in a different cover with the imprint of the official logo of the CME Church. The preface contains a chronicle of the musical history of the denomination, introduced with reminders of the Wesleyan tradition, and a contextualizing analysis of the contents that relates specifically to the African American tradition. The preface ends with "O Rapturous Scenes," the six-stanza hymn-text penned by Bishop Lucius H. Holsey, the third elected bishop of the CME Church. F. M. Hamilton, a minister and active leader of the CME

Church who was one of Holsey's contemporaries, composed the music of this hymn. Following this hymn is the traditional CME order of worship, leading into two opening hymns, "All Hail the Power of Jesus' Name" and "Holy, Holy, Holy," providing the only changes in the musical entries of *The New National Baptist Hymnal*. The hymnal includes eight Wesley hymns, which can be considered minimal for a denomination that declares a Methodist heritage. However, the historical and contemporary African American spiritual and gospel traditions are well represented, especially with the inclusion of "Lift Every Voice and Sing" and favorites from the repertoire of the civil rights movement. Also represented are songs from the evangelical tradition that are frequently used in CME worship.

Following the musical entries at the back of this hymnal are additional liturgical aids: responsive readings, aids to worship, the CME rituals for the sacraments of Baptism and the Lord's Supper, and a ritual to confirm and receive persons into the church. One reason given for adapting *The New National Baptist Hymnal,* which after its publication in 1977 was in use by numerous non-Baptist denominations nationwide and which contained a large repertoire of hymns utilized heavily by black congregations, was the inordinate amount of time and money that would have been needed to create a CME hymnal. Lawrence Reddick III observed in the news publication of the CME Church, *Christian Index*, "Though it would have been possible to spend the additional time and money to gather the church's musicians together, choose hymns, decide thematic structures for a hymnal, enter into negotiations for reproduction privileges and agree upon royalties with copyright owners . . . it could have proven a mammoth undertaking in money and time for this to succeed."[33] The process of adapting, adopting, and interchanging hymnals between denominations has a history that extends back many centuries, and will no doubt continue into a future that is ecumenically oriented.

Published Hymnals in Baptist Traditions

Church historians most often refer to black Baptists in relation to "movements" and "conventions," often avoiding the term *denominations.* This is done mainly to ensure that the local churches are able to maintain their independence. This concern has remained in tension as black Baptists have continually striven to maintain regional and national organizations. According to C. Eric Lincoln and Lawrence Mamiya, from 1815 to 1880, many black Baptists worked through existing national white Baptist organizations through their African Baptist Missionary Society. The earliest all-black Baptist associations were organized in the Midwest, although most of the churches were in the southeastern United States.[34] Black Baptists' hymnic history began with the organization of the National Baptist Convention, USA, in 1895. The publication of *Gospel Pearls* followed in 1921. Eileen Southern considers *Gospel Pearls* "a milestone in the history of the black church hymnody, ranking it with Richard Allen's 1801 hymnal."[35]

The denomination's hymnal committee and hymnal editors established an excellent tradition of black Baptist music for worship in *The New National Baptist Hymnal.* Published in 1977, it contains twenty-seven African American spirituals, songs from the repertoire of the civil rights movement, the "Negro national anthem" ("Lift Every Voice and Sing"), and other liturgical reminders of social concerns inherent in the gospel. In addition to the African American oral folk song tradition of spirituals now documented in hymnals, songs by black composers will be etched in the memories of worshipers. Among the gospel hymnists included are Charles A. Tindley, Charles P. Jones, Edward C. Deas, Thomas Dorsey, Lucie Campbell, Kenneth Morris, Magnolia Lewis-Butts, Roberta Martin, Andrae Crouch, and Margaret Douroux. Other black hymnists included are Anders T. Dailey, James Hendrix, and Juanita G. Hines.

The United Methodist Church

Songs of Zion, originally designed to be a supplemental resource for the entire United Methodist Church, has emerged as one of the leading black hymnals in terms of its content, longevity, and usefulness for the ecumenical church. This volume is the result of an urgent recommendation from members who attended a consultation on the black church sponsored by the Board of Discipleship of the United Methodist Church in 1973. The members recommended that a songbook reflecting the music tradition unique to the religious experiences of black Americans be compiled and published. In the preface of this hymnal, William B. McClain wrote:

> This songbook offers the whole church a volume of songs that can enrich the worship of the whole church. It is music that has nourished a people, soothed their hurts, sustained their hopes, and bound their wounds. It is music that will broaden the musical genres in worship in any Christian church. It is the songs of Zion to be sung by God's people, who are always strangers and pilgrims in any land they inhabit.[36]

Songs of Zion includes 249 musical entries, edited by J. Jefferson Cleveland and Verolga Nix, with numerous arrangements by both editors. Musical entries are divided into musical genres rather than theological categories, with essays of historical significance preceding under the following titles:

A Historical Account of the Hymn in the Black Worship Experience
A Historical Account of the Negro Spiritual
A Historical Account of the Black Gospel Song

The last section of the book includes songs for special occasions and service music.

The section under the rubric of "Hymns" includes 71 songs by black composers spanning the twentieth century, including Charles A. Tindley, Margaret Douroux, James Hendrix, J. Edward Hoy, William Farley Smith, Edward C. Deas, C. Eric Lincoln, J. Jefferson Cleveland, settings by Verolga Nix, and James Weldon Johnson and J. Rosamond Johnson. Included in the hymnal are songs by Charles Gabriel, Fanny Crosby, Isaac Watts, Horatio Spafford, and William Gaither. A significant inclusion is the "Prayer for Africa," which is the anthem adopted by the African National Congress and frequently incorporated in African American services of worship and civil gatherings. This Zulu song, initially titled "Nkos Sikelei Afrika," was composed in 1897 by Enoch Sontongo.

The body of spirituals is the largest category of songs included. In addition to considering their historical significance, the editors were careful to choose spirituals that can be used during the Christian liturgical year. The category of gospel songs covers each period of songs by representative composers. The section of songs for special occasions includes intricately composed and arranged songs that expand the musical abilities and repertoires of choirs, congregations, organists, pianists, and other instrumentalists. This plethora of styles broadens awareness of the varying levels of gifts of black Americans. The service music section includes introits, chants, a setting of the Lord's Prayer, offertories, prayer responses, benedictions, and choral "Amens."

Worship and conference planners particularly appreciated this volume because it includes music that is appropriate for a variety of ages and is useful for worship as well as for informal gatherings. Although it was categorized as "supplemental," it served a dual purpose of congregational testing prior to the publication of a new denominational hymnal, while at the same time fulfilling the urgent need of the black Methodist constituency. The *United Methodist Hymnal* did indeed incorporate many songs and hymns from the black song tradition. Apparently, *Songs of Zion* continues to fulfill needs and may remain in the United Methodist publication pipeline.

Church of Christ (Holiness), USA

Charles Price Jones is perhaps more familiar in relation to Charles Harrison Mason, both of whom were Baptists influenced by the Azusa Street revivals. Jones was self-taught and began preaching when he was twenty years of age. He was licensed to preach in the Baptist Church at the age of 22. He was drawn to the Holiness movement and was later dismissed from the Baptist Church (along with Mason and other Baptist ministers) because of legal matters regarding the name change of his congregation from Mt. Helm Baptist Church to the Church of Christ. Mason and Jones served together until they disagreed over the interpretation of some Scripture passages. They separated, and with their followers organized churches: Jones, the Church of Christ (Holiness), and Mason, the Church of God in Christ.

Jones also taught himself music, an art in which he would later become prolific as a composer and publisher. In 1899 he began to publish collections of his hymns. He published *Jesus Only* and then followed with *Jesus Only 1,* and another collection, *Jesus II,* in 1901. In 1906 he published *His Fullness* followed by *Sweet Selections and His Fullness Enlarged.* Since I own a copy of *His Fullness Songs*, the present official hymnal of the Church of Christ (Holiness), I will use this as a resource for evaluating the content and music of this composer who contributed to the foundational shaping of early black gospel songs.

According to an autobiographical sketch, Charles P. Jones experienced the empowering of the Holy Spirit when he gave himself to the Lord to be sanctified, after he sought to be perfectly holy by walking with God in the Spirit. One day he was talking with God alone, and the Spirit spoke to him and ordered him to write the hymns for the people. He walked to the organ and composed the song "Praise the Lord." In his own words, Price said, "I ruled off a tablet, set it to music, and sang it before I left the room."[37]

On the dedication page of *His Fullness Songs*, the committee of the National Convention of the Church of Christ (Holiness), USA, has reprinted the following information prepared by Charles P. Jones:

> *Jesus Only No. 1* was brought out in 1899. *Jesus Only Number 1* and *Number 2* in 1901, with *Select Songs* [published] later. The first *His Fullness* in 1906. The aim was not just to put another songbook on the market, but we had a special message in our souls concerning Jesus the Christ, the Son of God that had to be sung out, told out, suffered out; that men might know him in the power of his resurrection and the fellowship of His sufferings and be conformed to His death.[38]

His Fullness Songs contains 512 songs, with 310 songs carried over from the 1906 edition. Many of the songs are Christocentric, including Jones's compositions, most of which are written in the style of traditional white gospel compositions. All of the spirituals are his own arrangements. Although there is one song by Charles Tindley, there are no gospel songs from the "golden era" or modern gospel songs. After Jones's death, a committee determined which songs to include in the hymnal, so it is not clear what the voids communicate about the singing repertoire of the Holiness movement. Except for Jones's song "Jesus Only" on the first page of the hymnal, *His Fullness Songs* could easily pass for a typical white hymnal at the turn of the twentieth century and into the 1960s, with its inclusion of "O for a Thousand Tongues to Sing," "All Hail the Power of Jesus' Name," "He Lives," "Praise to the Lord, the Almighty," and lots of his own work.

Obviously, Jones gave high priority to gospel singing. Songs that are described as "familiar" in the hymnal were not part of my South Carolina upbringing in sanctified ("saved by God's grace": "consecrated" and "holy") churches. Perhaps the most familiar are "I Will Make the Darkness Light," "I'm Happy in Jesus Alone," "I Am Wholly Sanctified," "Deeper, Deeper in the Love of Jesus," and "I Have Surrendered to Jesus." "I Will Make the Darkness Light" is included in the Church of God in Christ hymnal, *Yes, Lord!*

Church of God in Christ

In 1982 the Church of God in Christ published *Yes, Lord!*—its official denominational hymnal. The Church of God in Christ had experienced years of successful growth as a denomination, with an oral music liturgical tradition far beyond any other. Admittedly, many of the "saints" of the church were opposed to the publishing of a hymnal. Students at the Charles Mason Theological Seminary at the Interdenominational Theological Center stated that they have had the hymnal available for twenty years and only used it once or twice to sing a Christmas carol. Therefore, they have no idea of the treasures contained in the pages of the hymnal. The contents are reflective of the ever evolving ecumenical nature of the church, including an openness to Euro-American liturgical music. The hymnal's compiler and major musical consultant, Iris Stevenson, credits the final agreement to organize the project to her persistence that the denomination's musical heritage and history must be documented, lest many of the instrumental and vocal discoveries would be "stolen."[39] Stevenson is a classically trained musician who brings to her tasks all of her musical gifts. The choices of music were informed and determined from a cross section of musicians and clergy who submitted songs for consideration. Under Stevenson's guidance, the committee of clergy, musicians, laity, and young adults evaluated the theological content of texts, their relationship to chordal progressions, and their accessibility to local congregations. Theological categories cover the basic range of denominational polity and practice. Theological themes are guided by the Pentecostal tradition from Charles Harrison Mason's experiences at Azusa Street to the musical offering at the yearly conference.

A brief introductory commentary posits the title of the hymnal in the practice of the founder Mason, who gathered his congregation in commitment and spiritual communication simply by chanting "Yes, yes, yes, yes, Lord!" any number of times until calmness and unity prevailed. This is written as a score, perhaps for the first time for congregational use, and is the first musical entry of the book. Other songs, hymns, and spiritual songs represent the traditional body of Protestant songs: evangelical, black and white gospel songs, and the black anthem, "Lift Every Voice and Sing." Spirituals are included, along with compositions from each of the golden eras of black gospel music, from Charles A. Tindley and Thomas A. Dorsey to generations of Martins, Andrae Crouch to Mattie Moss Clark, and Iris Stevenson to the Gaithers. Other religious song literatures include the Euro-classical tradition such as Beethoven, Bach, Mozart, and Handel, with a full choral setting of the "Hallelujah" chorus from Handel's *Messiah*.

Another exciting feature is the publication of the Church of God in Christ's melodic riffs in a variety of keys at the end of the book. There are a few aids to worship, models for prayers, and scriptural sources for the songs. *Yes, Lord!* is nothing short of a classic collection that will live well into the twenty-first century.

The Episcopal Church

The 1993 publication of *Lift Every Voice and Sing II: An African American Hymnal*, edited by Horace Clarence Boyer, is the second black Episcopal hymnal of the twentieth century composed for use in parishes that are composed largely of black worshipers. The first one, *Lift Every Voice and Sing*, compiled by Irene V. Jackson-Brown, is an excellent collection of 151 congregational songs, including spirituals, hymns, gospel songs by black and Euro-American composers, and other songs for worship, which were not duplicated in any other black hymnals available at the time. Both editions of *Lift Every Voice and Sing*, like other black song compilations published by Euro-American denominations at the behest of their black constituencies, serve a twofold purpose:

(1) to affirm and claim the musical repertoire used by African Americans in the liturgy of the Episcopal Church, and (2) to share some of the musical and poetic gifts that black people bring to the whole church. *Lift Every Voice and Sing II* includes music from the following genres:

- Negro spirituals
- traditional and contemporary gospel songs
- adapted Protestant hymns
- missionary and evangelistic hymns
- service music and mass settings in both traditional and gospel styles.[40]

The hymnal's introductory information includes an article, "Why an African American Hymnal?" by the Reverend Canon Harold T. Lewis, a member of the staff in the Office for Black Ministries. As in other Euro-American denominations, if songs from one's cultural tradition are not included in the regular denominational hymnal, the assumption is that they are not appropriate for the liturgy of the church. Black Episcopalians, according to Canon Lewis, did not sing their own songs, except outside of the regular time for worship. The civil rights and black consciousness movements provided the impetus for black members to rediscover the validity of "emotionalism" as a religious expression. *Lift Every Voice and Sing II* was published to be a resource for the whole church, not merely its black membership.

Horace Boyer provides an eight-page article, "Hymns and Song Performance Notes," based on African American religious performance practices. Carl Haywood follows the article with a section on performance notes for service music based on the *Book of Common Prayer*.

The Hymnal 1982, actually published in 1985, is the official Episcopal hymnal and the first hymnal published for U.S. Episcopalians since 1940. Despite the comment in the preface that this hymnal includes "texts and music which reflect the pluralistic nature of the Church . . . affording the use of Native American, Afro-American, Hispanic, and Asian material," a careful count reveals only seven African American songs—"Lift Every Voice and Sing" and six spirituals—and two Ghanian songs. Between *The Hymnal 1940* and *The Hymnal 1982*, two supplemental hymnals were published. *Hymns III* included one spiritual, "Go Tell It on the Mountain," which was listed as an "anonymous American folk hymn." The second, *Songs for Celebration*, included one spiritual, "Lord, I Want to Be a Christian," which was listed as an American spiritual.

Lift Every Voice and Sing II is a welcome addition to black published hymnals. The balance of materials from white evangelical sources are reminders of the traditional evangelical songs that have meaning for blacks, even though some of these hymns were excluded from traditional Episcopal liturgy. The choral arrangements of spirituals are first-rate in that they can be adapted by local congregations. The service music portion of this hymnal provides accessibility to liturgical settings by Episcopalians such as Lena McLin, Eugene Hancock, and David Hurd, as well as African American composers from the Roman Catholic tradition. In addition, *Lift Every Voice and Sing II* offers congregations a wonderful taste of liturgical settings by Glenn Burleigh.

The Roman Catholic Church

Not only were black Catholics the first black community in America (in 1565) and the first township to provide a home for runaway slaves, they were also at the forefront of addressing issues for the good of the community. Two orders of black nuns were founded before the end of the mid-1800s: the Oblates of Providence in 1829 and the Sisters of the Holy Family in 1842. Liturgically speaking, Roman Catholics and Protestants are indebted to the work of Father Clarence Joseph Rivers, who, during the 1960s, provided a model for liturgical inculturation in Catholic worship in particular and paved the way in general for the reclaiming of African cultural traditions among non-Catholics. Through liturgical gathering, scholarly dialogue, and publications as well as Rivers's musical compositions that incorporate musical gifts from Africa and the Americas, Rivers encouraged the tapping of resources that can enhance the spiritual vitality of the community of faith.[41] Rivers's ideas of black liturgy and his organized gatherings inspired the focus on discovering and recovering the African and early African American heritage of worship traditions at Interdenominational Theological Center.

The African American Catholic hymnal, *Lead Me, Guide Me*, published by GIA Publications in 1987, is alive with spirituals, gospel songs, hymns, service music, and music for the Roman Catholic mass, offering evidence that blacks can be both Catholic and "black." Without apologies, the twentieth-century composers whose works are included and used by both Catholics and Protestants express their faith through their experiences as black persons. In the preface to this hymnal, J-Glenn Murray says that "This hymnal, prepared by Black Catholics in the United States of America attempts to both meet the challenges of our faith and to incorporate the achievements of our centuries of vibrant life in the Spirit."[42]

Points of consideration include the importance of celebrating the Sacred Mysteries of the Liturgy, making sure that the worship is uniquely Catholic, in that everything that is done serves the ritual action of Word and Sacrament in keeping with the Roman Catholic liturgy. Murray acknowledges the variety of musical traditions among black Catholics, especially from African American musical traditions that were considered during the compilation process.[43]

Among the musical entries are African American spirituals, each of the categories of black gospel songs by Protestant and Catholic composers, Euro-American gospel hymns, and traditional hymns that are sacred to the black worship experience. There are a large number of settings of psalms, full settings of the Catholic Eucharistic Mass, and litanies of the Blessed Virgin Mary by black musicians. Special settings of services for Christian initiation of adults, baptism, reconciliation, anointing of the sick, marriage, funeral Mass, and service music are composed by black and Euro-American composers.

The Evangelical Lutheran Church in America and the Lutheran Church—Missouri Synod

In 1990, the African American Lutherans within the Lutheran Church, Missouri Synod (LCMS) conceived *This Far by Faith* in a "concept paper." After an exploratory phase that was extended to involve the Evangelical Lutheran Church in America (ELCA), the dream was shaped into an African American Lutheran worship resource that supplements the principal worship books of the churches. Initial financial support for the development of this resource was provided by two entities of the ELCA—the Division for Congregational Ministries and the Commission for Multicultural Ministries—as well as the Commission for Black Ministries of the LCMS. In September 1995, financial assistance was provided by the Lutheran Brotherhood Foundation, which enabled a more rapid completion of the hymnal, *This Far by Faith: An African American Resource for Worship.* Walking by faith and not by sight, the necessary committees were formed, a grant was received, and the committee worked from 1993 until the project was completed in 1999.

One of the many salient features of this resource is the introductory material that begins with a carefully researched reminder of the ongoing dialogue over the centuries between Christian faith and the cultural context in which faith is nurtured and worship is shaped. The succinct history of Lutherans in North America posits the early roots of black Lutherans in African soil, thus affirming the common heritage of Lutherans with other Africans enslaved in America. The repertoire of spirituals, "blackenized" Euro-American hymns, meter hymns, and the blues roots of black gospel music therefore carry the stamp of black Lutherans as well. Without sufficient records to the contrary, there is little doubt that Emmanuel, an African baptized in a New York Lutheran congregation in 1669, sang songs familiar to other Lutherans in seventeenth-century America. Weekday singing in the black community was no doubt quite different and perhaps not recognized or accepted as "sacred" by Lutherans, whose aural expectations were otherwise conditioned.

Following an excellent explanation of various methods that help facilitate the leading and singing of African American songs, the project development committee provided an excellent biblical rationale for the Lutheran *ordo,* the order and flow of the service. The first 118 pages of this resource are structured as follows:

Preface
Worship and Culture
[Information on] Leading African American Songs
"A Musical Time Line (From African Chant to Gospel Rap)," by Melva
    Costen
The Liturgy Is Biblical [an explanation of the flow of the liturgy]
Holy Communion (The Shape of the Rite)
Orders of Confession and Forgiveness
    Holy Communion (Setting One: River of Life)
    Holy Communion (Setting Two: Liturgy of Joy—James Capers)
    Holy Communion (Setting Three: A Pattern for the Service)
    Holy Baptism
    Service of the Word
    Service of Prayer and Preaching
    Variable Worship Texts
    The Way of the Cross
    The Journey of Faith—Prayers, Signs, and Blessings
        Young People Coming to Adulthood
        Marriage
        Blessing of Women and Men
        Blessing of Elders
        Burial of the Dead
    Witnesses to the Faith (Appreciation for the Ancestors)
    Psalms and Service Music [36 pages]
    Hymns and Songs [60 pages]
    National and Cultural Resources [5 pages]
    Commemoration of Martin Luther King, Jr.
    Celebration of Black History Month
    Juneteenth
    The Hurricane Season
    Kwanzaa
    Acknowledgment
    Copyright Holders and Administrators
    Topics and Themes
    Scripture References
    Alphabetical Listing of Tunes
    Authors, Composers, and Sources

The African American Heritage Hymnal

The idea of an ecumenical hymnal developed slowly but persistently in the mind of the Reverend Dr. Delores Carpenter, clergywoman ordained by the Christian Church (Disciples of Christ), theologian, Christian educator, and seminary professor. Such a hymnal can transcend denominational polities and get to the reality of mutual concerns and journeys as black Americans.

According to Carpenter's own account, the journey toward the development of the hymnal began within her own denomination. The Black Ministers Fellowship appointed a task force to investigate a hymnal for use in African American congregations. Carpenter, who was appointed chair, received the usual denominational reminder that a multicultural hymnal would be much more practical (an answer that always reveals one finger on the pulse of financial matters). Carpenter's adamant "no" came from her knowledge that African American contributions in a multicultural mix would be condensed into a few published spirituals, with no "down-home oral traditional gospels" that would cause the entire worshiping community to pat their feet, wave their hands, and even move toward a "ring shout"! When the denomination did not follow through with the hymnal development process, a former denominational executive suggested the possibility of producing a hymnal commercially. Thus a new process was set into motion.

Carpenter took the initiative to gather an ecumenical team, with the assistance of the Reverend Nolan Williams, a liturgical musician and concert artist. The impressive assemblage of pastors, theologians, musicians, cultural historians, and practitioners examined church music and the worship experiences of African American Christians with a view toward producing a document that would be useful well into the twenty-first century. National black publishers were not enthused, and in the process of investigating other publishing options, GIA Publications extended a contract offer to the team.

The initial title, *African Heritage Hymnal,* was assigned to coincide with the *African Heritage Bible*, which also involved an ecumenical group of a similar assemblage. As the contents were gathered, another look at the title called for a different name, since most of the musical material had evolved from a variety of African American sources.

The African American Heritage Hymnal is a liturgical document containing the following:

Introduction (Wyatt Tee Walker)
Essays:
"The Ecumenical Nature of African American Church Music"
    (J. Alfred Smith)

"African American Music and Freedom Movement" (Otis Moss)
Table of Contents
    Biblical Responsive Readings
    Litany Prayers for the Black Church Year
    Hymns and Songs
    Indexes (extensive)
Musical Entries (581)

The Current Status of Hymn Singing
in African American Congregations

The hymn, a major vocal genre[44] of music used in African American worship, has experienced a decline in usage since the last quarter of the twentieth century. One of the contributing factors has been the changing role of the African American congregation from the "authentic choir" in worship to their almost forced position as spectator-participants. A part of this paradigm shift is rooted in what can be identified as the "large gospel choir movement" initiated by Edwin Hawkins in 1969 with his choral adaptation and recording of "O Happy Day," a hymn by an eighteenth-century Englishman, Philip Doddridge. Gradually, the large choir assumed more and more leadership, providing evidence of carefully rehearsed repertoires of contemporary gospel songs, and gospelized arrangements of traditional spirituals and hymns. With increased support from congregations, the former auxiliary choir in some churches replaced, rather than augmented, traditional congregational hymn singing.

Admittedly, there are some advantages to this arrangement, as congregations are encouraged to hear and learn new gospel songs often composed by their creative music directors and other local musicians. An alternative view is that old and contemporary hymnic literature and songs from Africa and other global cultures are often neglected. In many instances, some of the carefully honed African American historical folk theology with reminders of God at work in the common struggles and rewards of unified social efforts are omitted from the good news. Obery M. Hendricks, an AME clergyman and former president of Payne Theological Seminary, in comparing the traditional spirituals with contemporary gospel music, highlights the importance of the "collective root experience" of composers of black music. I concur with his observation that these normative elements of black sacred music are not always present in current offerings: "Despite the empowering nature of the Black sacred music of the past in the dominant mode of Black religious music today—contemporary Gospel music—this prophetic voice, this biblical logic of justice, is all but stilled. Gospel music is heard everywhere today; yet . . . it does not press our suits of freedom."[45]

One of the results of the lack of continuity in African American religious history in music is reflected in the limited musical repertoires at ecumenical worship gatherings, including those at theological seminaries and other historically black universities and colleges. To move this observation to songs and hymns for the liturgical year adds another dimension to the problem of neglect of communal songs. Clergypersons who endorse the use of choirs have hastened the move away from congregational singing. Together both clergy and musicians could expand their knowledge of the many genres of liturgical songs and create a balance in the use of a variety of songs, while not neglecting the contributions that contemporary approaches to music in worship can make.

The current paradigm shift reflects an individualistic approach to music in worship by some choir directors, whose interest in the total worship service as a liturgical offering to God is suspect. Musicians are often encouraged to do their own thing—by directors who may be flaunting themselves, pastors who are on ego trips, and congregations that have been relegated to the role of an audience being entertained. Unfortunately, sincere and dedicated persons called into ministry are urged to perpetuate this pattern under the guise of "reclaiming their African heritage."

Chapter 4

The Evolution of Gospel Music

African American gospel music, also appropriately labeled "black gospel music," has black liturgical roots. Like the spirituals and other genres of black songs, its roots are in the nurturing soil and soul of Africa, and in the clandestine slave religious environment of Africans enslaved in America. In the ongoing evolution of black music genres and forms, gospel music emerged as a unique element of worship, appropriately understood as a viable part of the *liturgy,* "the work of the people." Gospel music in worship is in essence a liturgical offering from the black church to the world. As a prime example of the unity of sacred and secular in hearing and spreading the good news of the gospel, this section will include reminders of the role of gospel music as a liturgical form but also as a catalyst for the spawning of a variety of popular music genres during the twentieth century.

While affirming that music which emanates from the soul of African American people, expressing their current situation or *Sitz im Leben*, one must also consider the countereffects of having music released to communities outside of its existential situation of origin. This marvelous creation and concept of good news in soulful songs continues to have a powerful influence on young and restless seekers as they are driven to high moments and encounters with the Almighty. There are some who move from these encounters to acts of ministry—seeking justice, loving kindly, and walking humbly. And then there are those who sing and move to the slow or driving rhythms of gospel songs who have no idea of their initial intent as good news.

Black gospel music as a liturgical element has been vulnerable to misinterpretations and misuse from the time it moved out of the church to the stage and then back again. Truly the work of an African American people, the music evolved from the preached word, was given musical structure, and then was returned to the preacher for more theological shaping. Long before it became an acceptable form for a majority of worshiping congregations, it was viewed with suspicion because of its origin in the black Pentecostal (Holiness and sanctified) churches. Although it was embedded in personal experiences with the Spirit, some people were a bit suspicious of the kind of theology that motivated the singers.

It did not help that the words, with their obvious personal expressions and sometimes distorted interpretation of the biblical message, as well as the manner of delivery, would appeal to the appetites of people outside of the church. Although the early spontaneous creators and proponents of this music had a Christian basis for its origin and its energy, gospel was presented to the world and quickly took on elements of the world. These elements and resulting benefits propelled it into the commercial arena, where it has prospered financially. Gospel music has been literally taken out of the soulful context, reworked, put on stage as paid entertainment, and then returned as "music for worship," and the very grounds of its being have been affected. This chapter will approach the subject of gospel music through African American liturgical lenses and will address several questions. What is taking place when a liturgical form goes commercial and then returns to the liturgical source of its origin to become the controlling force in shaping the "faith, work, and walk of the people"? Can something be done by the black community, the source of soul that helped produce gospel music, to reclaim its liturgical essence?

Origin of the African American Gospel Genre

In this era when so many variations of styles and forms of African American gospel music are so prominent and public arenas are so often far removed from traditional sacred settings, it is not always believable that this genre has deep roots in the liturgical music and preaching of slaves. This twentieth-century genre was initially spawned by creative African Americans who sought and found ways to express good news because of, and in spite of, the bad times they experienced. The lyrics as well as musical forms were, fortunately, not bound by preconceived musical idioms or theological poetic devices. The nascent authors and composers were most often poor folk—persons living in poverty—who knew and understood how it felt to *wake up with a sound mind, and with blood running warm in their veins.* They knew the real world, the secular side of life, and they understood that such a life is not separate from religious life, for God is everywhere and will reach those in need *on time, in God's time.* Black gospel songs from their inception deliberately combined the sacred with the secular. Therefore, it would be expected that black gospel would find a home both in and outside of the liturgical space of black folks.

There is not a point in time when a clear line of passage from slavery to freedom for *all* African Americans can be marked. By now the record is clear that President Abraham Lincoln's paramount objective in 1863 was to save the Union rather than to abolish slavery. The Emancipation Proclamation declared that slavery was abolished only in eleven states. It was the Thirteenth Amendment passed by Congress on January 31, 1865, that abolished slavery throughout the United States and in areas subject to the jurisdiction of the United States. However, the "real world" of the slaves abounds in stories and oral histories by slaves who received the word from their slaveholders that freedom would come only in the next world. Thus, earthly freedom was never experienced by a large number of African Americans. June 19, 1865, is the day that the news of freedom reached blacks in Texas, which gave rise to the celebration in many states of "Juneteenth."[1] This brief digression is necessary so that the context of the development of gospel music as an urban black music genre can be determined as limited in boundaries, often in juxtaposition to latter years of the development of spirituals.

Black gospel music is one of many musical idioms developed over time in the life of African Americans. As slavery continued alongside freedom in a confused America, gospel music emerged within environments where spirituals and blues continued to thrive. An adequate explanation is that the gospel genre developed in an urban environment, where blacks had moved from rural communities. New situations and environments fostered and nurtured new musical sounds and religious expressions. Rather than having slaveholders confined to a few identifiable oppressors on a plantation, the new oppressor was the new nonblack society as a whole, which made freedom tenuous and places of refuge limited.

The urban environment of African Americans was broad enough to embrace the economic and spiritual realities of recently freed and uprooted African Americans seeking refuge in an imagined Promised Land. In keeping with the historical momentum of African people, existential situations, new and broader spaces to explore, a new land of problems and opportunities, and new forms of abuse and humiliation all fertilized and gave birth to new sounds. The story of these sounds is more than the story of a one-song genre; it is the story and process of a people seeking new directions, envisioning, and creating God-talk in the midst of struggles and spiritual fulfillment, regardless of setting. The new liturgical sound that developed in this environment, which had evolved from a number of other musical genres, was called black gospel.

By definition, black gospel music is both a *genre* (song form) and a *style* of performance, embodying the soulful expressions of the history of black people in and out of bondage and looking with joy to the future. As a genre, gospel began as a sacred, freely expressed perception of the good news of the salvation power of Jesus the Christ as experienced or envisioned initially by an individual, but offered as a shared experience for a people of faith and for potential believers. As a style of performance, gospel music reflects a sense of improvisatory freedom of expression that can range from simple and slow harmonic rhythms to complex harmonic tensions and complexities in the musical language of the blues. On the other hand, it can be expressed with a high-powered spiritual force with rapid changes in rhythms and increased intensity in presentation.

The uniqueness of this high-powered and deeply spiritual expression unfolded from the early 1920s to the 1930s, during which time it was given the name *gospel* by Thomas Dorsey, its credited founder. Since in its essence it was a liturgical expression in and of the black church, it was understood and treated as such. Due to the so-called secular overtones that gradually consumed performance practices, this new black musical idiom soon became popular outside of the church. Among the practices considered secular was an increased and often exaggerated emphasis on vocal rhythms and vocal textures to produce greater intensity, thus drawing more attention to the singer. This was often accentuated by body rhythms and physical contortions that further drew attention to the singer rather than to the divine power of the triune God. A further new dimension to the black gospel genre was the addition of the driving percussive rhythms of instruments, which often animated both the leading singers and the community of faith into a unified dance, not unlike the dives where jazz prevailed!

Before gospel music took its place as the genre that "has loomed from its status as the exclusive property of storefront African American Pentecostal churches to become a dynamic and driving force in the commercial industry,"[2] it reached out for the nurturing support of other sounds from the urban black community. The first of these new sounds has been labeled the blues, a genre that emerged out of the musings of freed slaves who expressed from a worldly perspective their insecurity, misery, and desire for stability. As the creators of the spirituals had done, the creators of the blues put their fingers on the pulse of their worldly condition and talked it over with themselves and others rather than denouncing it. Eileen Southern captures the eclectic process of making such music: "Blues singers, like the singers of the Spirituals, often draw upon songs that belong to the community repertory, borrowing from this one and that one, and refashioning the verses into a new song even as they are singing."[3]

Some spirituals communicate the same feeling of insecurity and misery as do the blues, in text, melody, and delivery style. This was obvious in some of the early spirituals and slave songs long before they were sorted into religious and nonreligious categories. This is one of the foci of James Cone in his classic work *The Spirituals and the Blues*.[4] The blues tend to be more worldly and specific, more direct in language, more expressive of an individual thought and a personal experience rather than the thoughts and experiences of a group.

Early African American performers of the blues across the nation contended that the blues have always existed. Buck Johnson, a pioneer bluesman, claimed to have played the blues since he was a child in the 1880s.[5] Gertrude "Ma" Rainey (1886–1936), who is considered the earliest professional blues singer, remembered hearing the blues sung by a young child in Missouri in 1902. At that time they were not known to her as the blues; the strangeness and poignancy of the songs attracted her. She later specialized in singing this kind of song, which she claimed to have named "the blues."[6] Dorsey was among the first to admit this as he recalled all the genres of black music available to musicians during the first two decades of the twentieth century.

In addition to the northern and southern styles of blues, there were traditional and "anthemized" arrangements of spirituals, slow-metered lined hymns, gospel hymns (Euro-American and those stylized by African Americans William Henry Sherwood, Charles Price Jones, and Charles Tindley), ragtime, and jazz. Out of the Azusa Street revivals there emerged Holy Ghost singing and dancing of the Holiness and Pentecostal churches, which greatly influenced the shape of gospel music. There were people such as "Professor" W. H. Nix, singer at the last session of the National Baptist Convention (Chicago, 1921), who demonstrated unusual improvisatory vocal skills and who inspired listeners, especially Dorsey. Nix was a member of the committee that compiled *Gospel Pearls* (see chapter 3). Nix's vocal embellishments seemed to "have assumed a crucial significance as a means for establishing expression."[7]

Black congregations should be examined for evidence of African influences in their music practices. In the early years, this African connection was not often accepted because of the "brainwashing" that had led many to believe that Africans were barbarians and that America was a civilized nation far removed from savage behavior. For this reason, even denominations and religious groups that endorsed and utilized black gospel in worship did not initially claim the African belief that there is no dichotomy between the sacred and secular. For many this was the Holy Spirit at work—as if the Holy Spirit did not function on the African continent prior to the departure of millions of its citizens![8]

African primal religion and musical traditions from the past found fertile ground in urban settings for developing new sounds to embrace existential realities. As newly freed slaves continued the process of reshaping concepts of Christianity to meet their faith and survival needs, they created a musical genre and a unique style of expressing the "good news" out of the things that constituted their environment. The late Pearl Williams-Jones noted quite appropriately that "the consistent and persistent retention in gospel music performance and practice of a clearly defined black identity growing out of the black experience in America is indicative of the indomitability of the African ethos."[9]

The African roots of jubilees, field hollers, moans, groans, spirituals, blues, jazz, and ragtime found their home in the late nineteenth-century and early twentieth-century Holiness, Pentecostal, and sanctified movements of African American churches. In this environment, the power of the Holy Spirit and the intensity of the natural African response were expressed in the exercise of charismatic gifts and in singing with the totality of one's being. The patterns of music making in traditional African cultures are highly evident in African American gospel music. Although rooted in the African American spiritual tradition and other oral forms of African American expression, gospel music differs in that authors and composers can be identified.

Black gospel music is also a *style*, a manner of musical expression that frees vocalists and instrumentalists to express feelings and emotions without being confined to opinions of hearers. Any genre of music can be recast or improvised in this manner—any song, hymn, anthem, aria, oratorio, cantata, or instrumental work. A "gospelized" song might be expressed slowly and soulfully with deep meaning, or joyfully with great vibrancy. In both instances, the presentation is enhanced and intensified by increased emphasis on vocal rhythms, a calculated use of vocal textures with percussive, bodily accompaniment. The musical structures and style of gospel music are on the same continuum as early African American liturgical singing, which is truly "the work of the people." The call-and-response structure is evidenced, as well as an intentional reworking or recreation of existing melodies, harmonies, and rhythms with all, or a majority, of the worshipers participating fully.

Historically, gospel music is an aesthetic form that can be appropriated from a hymn or spiritual, or it can be composed as a new song and performed in a variety of gospel styles. Williams-Jones, a multitalented gospel music specialist, often expressed the importance of the "intuitive" nature of the gospel music performing process:

> The performing process is so intuitive as to be almost unteachable. The greatest gospel artists are usually those who were born nearest the source of the tradition. . . . There are two basic sources from which gospel singing has derived its aesthetic ideals: the free-style collective improvisations of the African American church congregation and the rhetorical solo style of the gospel preacher. Inherent in this also is the concept of African American folk rhetoric, folk expression, bodily movement, charismatic energy, cadence, tonal range and timbre.[10]

Williams-Jones often demonstrated the truth of these words in her keyboard performances. As a gifted improviser, she was able to lecture on the performance process while skillfully performing on the piano or organ a piece by Johann Sebastian Bach. Then she would conclude her lecture, singing the words of a spiritual as a third layer above the others! She was one of the many African American musical geniuses who affirmed all ethnic music traditions while highlighting the unique contributions of African people to the music of the globe.[11]

Euro-American Gospel Hymnody

For the origin of the term *gospel music,* we must turn to the nineteenth-century American urban revival campaigns, conducted by two Euro-American evangelists, Dwight L. Moody and campaign music director Ira D. Sankey. A slogan used to advertise the arrival of the evangelist and musician highlighted the centrality of the gospel: Dr. Moody will *preach* the gospel and Mr. Sankey will *sing* the gospel! According to Ira Sankey, the phrase "to sing the gospel" was coined in Sunderland, England, in 1873, yet it was in the American environment that gospel hymnody had its initial impact.[12]

The first collection incorporating *gospel* in the title was *Gospel Songs: A Choice Collection of Hymns and Tunes: New and Old for Gospel Meetings, and Sunday School,* edited by Philip P. Bliss and published in 1874. *Gospel Hymns and Sacred Songs*, a second collection edited by Ira D. Sankey and Philip Bliss, followed the next year. The texts of these gospel songs were simple and to the point. African Americans frequented these revivals and contributed greatly to the fervent sound and spiritual depth of the singing.

Earlier foundations for gospel hymnody were planted in published collections of songs intended for use in Euro-American Sunday schools, and in the hymns of Lowell Mason and Thomas Hastings. It was important to the learning process that a large number of children could easily grasp the texts and that the music be simple and immediately accessible. It can be determined by the vast number of hymns included in black denominational hymnals of this era and in the repertoires of congregations in Euro-American Protestant and Catholic churches today that many of these Sunday school songs remain quite popular in African American liturgy. Many African American musicians, pastors, and congregations are not aware of their extended repertoire of nineteenth-century gospel hymns by Euro-Americans, and have in many instances claimed texts and tunes as originating in African American liturgical settings. A more accurate statement would be that the texts and tunes of these hymns have become *sacred* to African American liturgical traditions. The significance of the following list of a few of the gospel hymns composed and authored by Euro-Americans that have become a sacred part of black hymnody is simply a reminder of the African American gift for improvising, contextualizing, and, more specifically, "blackenizing" music from other traditions and claiming it for liturgical use. Thus, without a doubt, the "gospel style" of performance can be identified as uniquely African American.

Some Euro-American Gospel Hymns That Are Sacred to the African American Tradition

Title	Author	Composer
Sweet Hour of Prayer	William Walford/1845	William Bradbury/1861
Jesus Loves Me	Anna Warner/1860	William Bradbury/1862
My Hope Is Built on Nothing Less	Edward Mote/1834	William Bradbury/1863
Just as I Am	Charlotte Elliott/1835	William Bradbury/1849
Blessed Assurance	Fanny J. Crosby/1873	Phoebe Knapp/1873
Pass Me Not, O Gentle Savior	Fanny J. Crosby/1868	William H. Doane/1870
Jesus Keep Me Near the Cross	Fanny J. Crosby/1869	William H. Doane/1869
To God Be the Glory	Fanny J. Crosby/1878	William H. Doane/1875
Rescue the Perishing	Fanny J. Crosby/1869	William H. Doane/1870
I Am Thine, O Lord	Fanny J. Crosby/1875	William H. Doane/1875
Close to Thee	Fanny J. Crosby/1874	Silas J. Vail/1874
More Love to Thee, O Christ	Elizabeth Prentiss/1869	William H. Doane/1870
Shall We Gather at the River?	Robert Lowry/1864	Robert Lowry/1864
Nothing but the Blood of Jesus	Robert Lowry/1876	Robert Lowry/1876
Come We That Love the Lord	Isaac Watts/1707	Robert Lowry/1867
(Refrain) Marching to Zion	Robert Lowry/1867	Robert Lowry/1867
I Need Thee Every Hour	Annie S. Hawkes/1872	Robert Lowry/1873
All to Jesus I Surrender	Judson Van Deventer /1896	W. S.Weeden/1896

African American Gospel Music as
a Distinctive Genre and Style

The musical streams that joined in the creation of gospel music include the call-and-response traditions of Africans and African Americans; the slow, meter hymns of black congregations; the driving rhythms and percussive instrumental accompaniment of African American Pentecostal storefront churches; as well as blues, ragtime, and jazz. Additionally, the gospel music tradition has been enhanced by the efforts of composers such as William Henry Sherwood, Charles Albert Tindley, Lucie Campbell, Thomas A. Dorsey, and Roberta Martin.[13]

Charles Tindley is considered the pivotal force in the development of composed and published African American gospel songs. His compositions formed the foundation upon which the gospel music genre was developed. Lucie Campbell is credited with creating and nurturing a rich musical environment within African American Baptist churches. As a major songwriter and organizer, Lucie Campbell served as a crucial link among a network of new composers.[14]

A collection of songs that was decidedly cast in the African American spiritual, pre-gospel tradition is the 1893 compilation *Harp of Zion,* edited by William Henry Sherwood, a Pentecostal minister.[15] Sherwood appears to have been the first composer to take advantage of the return to the roots of the freed slaves who eventually flocked to Azusa Street.[16] One of Sherwood's compositions, "The Church Is Moving On," was included in *Spirituals Triumphant, Old and New,* published by the National Baptist Convention Publishing Board in 1927, which provides some evidence of the popularity of this song.

The National Baptist Convention, USA, established a music department in 1900, and singers were permitted and encouraged to introduce religious music at annual meetings. The publication of *Gospel Pearls* in 1921 by the Sunday School Publishing Board of the National Baptist Convention marks a significant event in the history of African American church music. In this book's preface, the Music Committee explained that by its name, this collection "tells the story and supplies the present day needs of the Sunday schools, churches, conventions, and other religious gatherings with pearls of songs suitable for worship, devotion, evangelistic services, funeral, patriotic, and other special occasions."[17]

This songbook of the National Baptist Convention, USA, was the first to use the term *gospel,* an indication that leaders in the black Baptist church accepted the practice of conveying the gospel through song. Prior to this publication, Charles Tindley incorporated black folk imagery into his songs, which interpreted the oppression African Americans faced as they settled in the cities of the North. Tindley is considered the first gospel hymn writer to have considerable influence on black gospel songwriters in general, most notably Thomas Dorsey. Tindley began to copyright his music in the early 1900s, and in 1901 sponsored periodic concerts of church songs, many of which he composed himself. In 1916 he published a collection, *New Songs of Paradise*,[18] which, due to its popularity, led to a seventh edition by 1941.

Chicago is often regarded as the center of the perpetuation of black gospel music, because by the 1920s its churches had produced many celebrated writers and singers. During this decade, Dorsey moved from blues to the style of religious music he called the "gospel blues." Building upon his exposure to the music of Tindley and the singing delivery style of W. M. Nix, Dorsey contended that altering the rhythmic values of notes helps to emphasize parts of the text, which enhances the meaning of the message. This is much like the musical aesthetics employed in the singing and playing of the blues.[19] By the spring of 1932, two apparent forms of gospel blues had emerged and were becoming acceptable modes of music in old-line black churches: the solo mode, wherein an individual can personally testify in song, and the choral mode, which broadens the testimonial opportunity. In both modes, the congregation can participate in an affirmation of the testimonial offering.

Dorsey led the way in shaping, notating, and printing solo music. His composition "Take My Hand, Precious Lord," prompted by the death of his wife and son, also led to a recasting of his spiritual journey. He was tempted first to return to the blues, but instead he found a resolution to his religious conflict by turning the use of blues idioms into music for worship. A prolific composer, Dorsey wrote nearly one thousand songs and published more than half of them. In acknowledging his contribution to the music of black America, Eileen Southern notes, "Although Tindley's songs inspired him, he wrote in a different style. To the religious intensity of the Tindley songs he added the melodic and harmonic patterns of the blues, and his experience as a blues-jazz pianist was reflected in the musical density and improvisatory nature of his accompaniments."[20]

During the 1920s and 1930s, certain traditions of gospel music were established that served to define it as a distinctive genre embodying a distinctive *style* of musical performance. As a genre, black gospel music is a twentieth-century, freely improvised musical expression of the good news in song, according to the intensity and black music aesthetics of contemporary African American culture. Inherent to the shaping of black gospel music is the concept of African American folk rhetoric, folk expression, bodily movement, charismatic energy, cadence, tonal range, and timbre.

As a distinctive style of performance, gospel music reflects the holistic understanding of the importance of the body *and* soul in spiritual expressions.

Performance practices will vary according to the manner of interpretation by the song leader and the freedom of the worship. The expectation of individual interpretation is one aspect of the black gospel music tradition that lies at the heart of the black aesthetic. Therefore, within the boundaries of control there is still a sense of freedom.[21] Nevertheless, there is a distinctive "gospel music vocabulary" and characteristic aesthetics that help determine the manner of delivery.

By the end of the 1930s, two categories of gospel performing groups had emerged: first, all-male gospel quartets that sang a cappella in "barbershop" style, adding percussive rhythmical accompaniment by slapping their thighs and snapping their fingers; and second, all-female gospel choruses dressed in choir robes or evening attire, and singing to the accompaniment of the piano.[22] Both groups attracted large audiences, and despite the emphasis in either the style of performance or the attire, the fervor and seriousness of the singing transformed the audience into a congregation, a community of faith.

The concept of gospel music as entertainment beyond the liturgical environment contributed largely to its categorization as music outside the bounds of worship. Long before the terms *liturgy* and *liturgical* were removed from the bonds of tightly framed, preplanned structure, black gospel music was not considered appropriate in some African American worship services. During the early years of the twentieth century, some African American Baptists and Methodists expressed concern that the gospel music of the sanctified or Holiness churches was not good for their image. One must keep in mind the various historical contexts of black music styles, and the fact that local preachers served as "gatekeepers" for the kind and quality of music used in worship. An examination of hymnals published prior to *Gospel Pearls* reveals a large number of Euro-American hymns. However, what was printed in the plethora of black hymnals was not reflective of the oral repertoire of the worship in the churches.

However, even *Gospel Pearls* provided an interesting perspective of the concept of music for worship in the black Baptist church. Of the 163 songs in the book, 143 are standard white Protestant hymns, plus American patriotic favorites ("My Country, 'Tis of Thee," "The Star Spangled Banner," and "The Battle Hymn of the Republic"). Included in the category of spirituals—*at the back of the book*—is one song by Tindley, "Stand by Me," and one song by Edward C. Deas, "Shine for Jesus." A second Tindley hymn, "A Better Home," appears immediately prior to the spiritual section. Other black composers included are Carrie Booker Pearson, Charles Price Jones, and Thomas Dorsey. Reprints of *Gospel Pearls* in shaped-note and regular-note editions as well as its use in black congregations across denominational lines indicate the popularity of the hymnal.

The importance of *Gospel Pearls* is first and foremost due to the prominence of women on the hymnal's editorial team: Willa A. Townsend, Lucie Campbell, Carrie Booker Pearson, and Geneva Bender Williams—all renowned composers. The volume has been significant because of its role in facilitating the spread of the use of gospel music in the liturgy of black congregations from the 1920s forward. Horace Clarence Boyer, whose study of black gospel music has added new dimensions to previous studies, explains the hymnal's success:

> Baptists no longer had to attend Pentecostal, Holiness, or sanctified churches to hear the music. They could now hear this music in their own churches on Sunday morning; for the shouting kind of gospel, they still had to go to the source. There were now two styles of singing gospel: one that emphasized singing in which the spirit dictated the amount of embellishment, volume, and improvisation that was applied, and a second that, while attempting to incorporate the dictates of the spirit, tempered the rendition to the musical taste of the Baptist congregation.[23]

Directly and indirectly, the popularity of *Gospel Pearls* spawned numerous gospel quartets. Among the famous ones was the Golden Gate Quartet, whose added harmonies, rhythmic accents, and swaying supported by finger snapping (an absolutely forbidden practice in worship) helped to push gospel onto the entertainment stage. Other popular quartets were the Southernaires, the Sallie Martin Singers, and the Roberta Martin Singers.

As a stylistic form, African American gospel music from the 1920s through the 1940s is characterized by the following:

1. The earliest texts are often subjective and filled with hope, thanksgiving, and lamentation, with acknowledgment of the blessings received or promised; some texts speak objectively of the triune God, with a strong focus on Jesus, the second person of the Trinity.
2. The improvised manner of the style of delivery is as important as what is sung. Melodies are freely improvised at the will of singers, often with spoken vocal injections and chanted testimonies.
3. Melodies often utilize flatted thirds and sevenths, demonstrating a close affinity with the blues.
4. Marked syncopation is common, as well as highly improvised, instrumental accompaniment that serves as a driving force in its production and as an integral part of the performance.
5. Songs are basically strophic in form, tending to be sixteen and thirty-two measures in length.
6. Certain techniques, such as arpeggios, passing tones, runs, chromatics, and glissandi, are used to "fill in" measures of rests.

Boyer adds to these observations his own experience as a gospel pianist and theorist par excellence:

> A gospel piano style had been developed based on the "rhythm section" concept, in which the middle of the piano is used to support the singers by doubling the vocal line in harmony; the left bottom portion of the keyboard serves as the bass fiddle, and the right upper portion acts as a solo trumpet or flute, playing countermelodies and "fill" materials at rhythmic breaks.[24]

Various keyboard techniques have evolved over the years, making the role of gospel instrumentalists—especially pianists and organists—more technically demanding. With a few exceptions, gospel pianists or keyboardists have tended to possess the gifts of playing "by ear" and improvising. Interestingly, gospel music keyboard techniques are now being taught in some church music degree programs and in nationally acclaimed gospel music workshops, thereby enhancing the skills both of music readers and those who structure chords and melodic lines according to the sounds they hear.

Major gospel concerts, whether in sanctuaries, concert halls, or public auditoriums, often involve the inclusion of a brief sermon that encompasses a scriptural text or a personal witness by the "lead singer" prior to the singing. The repetition of a portion of the chorus or the last portion of a song, called a *reprise,* is a common occurrence in gospel performances and is indicated by the continuous applause of an appreciative audience.

Historical Classifications of Black Gospel Music

Although gospel music is most often classified according to time periods and based on innovative features of its genre and style, it is not always given the same name. The most frequently used classifications of gospel music are: traditional, historic, or classical; the golden era; modern gospel; and contemporary gospel. No time period is considered self-contained in that there is always an overlapping from one period to another. Equally important are the developments in other musical arenas that, in turn, affect transitions in gospel music.

Traditional or Historic Gospel: 1920–ca. 1940

In the evolution and shaping of artistic genres and styles, dates are provided as approximate periods of time. The term *historic* denotes the beginning, the period of time when gospel music was established, with *traditional* symbolizing the foundational roots upon which future categories have been built. The term *classical* is often used to designate both the period of time between 1920–1940 and the lasting effectiveness of the powerful repertoire, to which many African Americans point when speaking of "the best of gospel music." All three terms apply to this era as an important transitional period in African American liturgical history. This is a period when African Americans struggled to accept their African heritage, where the secular and sacred came together even as they worshiped God.

This was the time of the Great Depression, which began in 1929 and brought chaos to the lives of black professional jazz and blues musicians. It was also a time when college-educated African Americans' exposure to the artistic side of Euro-American culture stimulated an interest for some and affirmed the established interest for others of new dimensions of religion and the arts. The Black Renaissance, also referred to as the Harlem Renaissance and the New Negro Movement, was well underway, with its focus on literature and other arts. Gospel music, despite its worldly or secular undertones, was after all religious music, and thus appropriate for the worship of God.

A portion of this era (1930–1945) is also called "The Dorsey Era" because of Thomas Dorsey's contributions to the music of the black church. In 1930 gospel music was endorsed by the National Baptist Convention. In 1932 Dorsey opened the Dorsey House of Music, which was the first music publishing company founded for the sole purpose of selling the music of black gospel composers. In this same year, Dorsey and gospel singer Sallie Martin organized a national convention of gospel choirs, thus adding gospel choir gatherings to other ongoing music conventions. With this focus on education it is of interest to note that in July 1919, the first convention of the National Association of Negro Musicians had been held, with an effort to raise the musical standards of the teaching profession.[25] Dorsey, along with Martin, had already organized the first gospel chorus at the Ebenezer Baptist Church in Chicago in 1931. In 1932, Dorsey, Thomas Frye, and Magnolia Lewis Butts formed the Chicago Gospel Choral Union, Inc., which met annually to offer workshops and provide a showcase for singing.

It was the Dorsey Era, indeed, for out of this era came most of his nearly 1,000 songs including "Precious Lord, Take My Hand," "When I've Done the Best I Can," and "There Will Be Peace in the Valley." As Wyatt Tee Walker notes, "Gospel music that was born with Thomas A. Dorsey as its chief architect . . . is the music of the Great Depression that details clearly and poetically what the religious mood of Black America was all about."[26] It is significant to note as well that this was the period when Dorsey promoted a "battle of songs" between Roberta and Sallie Martin and charged fifteen cents for admission. Although contests between musicians had taken place before in

the African American community, Eileen Southern contends this might have
been the first time that admission had been charged for a sacred music concert.[27] This era witnessed Rosetta Tharpe singing in concert at Carnegie Hall,
at Radio City Music Hall, and with the Dixie Hummingbirds and the Café
Society. According to Boyer, "[T]hese appearances were looked upon with
disdain because at that time Christians were admonished to follow the dictum
to be 'in the world but not of the world.'"[28]

Gospel's Golden Era: Mid 1940s–1969

By the middle 1930s black gospel music was well established in many African
American congregations and communities as a unique and significant musical genre. Male a cappella gospel quartets had established a performance style
that was preferred by black concert audiences, as the newly developing keyboard accompanying style was slowly becoming popular. Gospel choirs were
organized in the early 1930s and were already well established in black Pentecostal and Baptist congregations as well as a few black Methodist churches.
By the 1940s a new black sacred music was identified by its slow, soulful, and
deeply religious rendering, and by the jubilant expressions of praise, thanksgiving, and hope amidst urban poverty, new and intricately subtle forms of
racism and degradation.

The music reflective of this era is not at all complicated. The harmonies were
simply reminiscent of spirituals, hymns, and blues combined with personal testimonies, verbalized in a *down home* or African expressive *manner.* On the other
hand, some gospel music could be quite complicated, with driving rhythms and
complicated improvisations that invited worshipers into a highly emotional religious expression. Among the characteristics that ultimately led to the expression *Golden Era of Gospel Music* were the variety of vocal timbres and styles
evidenced among black gospel singers during this era, continuing into the
twenty-first century. There are the high shrill soprano and tenor voices, the low,
articulate, and also low, hoarse, and strained voice in all vocal ranges. Each
vocal expression reflects the passion and seriousness of a minister of the gospel.

During the golden era, gospel music became so popular that it reaped financial rewards well beyond the imaginations of any of its original pioneers. This
period was influenced by the Second World War and its aftermath, which
brought about unusual economic growth in the United States, through the benefits of the G.I. Bill of Rights, developments in technology, especially the
media, and black-owned recording industries.

Black gospel continued in liturgical settings, providing spiritual renewal for
congregations that were willing to continue a tradition that was rooted in the
black church. Spiritual inspiration continued not only for African Americans

but also for those in places far removed from the liturgical space of the African American worshiping sanctuaries, because of radio, recordings, and gospel concerts. The 1950s began with the first big all-gospel concert in history: the Negro Gospel and Religious Music Festival at Carnegie Hall in New York, with Mahalia Jackson as the "star attraction." Two observations about this big event can be considered antithetical to African American liturgical understanding. First, a distinction was made between *gospel* music and *religious* music, which might have been intentional. Second, the "star attraction" in black religious settings is not a human person, but the Almighty God in Jesus the Christ!

Gospel singers appeared on television during the 1950s, with Mahalia Jackson leading the way on the *Ed Sullivan Show,* followed by appearances on her own show in 1954. In 1957 the Newport Jazz Festival was the impetus that encouraged the Clara Ward Singers to move their music from black liturgical space to "center stage." Attention was also drawn to two historical "reversals": the organization of the first all-male gospel choir in history and the popularity of female quartets. Gospel radio also reached new heights of popularity in the mid-'40s as stations from New York to Nashville featured the *Gospel Hour.* Gospel recordings increased, but without the black artists ever receiving a fair accounting of or share of the money for records sold.[29] Thus, the golden era is so named because it is the time when gospel music was clearly recognized as a form of *entertainment*, judged more by record sales than by its liturgical function to edify congregations and build up the body of Christ. In order to offset losses incurred in the recording and selling of records, some singers moved from the "chancel stage" on Sunday morning after a "performance" and through the congregation-turned-audience to collect enough to cover expenses.

This was also the era of the civil rights movement, when African Americans led the charge to dismantle segregation and systemic racism. It was also a time when the African American spiritual tradition was reclaimed for civil rights "freedom songs." The choice of the civil rights theme song was the music and text of a hymn by Charles Tindley, whose gospel hymns had influenced the gospel songs of Thomas Dorsey. Tindley's "I'll Overcome Some Day" became "We Shall Overcome."

Bessie Griffin, who is credited with being the first gospel singer to appear in a cabaret, was the lead singer in the first gospel musical in history, *Portraits in Bronze. Black Nativity* followed in 1961 and became the first gospel musical to tour in both America and Europe. By 1963, gospel had its own weekly television show, *T.V. Gospel Time.* In 1969, James Cleveland organized "The Gospel Music Workshop America," which, like Dorsey's gospel music convention, brought together thousands of singers and persons interested in composing gospel music together yearly, thus increasing the number of persons exposed to this genre as well as to many new composers. Reading music was not a requirement for gospel music composers; only the gifts of hearing and reproducing chordal sounds and rhythms were necessary. By now, black gospel choirs were demanding and receiving their place on college campuses, creating tension with established music programs in historically black colleges, where reading music was (and is) required. However, there was personal security in knowing that whatever gifts one brought to rehearsals would be honed so that choral singing became more accessible to students of all races. Black students who were enrolled in traditional Euro-American colleges, universities, and seminaries were demanding the right to establish gospel choirs, many of which became very popular. Graduates of institutions of higher education, whether they were professionally trained musicians or not, hastened to Protestant and Catholic churches, where they often helped plant gospel choirs.

Changes that had occurred in the development of jazz reached a new height in the 1960s. Improvisational techniques were freed from a dependence upon fixed choral progressions. The first jazz mass to be performed in a Roman Catholic church as part of the liturgy was introduced in 1966 by Edward Bonnemere, a Catholic layman. Jazz was brought into the church through the Roman Catholic tradition, along with other folk music. Clarence Rivers, a Catholic priest, composed some of the first jazz masses, which aired initially at the Newport Jazz Festival in 1967. Duke Ellington, a major proponent of sacred jazz in the church, provided the impetus for the liturgical use of jazz through his concerts of sacred music. The first of these concerts was held at Grace Cathedral in San Francisco in September 1965, with a repeat performance and a recording of the concert at Fifth Avenue Presbyterian Church in New York in December 1965. The second performance was held at the Cathedral of St. John the Divine in New York in 1968, and the third at Westminster Abbey in London in 1973.

By 1975, due mainly to technological advances, church musicians experimented more rapidly with improvisational techniques, infusing more of the jazz elements into church music. This was the era when the Hammond organ reached new heights of popularity as an accompanying instrument for gospel music. During this time, old and new styles of jazz and gospel coexisted.

Modern Gospel: 1969–1980s and Beyond

This period of gospel activity in the African American church was marked by Edwin Hawkins's recording of "O Happy Day," a hybrid arrangement of a hymn by the Euro-American composer Philip Doddridge. More than two million copies of this recording were sold, as church choirs increased their efforts to model the "big choir sound" and the vocal tenacity of lead singers. The popularity of gospel increased at a more rapid rate in the last quarter of the twentieth century and into the twenty-first. Soundtracks are now readily available for congregations that want the big orchestral sound as background music for soloists and choirs. During this period, the gospel sound was heightened by the electronic organ, amplification of stringed instruments, and the addition of percussion, including conga and bongo drums.

Contemporary Gospel Music

Using the word *contemporary* to describe gospel music is at best a misnomer, since it refers to something that is happening concurrently or simultaneously, something that coexists within the same time period. Thus, all gospel music periods were contemporary in their time. However, the appellation with reference to gospel music of the late twentieth century refers to instrumental and vocal performance styles that originated in or are closely related to pop music, rhythm and blues, and jazz. While there have been infusions of blues and jazz since the beginning of the gospel genre, the so-called contemporary sound has removed some members of the congregation mentally and spiritually from the Holy Spirit–inspired, free expression of the church, to the jazz hall or bar, where attention to the Divine might be diverted to other things. Worshipers steeped in the sound and impact of the traditional and golden eras of gospel and modern-gospel-attuned worshipers might both be offended by this infusion of sounds.

Of course, creators and performers of gospel music since its inception have been constantly exploring new ways to express themselves. Eileen Southern calls this "a search for the expressive and the novel."[30] Composers experiment by combining elements of gospel with elements from other genres. Quincy Jones displayed eloquently what can happen in a significant way in his blending of a baroque musical form with gospel music elements in his setting of George Frederick Handel's oratorio, *Messiah.*

Unfortunately, many musicians have taken *contemporary* to mean "transient," "evanescent," "ephemeral," or "in transition." The problem persists with "crossovers" among gospel musicians, that is, church musicians who moved to pop music, perhaps to find themselves or for other reasons, but have continued some of the practices that are more at home in the church, and vice versa. Names that are usually associated with this era are Bebe Winan, CeCe Winan, and other members of the Winan family, Walter Hawkins, Tramaine Davis Hawkins (Walter's wife), Danniebelle Hall, Ben Tankard, Richard Smallwood, and the Smallwood singers. Their songs characteristically combine gospel with modern jazz, drawing upon rhythm and blues, pop, soul, reggae, and rap.

Gospel Rap and Hip-Hop

Gospel rap is rooted in "pop rap," the new music of the twenty-first century, which reflects the influence of a number of genres and styles, especially rhythm and blues, soul, and funk. Eileen Southern acknowledges Afrika Bambaataa, a disc jockey in the Bronx, as a pivotal force behind the development of music that later became known as *rap*. As an ex-gang member and a self-taught student of black culture, Afrika believed that the arts could be used to combat street violence.[31] Bambaataa is responsible for starting a youth organization (later named the "Zulu Nation") at Adlai Stevenson High School in 1973, which inspired the gathering of a number of young adults and teenagers from inner-city New York. His group started an art movement with activities including rapping, graffiti drawing, break dancing, and techniques of disc jockeying. While he experimented with rap as a way of "gang fighting," the term *hip-hop* emerged. Afrika began to use the expression, and before long it had caught on.[32] A few theologians in the 1990s spent some time discussing the theological implications of rap as a cultural means of expressing the reality of life.

Hip-hop is considered a culture, initially uniquely African American. Rap is an artful expression that has roots in Africa. It is present vocally in words and percussively and instrumentally by words that are produced melodically on "talking drums." This form continues in the percussive rhythms of some black preachers in order to gain the attention of the community.[33] It is in this context that gospel rap and hip-hop have been used in worship. A few pastors have presented the Word of God in sermons using this method, but the procedure apparently has not caught on as a regular form of communication in worship. This can also be attributed to the association of street rap with profanity and the demeaning of women in some rap music.[34]

With a new generation of young seminarians, it is to be expected that the theological environment would include members of the hip-hop culture. In fact, one of the large number of articles on hip-hop on the Internet was written by an ITC student. Concepts that have emerged from hip-hop generation students in relation to hip-hop and African American worship are the following:

- Hip-hop music encompasses different musical styles and patterns, and is *not* simply another musical genre.
- Hip-hop has its own rules and regulations for production and performance.

- Hip-hop serves as an educational tool for youth that extends beyond the attire that youth adopt from some of the leading hip-hop artists.
- Hip-hop is here to stay. The style of approach is dynamic, and thus, ever changing.
- It is possible that this will not become a standard worship form for African American worshipers but might be used to enhance some worship experiences.

Gospel Music as a Global Phenomenon

Although many gospel groups were known widely among African American audiences, the availability of recordings facilitated the recognition of this form of gospel music. As indicated earlier, by the early 1930s gospel music had moved outside the sacred walls of African American storefront churches to the city streets. In addition to gospel quartets and larger choral groups, this sacred music migrated with African Americans to the West Coast and around the world. Migration from the church into secular settings is attributed to "Sister" Rosetta Thorpe (Rosetta Nubin), who sang in a Cab Calloway show at the Cotton Club in New York in 1938. Shortly thereafter, she signed a recording contract with Decca Records, thus becoming the first gospel singer to record for a major commercial company.[35] In December 1938, African American gospel music was included in a secular concert entitled "From Spirituals to Swing at Carnegie Hall," which was a presentation of the black tradition from African tribal music to Kansas City jazz. It was produced by John Hammond, a Euro-American jazz enthusiast and record producer. This portion of the concert was labeled "Spirituals and Holy Roller Hymns," with performers Sister Rosetta Tharpe and Mitchell's Christian Singers, a male quartet from Kinston, North Carolina.[36] John Hammond also encouraged singers of gospel music to perform in nightclubs, a practice the African American church considered inappropriate and blasphemous. However, with gospel music continually surfacing in nightclubs and theatres, some African American congregations often looked upon this music with suspicion. In responding to this criticism, Clara Ward, leader of the Famous Ward (Gospel) Singers, maintained that her mission was to "evangelize rather than to entertain." As the earliest proponent of the "pop gospel" style that emphasized showmanship and elaborate dresses and hairstyles, Ward wrote, "Although perhaps there are many people who would not share my opinion on the subject, I now feel that God intended for his [sic] message not solely by those who attend churches, but also by the outsiders who in many cases never attend a house of worship."[37]

Mahalia Jackson, having experienced both the sacred setting of worship and the worldly setting of the nightclub, the latter of which supplemented her income, acknowledged an important distinction between secular and sacred music in her comparison of gospel music and the blues: "'Blues' are songs of despair; gospel songs are the songs of hope. When you are singing gospel you have a feeling there's a cure for what's wrong. When you're through with the blues you've got nothing to rest on."[38] An opposing position is offered from pop singer Della Reese, who acknowledged the entertainment dimension and financial profit from her performances: "We are not presented as holy singers; we are here to show that gospel is interesting music. We don't perform in nightclubs to save souls. . . . I like a comfortable apartment, a healthy bank account, and some good solid real estate."[39]

Any number of gospel music soloists shared the opinion of many African Americans that nightclubs were not appropriate for the singing of gospel music. However, some nightclub owners began to explore alternative strategies to encourage gospel singers to accept contracts with them that were basically geared toward financial remuneration. Thus, "gospel nightclubs" were established to take advantage of the mounting interest of Euro-American teenagers who had little interest in the liturgical origin of the African American style of gospel music. Clear evidence of the exposure and exploitation of African American gospel music was a redefinition of the sound, rhythm, and ultimately the style of popular music in America and around the world.

By the 1920s, two technological phenomena had expanded the sanctuary of this genre of African American liturgical music: the radio and the record industry. Recordings of African American gospel singers and preachers were available in the early 1920s. Major record companies recorded live performances in churches on Sunday morning radio broadcasts. By the late 1930s, popular African American groups such as the Southernaires and the Golden Gate Jubilee quartet regularly appeared live on radio in fifteen-minute segments. Thus, gospel music was made available outside of the church into the world, with the assistance of black-owned record companies. In addition to gospel music, these companies recorded the new "secular" music—rhythm and blues—and billed both genres in a manner that positioned gospel music as a secular form.[40] A radio program called *Hootenanny* successfully introduced gospel music around the nation during the 1950s and 1960s.

Radio and record publicity continued as a means for the global spread of gospel music until the advent and growing popularity of television. The one-hour national television program *T.V. Gospel Time* not only broadened the nonliturgical venue of gospel music but also provided an improvised "stage" upon which a provisional African American worshiping community could be viewed. The leader of a gospel group or a gospel soloist featured for the day functioned more or less as the preacher for the congregation. During the "service," the guest host stirred the congregation with three to four songs. Because this series aired in most locations on Sunday morning, a time when African Americans were in their own churches, ratings were low, and after two seasons the program folded.[41]

Gospel Music as a Foundation for Popular Music

From its initial foundation as liturgical music, gospel music developed into a complex form that embodies the totality of African American culture, life, and history. Due to the popularity of the diverse forms of gospel music, African American Christians and non-Christians recognized the power and magnetic effect of this style of music beyond worship. Thus, various marketing strategies were explored, and gospel music became a "big business" venture, even for some of the liturgical settings in which it started. One business strategy was to "showcase" gospel music in places where entertainment music was traditionally performed. In this context gospel music began to change, subtly at first, but overwhelmingly in the long run. It was an "attraction," to be enjoyed by an audience, and the message that lies at the heart of gospel gave way to the medium of performance. Often in the style of performance, many texts are hard to distinguish from the texts of pop singers.

Along with its rise in popularity, gospel music was exploited by the music industry to spawn new and emerging consumer markets. Portia Maultsby, ethnomusicologist and gospel music scholar, observes, "Repackaged and promoted as entertainment to a cross-cultural and non-Christian audience in nontraditional arenas, the spiritual message and cultural aesthetic of gospel were subordinated to the money-making interest of the music industry."[42]

The radio and subsequent audio and visual technology contributed to this venture as a major arena for promotion and publicity. With a plethora of available recordings and support of the media, "the gospel sound and its beat led to appropriation of this music by purveyors of popular styles."[43] The major consumers were African American teenagers, and thus the entertainers determined that the performance of popular music was a quick and easy way to earn money. Maultsby identifies 1949 as the year that the term *rhythm and blues* was applied to all post–World War II forms of black popular music. This term was changed to *soul* in 1969, and through the 1970s, soul music was transformed into *funk* and *disco*.[44]

Gospel music has a magnetic power to draw people in. There is an attraction to the musical sounds and rhythms, and the personalized message draws listeners into the story. The vocal and physical delivery of the singers help you to hear and understand that you still belong to someone despite your status in life. It is the simplicity of the phrases and repetition of words and rhythmical devices. It is the depth of feeling that is evoked with each musical phrase, the memorable lines that one can recall long after the music stops. It is all of these and more that provide the magnetic appeal of gospel music.

Popular songs that incorporate the gospel sound, beat, feeling, and style have a "religious sound" based on aesthetic principles essential to African American musical performance. Gospel singers who cross over into popular music and are imitated by the popular music culture have facilitated this process. In addition to vocal techniques, timbres, and delivery style, popular music idioms such as rhythm and blues, soul, and funk have borrowed and feasted upon rhythms, improvisatory instrumental and vocal styles, emotional spirit, and energy that are characteristic of gospel music. Each of these characteristics functioning simultaneously, or alone, continues to influence the music of America and the world. As these characteristics combine and form new techniques and expressions, they are then "recycled" back into gospel music, and ultimately back into the African American liturgical setting, where they are reworked and returned to the secular environment. It could be said that the African unity of sacred and secular has returned for "testing," as a liturgical music form and style was thrust into the world and became the seed for the formation of new forms outside of the church. Artists who cross over from sacred to secular and from secular to sacred are simply reminded of the world of the artificial dichotomy established by a culture that has probably changed its mind about dichotomizing life!

The pop and gospel connection has reached out to and embraced a young African American generation whose existential situation in a technological age differs greatly from any of the previous African American liturgical periods. Numerous problems exist. First, there is the danger of an elusive faith grounding that is often unclear in texts composed by persons for whom monetary gain might be of utmost importance. Even where texts are theologically well grounded, the rhythm, beat, and melodic sound might overshadow the words. In addition, there is concern that one day gospel music will no longer belong to the church, but to increasingly large business corporations.

Gospel Music in the Liturgy:
Joys, Problems, and Possibilities

Throughout the centuries people have responded to God through music in a variety of musical genres and styles, and they will continue to do so. Black gospel music combines songs, emotions, thoughts, faith, physical movement, and thus the entire body in an offering to God in Jesus the Christ. Because of its emotional appeal, gospel music continues as a significant form and style of music to free the people to hear and feel the presence of the Almighty. Therefore, it can function effectively during any worship service, especially special services of evangelism.

In her dissertation on "The Black Gospel Music Tradition: Symbol of Ethnicity," Mellonee Burnim, a gospel musician and noted scholar, highlights ongoing possibilities of black gospel within the context of the performance event. Her study effectively utilizes the thoughts, ideas, and concepts held by carriers of the tradition, a vantage point from which she speaks. Although music as an act of worship is not the focus of her study, much of the information is transferable to ritual actions in worship. First among her seven findings is that black gospel music "transcends boundaries of age, denomination, and geographic locales."[45] Although Burnim emphasizes the "communication of blackness" as the single factor that unifies this tradition, it is important to focus on the intergenerational nature of her findings. Gospel music's ability to transcend the boundaries of age and level of vocal skills makes it an important factor in affirming the good news in worship and beyond. Admittedly, problems have occurred and continue to do so as members of the congregation, steeped in traditional gospel and other music genres, are not totally enamored over contemporary gospel as a worshiping genre. Still, gospel music has a much broader acceptance as an offering to God. Since the congregational dimension of music for worship is vital, it is important to observe also how a combination of age levels in the choir can facilitate the acceptance of gospel music as an act of worship. This is particularly true when the choir functions as *leaders* of worship rather than as *performers* in church.

Another conclusion from Burnim's study is that as a uniquely cultural form, gospel music is reflective of the gathered community's history, ideology, aesthetics, and behavior.[46] As autonomous worshipers separated from Euro-Americans, whether in black congregations or in independent black denominations, the gospel tradition represents more than musical sound; rather, "it is a unified system of meaning holding maximum relevance only for those immersed in the tradition. And finally, gospel music in worship symbolizes ethnicity, and is a unique expression of Black values, experiences, and beliefs."[47]

Other significant factors from this study related to worship are enumerated below:[48]

- Choirs (as well as congregations) symbolize ethnicity in the actual performance as meaning is conveyed (symbolically) through elements of sound quality, delivery style, and performance techniques. Burnim suggests that the diacritical features of dress, language, and gestures represent auxiliary symbols of ethnicity in the gospel tradition. Basic value orientations are evident in the designation of gospel music performance events as ritual, and in the specific technique through which factors of timbre, time, and pitch are manipulated in performance.

- The black gospel music tradition is multidimensional in function: It is designed to evoke a response, and it is a black cultural form of artistic expression as well as a religious phenomenon.
- The black gospel music tradition operates according to a cultural frame of reference that encompasses both sacred and secular music forms, and nonmusical forms of expressive behavior as well. According to Burnim, proponents of gospel music uniformly articulate the same aesthetic values whether judging performances of gospel or soul music, preaching, or "speaking" (talking), dancing, walking, or even simple everyday choices of clothing. Distinctions between sacred and secular are often merely a matter of intent or function, for the outward manifestations of these distinctions are often extremely subtle, and indeed in the minds of some listeners, nonexistent.

One of the dangers that gospel music has already experienced is that once the genre left the church and went on stage, it returned to the liturgical setting insisting that it should remain in the performance mode that it was thrust into outside the church. Often when gospel music is led by choirs or soloists, the congregation is relegated to the status of audience rather than as active participants who are open to hearing and receiving the good news "in spirit and in truth." Since gospel soloists and choirs need support from an audience, the congregation is drawn in, and assumes that role. Words from the song leader encouraging the congregation to participate, such as "Come on y'all," or "Put your hands together," are indeed engaging invitations. Once the congregation-turned-audience is drawn into the clapping, swaying, and repeating of words and phrases, however, these actions and verbal responses often become the focus rather than the intentional worship of God in and through Jesus the Christ.

Gospel music as a genre extended from the church during the 1930s as "the work of the people offered to God in praise" with evidence of the people's involvement in the world. Off and on gospel music returns from the world to the people in worship without deliberate and careful theological scrutiny of the texts by pastors who can discern the message and determine where a song can serve the Word. The emphasis is too often on the correctness of the sway and exactness of syncopated rhythms, and if there is a word from the Lord it may not be heard!

There is always the danger of persons or even authentic musical expressions returning home with the "smell of life upon them." The "aroma" that emanates from the prodigal now returned home is filled with financial rewards and marketable inveiglements that encourage church musicians to record and sell their CDs for personal gain. The people, the worshipers themselves, need to reclaim this genre and make sure that when and if it returns to the people that it has the aroma of praise to God and edification of spiritual life of the people upon it. Pastors should take the lead in determining how this and all musical genres enhance worship and serve as a means of glorifying and praising God rather than as a way to glorify performers. As with all other elements of worship, the purpose should be to the glory of God rather than the glorification of singers. The texts of the songs should reflect the Scriptures used in the service for the day, and the singers should understand this. Obery Hendricks, an AME minister and former president of Payne Theological Seminary, speaks to this issue most eloquently:

[D]espite the empowering nature of the Black sacred music of the past, in the dominant mode of Black religious music today—contemporary Gospel music—this prophetic voice, this resistance voice, this biblical logic of justice, is all but stilled. Gospel music is heard everywhere today; yet, unlike the Spirituals, it does not press our suit for freedom, it does not call, as the Spirituals, for "Moses, way down in Egypt land, Tell Ole Pharaoh to let my people go."[49]

During the early years of gospel music, poet Langston Hughes voiced his concerns about the irreverent use of spirituals in nightclubs, whether sung or played, "in live rhythms for the amusement of cabaret revelers." It can be concluded from his observations that this practice emerged when gospel music became an entertainment form outside of the church:

I do not think religious songs with their deep meanings for many people are a proper part of night club entertainment where folks are out for fun and drinking. Nor do I like the idea of dance bands making swing records of our Negro Spirituals. I never hear them jazzing up "Onward Christian Soldiers," or "Eli Eli," or "Rock of Ages." Why should they so desecrate "Deep River" or any other beautiful religious song?[50]

A second concern voiced by Hughes was about the "theatrics" of gospel singers who return to the church as highly prized entertainers. Noting the huge placards advertising church theatrical entertainment, his observation provides a glimpse of similarities between churches of the 1940s and some in the early part of the twenty-first century:

These placards set me to thinking how nowadays the theatre has invaded the church and has taken over various aspects of show business. . . . I had intended going to church the Sunday they [Maxine Sullivan and Marie Bryant] were billed just to see what sort of entertainment they would offer a Sunday evening congregation. The churches have so many expert entertainers in their own ranks that I do not quite see why they need to draw upon the theatre. . . . I remember last winter in Chicago hearing Elder Beck stand up in the pulpit and swing out a trumpet in a manner that would do credit to Louis Armstrong himself.[51]

Enough published concerns exist from throughout the twentieth century in the writings of musicians and pastors in historically black denominations to debunk the evaluation of some who have said that those who commented about the abuses of music in worship wanted to emulate the Euro-Americans. A careful reading of all of these concerns reveals the deep hope that authentic worship in the African American church will not be destroyed. A quote from the late Wendell Whalum captures the concern of a number of persons who take music, theology, and the church seriously, and also reminds us that there is work yet to be done:

Members of the clergy sometimes are guilty of misusing the music portions of the church service. Not possessing even the ability of a good layman [*sic*] to appreciate music, they will impose inferior standards, for various reasons, on their congregations. They do not use hymn books of good solid reference, and their choirs are made to serve as fund-raising organizations rather than to enhance the worship service.[52]

Whalum affirms the importance of the concept of gospel music but chastises ministers who have allowed a misuse of a viable African American musical genre. He states:

Gospel choirs today, though often very talented and entertaining, sometimes turn the act of worship, which is at best well-planned drama, into a religious circus in which the profane often exceeds the religious. *But the choirs, themselves, are not wholly to blame here. Blame must also be directed towards the ministers who have allowed a musical hodge-podge to develop.*[53]

We return now to the first question raised at the beginning of this chapter: What is taking place when a liturgical form goes commercial and then returns to the liturgical source of its origin to become the controlling force in shaping the faith, work, and walk of the people? The answer lies not so much in the form as in the persons responsible for worship. It should always remain clear that the Word of God in Scripture is the determining factor for the "work of the people," the liturgy of the church. God uses the worship planners, the team that will take seriously both God's Word and the needs and concerns of the people, to help maintain the balance. There is no African American liturgy without God and without the people who have always relied upon the almighty power of God to keep in tension the innate power of African American music and God's call upon the people to praise God through artistic forms.

And to return to the second question: Can something be done by the black community, the source of soul that helped produce gospel music, to reclaim its liturgical essence? There are some who would say that the liturgical essence of gospel music has not been lost after its journey into the world and around the globe. This depends upon the vantage point from which the person or community of faith speaks when responding to this question. There are many who would express joy that the world of popular music has depended upon the gifts of African Americans. There are some who are concerned that much of our music has been "stolen" by others, for which they are reaping the greatest benefits. Still others observe that much time has elapsed since gospel music originated, and few would know exactly what took place in the 1940s except from examining historical records.

In all instances, one must return to the actual worship setting, remembering that the line between the sacred and secular is an imaginary division placed there by humans in every age. Furthermore, human hands cannot control the "crossing over" of artistic forms from the sanctuary to the world. Our prayer should be that all our music and all our artistic offerings be used to the glory of God.

And so, what is the "smell of life" that can so boldly return to the sanctuary at will? It is the smell of human life that enters, prays, offers praise, blesses, forgives and seeks pardon, contributes 10 percent of income, receives blessings, is sent forth, leaves and then reenters the world, only to return to the sacred place of the sanctuary, knowing that we all fall short of the grace of God. If humans can ask and receive forgiveness and newness of life from God the Creator, is there some reason that God will not do likewise to a sacred art form? In this cyclical rather than linear movement, the music will leave again and return to the secular environment having been made new again, or "resacralized." After all, cyclical rhythm is basic to African primal worldviews.

The gospel genre, interactively with other black folk music genres—such as blues, jazz, and spirituals—allows performers and congregations different dimensions of *freedom*: freedom to improvise, recreate, and personalize without distorting the symbolic unity of the community, and the freedom to react to the artistic embodiment of struggles and fulfillment. Gospel music, like other aesthetic expressions, helps one to become disembodied, capricious, impulsive, renewed, and invigorated.

Gospel music has persisted within African American worship traditions because of the vital role that it has played and continues to play into the twenty-first century. While recognizing its contributions nationally and globally, the urgency is that its liturgical integrity will be in constant reflection of the spirit and truth of its origin.

Chapter 5

Instruments in Worship

At the beginning of the twenty-first century the dominant sound in many African American congregations comes from small and large consorts of percussion and keyboard instruments. Such sounds that now dominate sacred spaces of worship have not always been possible for African people in America. The process of stripping African slaves of their humanity included taking away the drums that were so basic to life, especially in West Africa. From the seventeenth to well into the nineteenth century, instruments were impractical for worshipers who were required to "steal away" and worship in secret. Persons of African descent initially made use of a most important gift: the human body, with its divinely structured instrumental capacity to produce sound.

On the continent of Africa, the sound of the voice, created by human breath, lungs, tongue, and supporting diaphragm, provided clear, unaccompanied sound. Thus the human body was the initial instrument that would be used to offer praise to God in worship. In a strange and alien land where brush harbors or bush harbors, gullies, woods and cabins, and other hastily prepared places served as gatherings for worship, an enslaved people moaned and groaned as well as created melodies and harmonious sounds as a means of offering praise to God. Handmade quilts would be saturated with water and used to muffle the sound so that it would not be heard by plantation owners. These same sounds, unmuffled, provided a means for "sounding musical alarms for freedom." Knowledge of African people assures that these sounds were accompanied by physical movements such as clapping and stomping that "sounded" in rhythm as an integral part of the vocal sound. With soft taps, claps, and grunts, such worshipers must have utilized their bodies as a means of internalizing and expressing feelings about the presence of the Holy Spirit. Surely it was not difficult for a people so familiar with the sound of the drum to express the various percussive sounds by employing their total being as they sang, prayed, and responded to the preached Word.

Evidently, a few drums were imported by Africans to the West Indies and to a lesser extent to mainland North America during the seventeenth and early eighteenth centuries.[1] According to judicial records of Somerset County, Maryland, in 1707–1711, there was a complaint that slaves were "drunk on the Lord's Day beating their Negro drums by which they call considerable numbers of Negroes together in some certain place."[2] Eyewitnesses to the Stono insurrection in South Carolina in 1739 reported dancing, singing, and beating of drums, which, considering the circumstances and period of slavery, must have been African drums.[3] It is of more than passing interest that slaveholders were accused of facilitating disruptive behavior, such as the beating of drums on the Lord's Day, by denying Africans an opportunity to learn about Christianity.[4] Visible evidence of an African drum on mainland North America is provided by an African hollow-log drum from eighteenth-century Virginia, which is now housed in the British Museum.[5] This drum is much like other *mpinti* drums of the Ashanti in Ghana, as well as the *apinti* drum of Guyana. Other African instruments found in the Americas that likely crossed the Atlantic with African people are the *bonjour*, a kind of guitar; a *cotter*, played by beating sticks over the strings; a drum called a *gomba*; various kinds of wind instruments; and the *balafo*, an ingeniously constructed African xylophone with gourds underneath the wooden keys, which serve as resonators.[6] The size of the *balafo* made it much more cumbersome to transport. Thus, it is likely that some might have been constructed in the Americas. Africans in the West Indies and South America often ignored a law that prohibited the use of drums, a law intended to avoid communal gatherings and dancing to forestall the possibility of communication and to subsequently discourage insurrections. With prohibitions on the mainland being strictly enforced during this era, there is only minimal evidence of the presence and use of African instruments. There were no portable stringed instruments to "hang on a willow tree." Instead, the songs of their souls poured out through their voices with the accompaniment of their physical bodies as they claimed God's gift of human flesh as *idiophones* (self-sounding instruments; see chapter 1). The gathered community in the American Diaspora was from the beginning a symphony of divinely created self-sounding instruments, subjected to but unscathed by "false winds" that attempted to destroy the "humanity" of the instruments. Instrumental sounds were liturgy—the work or action of the people.

The early community was busy calling each other to worship, gathering, listening for a Word from the Lord, and responding as the Spirit dictated in prayers, songs, sermons, testimonies, and dance. Sentinels stood guard, listening for intruders who would dare disturb these precious moments. Any imported instrument other than their own voices and their fatigued, over-worked bodies would reveal their location.

The total human body was the starting point for instruments in African American worship. By the time the earliest visible and legal African American congregations and denominational churches were established, human sounds—vocal and physical—were being used regularly as instruments of worship. There were indeed skilled African instrumentalists within the slave community, whose unusual talent did not go undiscovered. Their gifts were included as part of the advertisement for runaway slaves, providing researchers primary sources of information about many talented Africans. Unfortunately, there are no written records to indicate whether their talents were used as part of early worshiping experiences. The church was, in fact, among the first nurturing arenas for musical talent, the first concert hall for blacks, and the launching pad for musicians who would make a career of instrumental and vocal music.

The African Instrumental Heritage

As noted earlier, the voice is the basic musical instrument for worship. Vocal sounds—hums, moans, cries, and modulated expressions—are the primary means of offering praise to God. Vocal forms were shaped as humans imitated sounds of nature and sounds of their inner beings. The voice, therefore, takes priority over other instrumental forms. Singing with one voice or in unison was for the early Christians symbolic of their unity and togetherness, which are so important to the faith. This concept originated in the so-called secular world, where unity was understood as good and duality as evil, and thus unity was to duality as harmony was to disharmony.

Next in the natural sequence of sound-producing instruments is the human body, from which God's gifts of rhythm and feeling emanate. Just as the voice imitates sounds in the universe and returns these sounds as offerings of praise to the Creator, the rhythmic pulse of the heartbeat can be imitated by movement and the percussive sound of the physical body. The body is useful, therefore, as a percussive expression of the inner sound emanating from within oneself. People offer their praise through bodily movement—dance, swaying, handclapping, facial expression, and foot stomping (but not snapping the fingers).[7] In this manner, the human body itself can be placed in the category of folk instruments identified as *idiophones*. Broadly defined, the idiophone is any instrument upon which a sound may be produced by striking or pounding without the aid of a stretched membrane, a vibrating string, or a reed.[8]

From this perspective, African American worshipers function holistically and "instrumentally" out of the African primal worldview that understands that music is an umbilical cord that links one to the extraordinary power of God. With voice and body in a natural linkage to the Creator, the body can become or can be used as an instrument. In this way, all worship includes instruments in African American worshiping communities. This is also a way of affirming the importance of holistic worship, where our whole being is offered to God in adoration, praise, confession, thanksgiving, and submission.

The gift for improvising, making use of what is available, so prevalent in African traditions, is connected to instrumental resources that are at the disposal of African people. There are nomadic societies in Africa, for instance, that are without the natural means to create idiophones such as log drums (because there are not enough trees) or *membranophones*, which require certain animals for the different types of drums needed. Making certain instruments may be further complicated because of the uncertainty of time in any location, and animals must be killed and the skins dried before they are serviceable. Rhythmical interests are displayed in handclapping, simple and complex bodily movements, rhythmic stamping, and, of course, the use of vocal-percussive grunts.[9] Improvisation is one of many gifts that continue wherever Africans are in the Diaspora. On the strange and alien soil of what would later be called the United States of America, Africans imported as slaves were not permitted to have drums because they allowed Africans to communicate with each other across long distances. The body, nevertheless, is a personal idiophone and available for use by the individual encased in the body.

Needless to say, even the use of one's own body as an instrument of worship can create problems. At different times in history and at different points in sociological tolerance, some congregations have discouraged physical expressions. The twenty-first-century pattern continues to be varied within and across denominations, with the Pentecostal denominations continuing the freedom and openness of physical expressions since their founding. During the latter half of the twentieth century, churches began to accept and appreciate the ritual actions of others in an effort to avoid stereotyping denominations according to presupposed ritual practices.

The memories of seventeenth-century Africans in America were surely filled with the sounds of instruments in their homeland, for theirs was a land of musical sounds that expressed the aliveness of African life. African and other non-European instruments were grouped according to certain classifications established in the early twentieth century.[10]

Although music is an integral part of African life, it does not mean that every black African must be a musician. Another fallacy is that all Africans are so rhythmically astute that any one of them can beat a drum or play another instrument by virtue of his or her ability to accent in the right places at the right time. Bebey notes that most Africans do have a natural sense of rhythm. This instinct for rhythm not only produces a large number of percussionists but also enables many Africans to master the techniques of more complicated melodic instruments.[11]

A strong tendency to feel rhythmic pulses does not naturally grant African musicians the right to play any instrument. Strict rules govern the choice of instrument and the specific occasions for which persons are allowed to use particular instruments. Bebey provides an example from Rwanda, where the privilege of playing the six royal drums—the royal emblems of the Mwami (the king of the Tutsi people)—are reserved for one particular musician.[12] In other communities, only young, talented musicians can fill the place vacated by the death of one of the official drummers.

The *kora* (*cora*, or *seron*) in Guinea, a chordaphone that has been described as one of the most beautiful musical instruments, both visually and aurally, is one of many examples of African instruments that predate a number of Western instruments. It is available for all persons to learn and to master. One of the lessons from African people is that the ability to play an instrument is virtually a form of communication or "communion" between the musical instrument and the musician. Musicians must learn to speak the same language as that of the instrument that they play.

The amount of time spent on the idiomatic use of the body as an instrument in worship is due to the continuity of this practice among African people in the Diaspora through the centuries. It is seldom discussed as an African primal inheritance. The emphasis on the African instrumental heritage is also a deliberate reminder that the various sounds of instruments permeate our understanding of their offering praise to God.

Although the human body and the voice can be considered instruments, another definition can be considered when examining instruments in worship. Instruments can be understood as devices or mechanisms for producing musical sound that can facilitate or enhance worship and can be used to offer praise to Almighty God.

Biblical Foundations

Hebrew Bible

Throughout the centuries, tensions over the use of instrumental music have continued as worship leaders and theologians with interest in church music have used biblical references both to condemn and to condone the use of instruments in worship. On the one hand, the Hebrew Bible provides the church with rich sources of information and justification for the use of instruments. While the New Testament is not totally silent on the matter of instruments, there seems to be a different mode of reference to music that may ultimately point to the fullness of the sound of the heavenly hosts as indicated in Revelation. Consideration must also be given to the difference in the time spans of the two records. The Hebrew Bible describes events in the life of a people for 1,500 years or more, while the New Testament covers only approximately seventy years. Those who seek to condemn the use of instruments according to New Testament content are often overlooking differences in the course of time and focus of information.

The first reference to music in the Hebrew Bible includes an acknowledgment to the ancestor of instrumentalists and is mentioned with the ancestor of those who are responsible for livestock: "Adah bore Jabal; he was the ancestor of those who live in tents and have livestock. His brother's name was Jubal; he was the ancestor of all those who play the lyre and pipe" (Gen. 4:20–21). Although this passage does not concern Hebrew words directly, the parallel references are reminders of offerings in worship, both requiring the best form from the people of God. This pairing in the Hebrew community could have provided a foundation for music to be the best possible offering by congregations and instrumentalists to the glory of Almighty God.[13] There are some, however, who argue that the music through the lineage of Jubal was profane.[14] There are accounts in the Hebrew Bible of the effects of instruments on healing and prophesying and transporting worshipers into supernatural experiences of God:

> And whenever the evil spirit . . . came upon Saul, David took the lyre and played it with his hand, and Saul would be relieved and feel better, and the evil spirit would depart from him. (1 Sam. 16:21)

> Elisha said, . . . "But get me a musician." And then, while the musician was playing, the power of the LORD came on him. And he said, "Thus says the LORD . . ." (2 Kgs. 3:14–16a)

Instruments were necessary in signaling worshipers to come to the temple, according to the Lord's specific instructions regarding the making of silver trumpets (Num. 10:1–2). The epitome of Hebrew worship and the use of instruments emanated from David, who was an instrumental performer and composer: "David also commanded the chiefs of the Levites to appoint their kindred as the singers to play on musical instruments, on harps and lyres and cymbals, to raise loud sounds of joy" (1 Chron. 15:16).

Instruments also were used in temple worship itself, especially to accompany the Psalms. Many of the instruments were of African ancestry, especially Egyptian. The most frequently referenced instrument was the *kinnor*, a lyre played with a plectrum, which is similar to the Greek *kithara*. Other instruments of Egyptian ancestry are the *nevel* or *nebal*, a large harp that is played with the fingers. Some evidence suggests that this instrument may have been a larger and lower-pitched *kinnor*, similar to the lute.[15] Jeremy Montagu notes that *kinnor* is the modern Hebrew name for the violin and the archetypal string instrument of the Bible.[16]

It is important to note references to times that the Hebrews silenced their instruments during the Babylonian exile. Psalm 137:1–4 is perhaps the most familiar:

> By the rivers of Babylon—
> > there we sat down and there we wept
> > when we remembered Zion.
> On the willows there
> > we hung up our harps.
> For there our captors
> > asked us for songs,
> and our tormentors asked for mirth, saying,
> > "Sing us one of the songs of Zion!"
> How could we sing the LORD's song
> > in a foreign land?

The following passages from the Psalms command the playing of instruments: 33:1–3; 81:1–4; 92:1–4; 144:9; and 150:3–5. The prophets Isaiah and Amos denounce the use of instruments in the following passages: Isaiah 5:11–13; Amos 5:21–24 and 6:1, 4–7. Although the story of Shadrach, Meshach, and Abednego is among the favorite Hebrew stories of African Americans, many may not be aware that their furnace punishment was due to the fact that they did not fall down and worship the golden image at "the sound of the horn, pipe, lyre, trigon, harp, drum, and entire music ensemble," as King Nebuchadnezzar had ordered (Dan. 3:4–5).

The shofar, a ram's horn, used for signaling, is the only ancient Israelite instrument that is still used today. Other signaling instruments are the *magrepha*, a forerunner of the pipe organ used to call the Levites to duty; the *chatzotzra*, a silver trumpet; the *tof* or *toph*, a small hand drum or tambourine; and the *tziltzal* or *zelzelim* (cymbals). In addition to calling the Levites to duty, signals were needed to announce the entrance of the priests and to indicate when the congregation should prostrate or stand. Bells on the hem of the priest's robes were used as percussion instruments.

At its peak around the beginning of the Christian era, music in the Jewish temple was quite elaborate. Large choirs of trained male singers were utilized, with occasional additions of young boys, accompanied by skilled instrumentalists, especially during times of sacrificial offerings. According to the Mishnah (which was compiled about 200 C.E.), each day of the year there was a solemn sacrifice in the morning and another in the afternoon. On Sabbaths and feast days there were additional sacrifices. Gelineau notes that ritualism and magic are two inherent dangers in the use of instrumental music in early Jewish worship, and contends that sacred instruments were confined to the liturgy of the temple. Only the shofar remains, with its sole purpose of giving a signal, rather than providing musical accompaniment.[17] Instrumental music associated with temple worship apparently ended after the temple's destruction in 70 C.E., when the practice of sacrificial offerings also ended.

New Testament

The early Christians in Jerusalem no doubt continued their Hebrew singing legacy in the temple and in musical practices of unaccompanied Jewish chants in the synagogues. Singing continued in the New Testament churches through the centuries with the blending of Jewish and Hellenistic musical practices. Therefore, song has always been considered foundational to Christian worship. It is believed that the entire worship service was a combination of textual intonations and cantillation, so it was practically impossible to characterize music as a separate element of worship. The emergence of instruments as a problem occurred with the spread of Christianity, as various cultures added their local musical instruments. There are only a few New Testament references to instruments, and they are indicated as follows:

- Matthew 9:18–19, 23–25—The *aulos* (flute) is used after Jairus's daughter dies.
- Matthew 11:16–17—Jesus compares his generation to children playing the *aulos*.
- 1 Corinthians 13:1—Paul uses instruments metaphorically.
- 1 Corinthians 14:6–19—The reference to instruments is followed by the comment that instruments cannot produce words. Some interpreters of this passage have used it as an argument against the use of instruments in church.
- 1 Corinthians 15:50–52—The "last" trumpet will sound, which shall awaken the dead.
- 1 Thessalonians 4:13–18—The trumpet of God will awaken the dead.
- Revelation 8–9; 11:15—Seven angels blow their seven trumpets.

- Revelation 18:21–24—An angel announces that the voice of the instruments will be heard no more.
- Revelation 5:6–10; 14:1–3; 15:1–4—Instruments are used in heavenly worship.

John the revelator envisions a voice speaking like a trumpet, flute, harps, and ultimately seven trumpets sounding alternately with peals of thunder, rumbling, flashes of lightening, an earthquake, hail, and fire. African American slaves found great comfort in these references as they were adept at thinking in pictures, as demonstrated in many of the spirituals: "I looked over Jordan and what did I see . . . a band of angels coming after me." "My Lord calls me, he calls me by the thunder, the trumpet sounds within-a-my soul."

Instruments in Worship in the Early Church

The early Christians who worshiped in the synagogue and in gatherings to celebrate the risen Christ continued singing, as was the Jewish custom. According to New Testament accounts, the new communities sang to express praise "with one another" as reflected in the words of Clement of Rome (ca. 96): "Let us, therefore, gathered together in concord by conscience, cry out earnestly to him as if with one voice, so that we might come to share in his great and glorious promises."[18]

The concept of one voice in song—without instrumental accompaniment as a communal expression of praise—was more than a style of expression. It was a concept of unity among all people so that Jew and Gentile and male and female would be one in Jesus the Christ. In the first centuries after the death and resurrection of Christ, Christians were forced to meet in secret; therefore, they often met in private homes. As instruments were introduced into worship, the major opposition was due to their association with secular activities in the world.

In 313, the Edict of Milan granted legal recognition to Christians, at which time their religion was made equal to all other religions in the Roman Empire, giving them freedom to worship legally and openly. Constantine later made the Christian religion superior to all other religions.

As persons were evangelized and baptized into the church from cultures that incorporated the use of instruments in other aspects of life, instruments were gradually used in some portions of the worship services. Numerous church fathers voiced their opposition to the use of musical instruments in worship in the Western (Roman) Church. Clement of Alexandria (ca. 150–215), a convert to Christianity, is one of the earliest voices to associate musical instruments with war:

> We . . . make use of but one instrument, the word of peace alone by which we honor God, and no longer the ancient psaltery nor the trumpet, the tympanium and the aulos, as was the custom among the expert in war and those scornful of the fear of God who employed string instruments in their festive gatherings, as if to arouse their remissness of spirit through such rhythms.[19]

Like other opponents of the use of instruments in worship, Clement associated instruments with idolatry and immortality:

> Let carousing be absent from our rational enjoyment. . . . Let lust, intoxication, and irrational passions be far removed from our native choice. . . . The irregular movements of auloi, psalteries, choruses, dances, Egyptian clappers, and other such playthings become altogether indecent and uncouth, especially when joined by beating cymbals and tympana and accompanied by the noisy instruments of deception.[20]

Tertullian, a brilliant lay Christian writer who later became a Montanist orthodox bishop, voiced his opposition in a booklet called *De spectaculis.* Tertullian equated instrumental music with the theatrical music of shows and circuses and therefore on par with human lust for pleasure. Such music and any music that produces strong excitement and emotional desire was considered by him as idolatrous in that it would not evoke Christian conduct.

Several years later, the theologian Eusebius offered an alternate opinion by suggesting that human beings personify divine instruments in their manner of Christian living. Instruments for Eusebius are symbolic personifications of Christian grace:

> We sing God's praise with living psaltery. . . . Far more pleasant and dear to God than any instrument is the harmony of the whole Christian people. . . . Our cithara is the whole body. By whose movement and action the soul sings a fitting hymn to God, and our ten-stringed psaltery is the veneration of the Holy Ghost by the five senses of the body and five virtues of the spirit.[21]

The value of the unaccompanied voice was affirmed by Basil the Great, bishop of Caesarea, and John Chrysostom, a powerful preacher and leading voice of his day. The controversy surrounding the use of instruments led to legislation against their use. One rather harsh legal tradition even denied baptism to persons who played the *aulos* and the *kithara* unless they renounced their trade. A law in Alexandria, Egypt, fixed excommunication as the penalty for a cantor (singer) who learned to play the *kithara.*[22]

Most of the writings of the early church cited by researchers in the Western Church tradition tend to condemn the use of instruments in worship, including the use of the body as an idiophone and hence clapping and dancing as well.

There is, however, another side of the story. This side concerns worshipers of African lineage from both North Africa and the Sahara region. Although a direct line has not been established between the Egyptian and Ethiopian churches, there is evidence that cultural patterns were incorporated in Christian faith communities. The music of the liturgy, especially the continuous use of instruments over the centuries, and the deliberate program of church music in these communities, provides an excellent example of liturgical continuity across the centuries. (See chapter 1 for a discussion of the Coptic and Ethiopian churches and the place of music in their respective worship traditions.)

The information about African traditions demonstrates the importance of incorporating cultural expressions of a people in the shaping of rituals. As far as can be determined, music occupies a central place in all cultures. Before written music was available, oral acquisitions facilitated the learning process. The oral tradition was the strongest cultural link binding and unifying many voices so that they might become "one." At the same time, vocal and instrumental music in various forms occupied a central place in the mythology and religious systems of most ancient cultures. The immense power of music in general and the diversity of responses that music provides in the worship of the church are predicated on primal perceptions of the symbolic value of both voice and musical instruments. In addition to the Ethiopian liturgical history, which is steeped in the oral tradition of Ethiopian culture, current research by ethnomusicologists has determined that there are distinct cultural differences in the way instruments are used in worship. There are also differences in the cultural understanding of which instruments can be brought into the worship space and which should remain outside the sanctuary.[23] All of this relates to an outside culture imposing actions or non-actions on a group as a determination for what is good or bad according to taste and practice.

Euro-American Tradition

After many years of unaccompanied singing in worship, the exact year, the place, and the reason that instruments were finally used and accepted in the Western tradition of Christianity remain a mystery. The rejection of instruments in worship by the early church and the church's mistrust of any form of instrumental music is hardly believable in the twenty-first century, where instruments pervade much of the worship. Early rejection has been traced to the Roman *hydraulis*, or water organ, a forerunner of the medieval organ. This instrument was linked to nonreligious activities such as rites, games, and the theatre. Christians opposed any music that promoted moral decay, especially if it could be linked to the pagan cult of the idols.[24] Even Augustine, who encouraged the use of all the arts in Christian life, only permitted the *kithara* and other instruments that he believed served to help grasp spiritual things and to understand Scripture.[25] In the Western Church tradition, the use of instruments in worship did not become a common practice until the Renaissance. However, Roman Catholic ecclcsiastical authorities remained reluctant to use instruments until well into the twentieth century.

The organ was probably the first instrument to be introduced into worship in the Western Church, apparently between 1000 and 1300. Constantine Copronymus, emperor of Byzantium, gave an organ as a gift to Pepin, king of the Franks. The organ evoked concern because of its imperial connotations: It played a central role in ceremonial occasions at the Byzantine court; therefore, it was a symbol of the emperor's "imperial majesty." This organ was later destroyed, but a Venetian priest trained in the art of organ building constructed a replacement. At first it was not used to assist with the liturgy. Gradually it became acceptable, and by the thirteenth century most major churches in Europe possessed an organ. By the fifteenth century many churches had two organs: one for solo performances and a smaller one to accompany and support choral singing.[26]

The Pipe Organ as an Embodiment of Cosmic Harmony

The gradual popularity of the organ is based on its close connection with the classical Greek understanding of the quadrivium—an embodiment of the cosmic harmony. According to the traditional Greek worldview, the cosmos is pervaded by *harmonia,* a quality that causes all things to be related and interconnected and manifested to humans through music. For Plato and later Neoplatonic thinkers, music was of divine origin. It was the means by which humans could contact and absorb into their souls the balance and perfection of cosmic harmony. For the Western Church, Platonic teachings on music were not only embedded in the quadrivium, but they also supported the suspicious attitude toward the sensuous enjoyment of music. Therefore, there were strict regulations and restraints placed on musical expressions. This attitude eventually led to and fostered a music that can be considered sacred. Characteristics of sacred Christian music include ascetic severity, subtlety, rhythmic reserve, serene balance, and repose. This attitude persisted throughout the Middle Ages, governing and energizing all facets of musical activity in the church. Evidence of the organ's symbolic representation of cosmic harmony are summarized in these words by St. Aldhem, an English poet and scholar:

If a man longs to sate his soul with ardent music
And spurns the solace of a thin cantilena
Let him listen to the mighty organs with their thousand breaths,
And lull his hearing with the air-filled bellows
However much the rest [of it] dazzles with its golden castings.
Who can truly fathom the mysteries of such things,
Or unravel the secrets of the all-knowing God?[27]

Although cosmic harmony is reflected in the organ's many parts and passages for a variety of notes, it is whole in substance. Bishop Baldric of Dol, who was not particularly fond of the sound of the organ, noted that the organ encouraged him as he thought of the resulting single melody that emanates from air blown through different pipes of different size and weight. This he compared with humans of different varieties who are organs of the Holy Spirit who can unite in a single purpose. The introduction of organs in church might have been for music making, but also because this instrument was the material embodiment of cosmic harmony, because it provided a visible "sermon" on harmony. Thus, for centuries the organ has been held in high esteem in Roman circles for its support of the liturgy and for its visible grandeur and majestic sounds.

Use of the organ peaked during the Renaissance period. Then during the Baroque Era, the use of the organ in worship was declared contrary to the law of God, and subsequently its use declined. Less music was written, and theological perspectives of Calvinism urged the demolition of organs, images, and all manner of "superstitious" monuments in cathedrals and parishes.

Organs in American Worship

The history of church organ music in the United States began not among the Puritans and Pilgrims but among Spanish Roman Catholic missionaries from Mexico, in the sixteenth century. No doubt because of their rich musical heritage, these missionaries realized the valuable role of music as a means of teaching the faith as well as for introducing religious rituals and ceremonies. It is no surprise then that the missionaries focused on the teaching of music in order to teach European music theory, which facilitated the introduction to liturgy and to the music of the church. Pedro de Gante founded a music school in Texcoco, Mexico, and with twelve Franciscan missionaries provided instruction for the Mexican natives. Organ builders were active in Mexico throughout the seventeenth and eighteenth centuries. With motivation and support from church officials, missionaries were successful in obtaining organs for their new churches in the area that later would be known as New Mexico. Franciscan missionary Cristobal de Quinones holds the distinction of installing the first organ within the boundaries of what would later become the United States, in 1609.[28] Quinones's success is noted in his insistence that the organ is important and valuable in the service of the church, and in his persistence in learning the language of the Queres Indians so that he could communicate with them. By 1641, seventeen of the twenty-seven churches in the mission had organs.[29]

Puritans' objections to the use of instruments precluded their use in Congregational and independent churches. Anglicans, German pietists, and settlers from Europe who were not influenced by the Reformed tradition of Geneva were the entry places through which the use of organs in worship would begin. Large numbers of German pietists arrived in Pennsylvania during the late seventeenth and eighteenth centuries. Among the early German settlers was Justus Falckner, who suggested that an organ would be an effective means of "evangelizing the Indians and retaining youthful church members."[30] This might have been the beginning of a form of musical enticement to enhance church growth among Euro-Americans. Falckner's concerns are cited here as an important reminder that such thoughts have roots that extend far into America's past:

> Instrumental music is especially serviceable here. Thus, a well sounding organ would perhaps prove of great profit, to say nothing of the fact that the Indians would come running from far and near to listen to such unknown melody, and upon that account might become willing to accept our language and our teaching and remain with people who had such agreeable things. . . .
>
> If such an organ-instrument [*Orgel-werck*] were placed in the . . . church . . . it would prove of great service to this church. As a majority of the Swedes are young people, and mostly live scattered in the forest far from the churches, and as we by nature are all inclined to do good, and above all to what may we serve our souls, such as the Word of God which is dead and gone, so are especially the youth. . . . When they have performed heavy labor for the whole week . . . they would sooner rest on a Sunday, and seek some pleasure rather than perhaps go for several miles to listen to a sermon. But if there were such music there, they would consider church-going as a recreation for their senses.[31]

Falckner continues his spiel with reminders that Luther had the same idea and employed the organ and sacred music for this same reason: to induce people to listen unto and then receive God's Word. In 1763, an anonymous Presbyterian writer from Philadelphia justified the use of instrumental music in a pamphlet titled "The Lawfulness, Excellency, and Advantage of Instrumental Music in the Public Worship of God." His intent was to encourage Baptists and Presbyterians to reevaluate their objections to instruments to worship. In addition to pointing out references to the use of instruments to the glory of God in the Hebrew Bible, he encouraged opponents to listen to the organ without prejudice to a service of worship where the organ was played well.

Since Pennsylvania was the center of free Africans and African American worshipers who were quite vocal about racism in the context of segregated places, as well as the center of the development of African American congregations and denominations, it is expected that they would have been exposed to the sound of the organ. The inclusion of the organ in worship was no doubt predicated on its sound, which enhanced the sacredness of worship, rather than on their desire to worship like Euro-Americans. An African American Christian most often makes a choice to serve God from that vantage point rather than from his or her desire to emulate a particular culture.

Africans enslaved in New England during the early eighteenth century might have heard the sound of an organ in the private homes of rich colonists. The history of church organs among Protestants in New England likely began at the home of Thomas Brattle, a wealthy Bostonian. The exact date of the arrival of Brattle's organ is uncertain, but Samuel Sewell, whose diary entries have provided helpful information about the musical activities of Africans in America, records its use in 1708.[32] At this time organs were not used in churches because of their perceived connections to Roman Catholic worship. According to William Arms Fisher, Thomas Brattle willed the organ to the Brattle Square Church with a provision that if the church declined it, the organ was to be given to Queen's Chapel, which was later named King's Chapel. Following his death in 1713, the church declined the organ, so it was sent to King's Chapel. It was not accepted there immediately, however, so it remained on the porch of the chapel for seven months before it was unpacked. This single-manual organ of only forty-nine keys was finally installed in 1714,[33] and it served the chapel for forty-two years.[34]

Africans in America were likely exposed to the sound of the organ through a variety of ways. It seems probable that some had heard the organ in Africa or England, considering the range of years that slave trading continued. Early in this history, small one-manual organs with no pedal boards were the norm. Many of the organs in this period were imported from England, with a few from Germany. Some congregations were still reluctant about installing organs in their churches, however, and there were so few prepared organists available, even to accompany congregational singing.

In an attempt to make organs economically accessible to a larger church population in America, a keyboard reed instrument was designed. Its sound was produced with the aid of a thin elongated piece of cane reed, metal, or other material that was fixed at one end and free to vibrate at the other end. This organ, also called a melodeon or a harmonium, was inexpensive, easy to move, and required minimal upkeep. Shrinking and swelling, which often plagues pipes, does not occur in reeds. As the method of voicing reeds improved, so did the sales of the instrument.

By the eighteenth century when African American churches were becoming visible, the organ had become more common, except in Puritan churches where reservations about instruments persisted into the nineteenth century. Not only did African Americans hear sounds from the organ, some helped to create the sound by pumping the air into the pipes.

The use of electricity in connection with organs didn't occur until the nineteenth century. By 1869, organists in America did not require a person to pump the hydraulic motor, which no doubt forced a number of African Americans out of jobs as organ pumpers. The use of electricity also opened the possibility of other innovations for the organ. Early electric actions utilized batteries for power. Hilborne Roosevelt is credited with providing a new direction and momentum to organ design toward the style associated with the twentieth century. His interest in science, innovations, and especially electricity led him to experiment and to conduct other activities related to changes and advancements in other aspects of the organ. Orpha Ochse notes that his use of electric action made possible experiments in the placement of the tonal divisions of the organ. Hilborne Roosevelt, first cousin of Theodore Roosevelt, has been acclaimed as the first person to exhibit an organ with electric action in the United States, which he did in 1869.[35] Roosevelt built 358 organs in two decades, and achieved fame as the builder of one of the world's largest organs, located in the Cathedral of the Incarnation in Garden City, Long Island.

Electronic Organs and the Emergence of the Hammond Organ

Experiments in producing sounds electrically had occurred before the end of the nineteenth century. However, interest in relating electricity to organs increased significantly after a sequence of inventions, beginning with the invention of the Telharmonium in 1904 by Thaddeus Cahill and concluding with Richard H. Ranger's Rangertone in 1932. According to Ochse, it was not until 1932 that the possibilities of electronically produced sounds were brought to the attention of organists in a practical form.[36] When this was demonstrated successfully in 1934 during a performance of Johannes Brahms's *Requiem,* it was noted that electrically produced sounds opened up the possibility of expanding the use of organs in places that previously had found them too expensive and too large to transport.

The Hammond organ, the most popular instrument in African American congregations, was developed by Laurens Hammond, owner of the Hammond Clock Company in Chicago, and was first presented to the public on April 15, 1935. Hammond's professional background was in science, engineering, and mathematics. He did not play any instruments, nor did he attempt to answer musical questions. Unfortunately, the promotion of his invention was not received well by producers of pipe organs. Advertising practices by the Hammond Company caused a stir among pipe organ builders, who accused Hammond of false advertising. Of special concern was Hammond's claim that this electronic instrument was "an organ" and that it could produce the effects possible on a pipe organ. Despite this conflict, by August 1936, the company claimed to have placed the $1,250 instrument in 567 churches. That same year a court case ensued, with the Council of the American Guild of Organists questioning Hammond's use of the word *organ,* as well as charging that the Hammond Company misrepresented both the instrument's tone quality and the value of the company. After numerous experiments, it was revealed that the Hammond could not produce the sound of pipe organ music. The Federal Trade Commission ordered the Hammond Company to cease its claims.

In spite of the fact that the Hammond organ cannot reproduce the sound of pipe organs and that its sound and associations are more nearly aligned to music for entertainment, this organ has maintained a reputation as the basic instrument for many African American congregations. This is especially true of the Hammond B-3 model, which gained its popularity during the 1950s and 1960s as a jazz improvisatory instrument and also as an instrumental accompaniment for black gospel music both in churches and in other public arenas. The sustained quality of the pipe organ that supports and encourages congregational singing is not always the operating principle in African American congregations, where rhythmical accompaniment ignites and sustains participation. The Hammond's association with the entertainment world did not limit its possibility as an instrument for worship except in African American communities and congregations where pipe organs have flourished and are preferred. Having additional options available and more affordable electronic organs has helped African American congregations that prefer the sustained pipe organ sound to purchase instruments. Electronic instruments that serve both purposes in one instrument became popular in the 1980s.

One cannot overlook the availability of skilled African American organists who have the facility and in some instances college and graduate degrees in organ techniques. Some are able to handle both forms and can adjust to local congregational needs in this area. Despite the tendency for skilled organists to be challenged by some who assume that to be gifted as a sight-reading keyboardist is to deny the African American heritage, the number of African American musicians seeking professional music degrees with a focus on the organ is increasing.

Organs in African American Worship

In 1828, African American Episcopalians installed a pipe organ in the St. Thomas Church in Philadelphia which, as far as can be determined, was the first organ to be installed in a black church. There is no evidence that this event disturbed the worshiping community, but it evoked concern from news reporters, who noted that the organ had been purchased and that a young female, Ann Appo, had been employed as an organist. According to Eileen Southern, these concerns might have centered on matters of economics.[37] One wonders, however, whether the employment of a female might have raised eyebrows. Nevertheless, St. Thomas persisted in the use of the organ to accompany the congregational singing of hymns and to provide accompaniment to choral performances of anthems and oratorios.

By the 1830s, the use of the organ had become a tradition at St. Thomas and other African American congregations. This attitude engendered support for trained instrumentalists and choirs with music reading abilities, and subsequently for the incorporation of published anthems, oratorios, and cantatas in church music repertoires. Among the other black congregations identified as "progressive" promoters of quality music and trained musicians were St. Philips Episcopal in New York City, First African Presbyterian Church in Philadelphia, and the Belknap Baptist Church in Boston. An 1849 survey by the Society of Friends indicated that in a black population of 9,076, thirty-two *men* were professional musicians, whose livelihood depended entirely upon their musical activities.[38] Other extant records confirm that there were a number of black musicians in other cities who supplemented their income as part-time members of the music profession.

Closely aligned to the use of instruments in worship during this early period were the black sacred music concerts sponsored by or held in black churches. These concerts included small and large instrumental ensembles, basically to accompany full choral works or excerpts from oratorios. According to an announcement by the African Harmonic Society of Philadelphia, the first concerts were apparently held during the mid-1820s. The society announced that it was holding its second sacred concert on April 13, 1827, at the First African Presbyterian Church. In September of the same year, St. Philips in New York sponsored a concert of sacred music.[39] The performance repertoire indicates that urban African Americans were familiar with the choral works of black composers such as William Appo, Francis Johnson, and Robert C. Jones. Compositions by European composers included such names as Chappell, Handel, Mozart, Gluck, Bellini, and Haydn.

In 1841, the First African Presbyterian Church in Philadelphia hosted a performance of Josef Haydn's *Creation.* The large number of musicians involved in this production included a fifty-piece orchestra conducted by Frank W. Johnson and a chorus conducted by Morris Brown, Jr.[40] Clearly the "singing schools" sponsored by black congregations had been successful in helping to prepare choristers for this and the many other sacred music concerts. Instrumentalists and vocal soloists no doubt studied privately in music centers that were available to blacks in New York, Boston, Washington, D.C., Philadelphia, and Baltimore. The church continued into the twentieth century as a major arena in which to present black talent to the community.

Information about free blacks in cities affirms the diversity that existed in America in general and in worshiping congregations in particular. Laws enacted in 1778 offering freedom to slaves who served in the American army for a number of years, and laws enacted from 1780 in Pennsylvania through 1783 in Massachusetts providing for the gradual abolition of slavery affected black persons socially and economically. Newly freed slaves saw the possibility of a better life, and many were able to take advantage of the opportunity. Some had already learned to read and write; others had to find ways between jobs to do so. There were two or more worlds in process at once. African Americans who were still enslaved created and sang their own folk songs, while others, free according to the law, struggled to establish themselves as professional musicians. America needed music teachers, and according to Southern, in some places the color of a person's skin was less important than the ability to impart instruction.[41] Blacks were composing and performing, and Euro-Americans were so anxious to evaluate the black artists one generation removed from slavery that they attended performances out of curiosity. While applauding the unusual talent, they were also keeping a finger on the pulse of folks who emulated their "former" oppressors.

Much of the musical activity from 1820 forward took place in the black churches that were established. By the middle of the nineteenth century, those churches had tripled in number. Most of the black city churches organized Sunday schools for adults and children and weekly schools for children and young people. They also sponsored sacred music concerts for adults and children as well as lectures on music, especially in Philadelphia. No doubt Sunday's music for worship was easily reflective of the concert music that had been heard in the same space earlier that week. Active among the concert artists were Elizabeth

Taylor Greenfield, a well-known soprano who was also called the "Black Swan," and Thomas Bower, who was called the "colored Mario" because of his operatic tenor voice that reminded many of Italian opera singer Giovanni Mario. Among the instrumentalists of note was Francis (Frank) Johnson, a black trumpeter who was the first black musician to win wide acclaim in the nation and in England. He was the first black musician to publish sheet music in 1818, the first to develop a school of black musicians, the first to have five formal band concerts, the first to tour widely in the nation, and the first to take a musical ensemble to Europe.

By 1848, while many of the Philadelphia churches were opening their doors to instrumentalists, the AME Church found itself in the midst of another form of musical tension. This time the location was Baltimore, Maryland, rather than Philadelphia, where the use of instruments in the church caused conflict among the members. The occasion was a concert of sacred music directed by James Fleet of Washington, D.C. Earlier, in 1841, the Bethel Church in Philadelphia had set aside a gallery for a choir to sing for the dedication service. Later, when these members attempted to introduce choral singing into the regular service there was resistance, especially from the older members. Their concern was both having a specially trained choir and the fact that the singers were reading notes from a score.

It can be assumed that there were many interactions between the church and the public life of blacks interested in music. In the southeastern coastal section of the United States, Africans were still being imported through the West Indies or directly from Africa. According to the five available black newspapers and some of the Euro-American papers, middle-class blacks were emerging from cities with different musical tastes. Free blacks who could afford homes also bought pianos, held parlor parties, and incorporated social activities that included music. A large percentage of the social and cultural activities pivoted around the church.

African Instrumentalists

In addition to letters, court records, and journal accounts of the unusual musical gifts of Africans in America during the colonial era, there are numerous references to skilled instrumentalists and singers in newspaper advertisements for runaway slaves, slaves to be sold, or slaves for hire. The most detailed collection of advertisements is descriptive of the high level and quality of musicianship that Africans possessed. Phrases used frequently include the following: "plays extremely well on the violin," "is an exceptionally skilled fiddler," "plays exceedingly well on the fife."[42] Their level of musical skill, combined with other skills, and their ability to do additional work often determined the "market value" of slaves.

The fiddle, as used in these advertisements, is apparently the colloquial name for the four-string violin, which was commonly used during this era. However, one of the important and popular West African instruments during this era was the one-string fiddle that was no doubt in common use among the slaves.[43] Additional instruments identified in this excellent primary source are the French horn, trumpet, drums, and one reference to a skilled player of the German flute.[44]

Bits of helpful information to confirm the instrumental gifts of some of the slaves are also found in local town journals, court records, and writers of the eighteenth century. According to a local historian, a gifted slave musician named Nero Benson served as a trumpeter in the company of Captain Isaac Clark in Framingham, Massachusetts, in 1723.[45] One of the most detailed accounts of the music among blacks in the North from the late seventeenth to the early eighteenth centuries is the diary of Samuel Sewell of Boston, who was a song leader in his congregation and a judge.[46] In addition to his documentation of music practices during the time of the early settlers, Sewell discloses some of the musical activities of blacks relative to their participation in the community.

The major accounts of the musical skills of Africans in the southeastern part of the United States are from missionaries' letters to their English supervisors and the diaries of Euro-American observers. These references are basically about the African gift for singing rather than any obvious instrumental skills. The assumption is that most Africans were innately artistic and were self-taught. As to where they obtained their instruments, there are two documented possibilities: They made them from materials at hand or they were gifts from a caring planter. A Philadelphia Quaker wrote in 1719:

> Thou knowest Negro Peter's Ingenuity In making for himself and playing on a fiddle without any assistance. As the thing in them is Innocent and diverting and may keep them from worse Employment, I have Encouraged in my Service promist him one from England. Therefore, buy and bring a good strong well-made Violin with 2 or 3 Sets of spare Gut for the Suitable strings.[47]

There is also evidence that some rich Euro-American students in South Carolina took slaves with them to college to be servants as early as 1693. In this environment, Africans might have learned by overhearing the music of students, or they might have gained minimal skills directly from some of the students. There were only a few schools where slaves received professional training in urban places in the South such as Charles Town, which later became Charlestown. Opportunities to demonstrate and develop instrumental skills occurred during "Lection Day" festivities, "Pinkster Day" (Pentecost Sunday) celebrations, New Orleans festivals, and other slave gatherings where for a Sunday, Christmas, or other brief periods of time Africans in the Diaspora experienced moments of freedom.[48]

There is ample data to suggest that instruments were used very early in black worship gatherings. Except for worship in the "invisible institution," where secrecy was necessary, there were hardly any reasons for African people to avoid instruments in worship. There is certainly evidence that instruments were used in African primal worship rituals. An array of instruments was used for invoking and healing and in postfuneral rites; the latter, of course, continued in the Creole area of New Orleans and then became the foundation for jazz and ultimately black gospel music.

The presence of skilled musicians among the early Africans in America, the use of the organ in worship as early as 1828, and the role of music in the life of free blacks suggest that instruments were available for worship in some communities. From 1827 forward, newspapers by African Americans facilitated communication between black communities, especially those along the eastern seaboard, and announced the location of vocal and instrumental concerts by black artists. Music not only played an important role in the lives of urban African Americans, but it also provided substantial income for musicians. By 1849 there were professional musicians whose livelihood depended entirely upon their musical activities. There were bands and orchestras and orchestral equipment for performances of sacred music concerts, but there are no extant records indicating that instruments were considered necessary in worship. On at least one occasion, March 14, 1841, a full performance of Haydn's oratorio *The Creation* was performed with the musical support of a fifty-piece orchestra at First African Presbyterian Church in Philadelphia. Congregational songs soared without accompaniment, except for the use of the feet and other parts of the body to keep time. We can conclude, however, that the piano and organ were available, as congregations desired to use them in worship.

Instruments into the Twenty-first Century

Diversity is perhaps the best way to describe the use of instruments in African American worship, not only at the beginning of the third millennium but throughout the history of African American worship. Acknowledgment is made here of the small number of black congregations in denominations whose history and polity reject or refrain from the use of any human-made instruments in worship. The Churches of Christ are among these denominations. The reasons for refraining from the use of instruments include Deuteronomy 12:32: "See that you do all I command you; do not add to it or take away from it" (NIV). In harmony with the Scriptural principle, whatever is not commanded is forbidden.

2 Chronicles 29:27–38 provides the reminder that instruments were commanded in direct connection with the sacrifical offerings of the ceremonial law. When sacrifices ended, the offering was completed.

There is neither command nor example given by Christ or the apostles of the use of musical instruments in worship.

Where the use of instruments is permitted, there is evidence of the influence of the electronic age and technological innovations. Many of the innovations, including radios with greater amplification, occurred after World War II. Other influences include the media, TV evangelists' services, popular culture, Christian contemporary music, praise teams, and generational and intergenerational diversity. This means that a church may have two organs: a traditional pipe organ and an electronic one, such as a Hammond B-3. They may be supplemented by one or more electronic keyboards with synthesizer capabilities, and a regular six- to nine-foot grand piano. There may be drum sets, including African drums, and other African and orchestral instruments, including the harp.

Over the years, a number of small and large instrumental groups have been involved in worship. A few congregations have incorporated instruments from other cultures, in addition to those from Africa. The use of so many different instruments creates varying degrees of controversy in congregations, especially if there is no conversation regarding the purpose and role of instruments in glorifying God. One problem may be the varying degrees of knowledge and skills of the instrumentalists. Many musicians have a tremendous gift for playing by ear and improvising but cannot read music from a score. Many have little or no knowledge and experience of the theology and practice of worship and church music. Some combine this with a lack of understanding of the role of congregational involvement in singing, so instrumentalists often concentrate on their own performance skills and charge dearly for this.

Confusion is greatest when the reason for using particular musical instruments or styles of music in worship has more to do with connecting the congregation with cultural lifestyles rather than glorifying God. Another way of expressing this critique is by employing the well-used concept of entertainment. If entertainment, human pleasure, and enjoyment are the basic reasons for the choice of music and instruments, then the future of worship is at stake. Churches that opt to offer entertainment often experience growth in numbers and congregational energy, but they are also generating an illusion and a misrepresentation of spiritual vitality. Efforts to evangelize a particular generation or age level have created revolving doors for newcomers, who will leave if their musical expectations are not constantly met. Some congregations have made music rather than the worship of God and spiritual edification their chief attraction.

Another problem is that the extended age of electronics has heightened the use of "background music" as a facilitator for everyday living. Music of some sort is playing in the background in stores, at recreational centers, and sometimes at work, subliminally guiding our lives. We seldom travel without the accompanying sound of some sort of recorded music. We have become acclimated to background music and rhythms that propel us into each moment. This use of sound can be considered part of an "assault of sound," especially if it is outside the worship setting and reveals the impact of noise. Daniel Frankforter observes that the assault of sound

> compromises our ability to focus on it [sound] as an artistic experience and a form of intellectual communication. . . . As a visceral experience and a prompt to bodily sensations, the louder the music is, the better it works. Electronically generated and amplified sounds are preferred to acoustical instruments, for they are more effective at overwhelming listeners and submerging them in a sea of sensation.[49]

Audiotapes and CDs became acceptable church instruments in the latter part of the twentieth century. The artificiality of using recorded orchestral or stage band accompaniment for solos, ensembles, and choirs has become commonplace for some and problematic for others. Since recorded sound is available for some electronic organs, congregations may soon learn to adapt to this form of instrumental enhancement for use in worship.

The twenty-first century will no doubt remain an adventurous era for congregations as a variety of instruments are available for the diversity of traditions and the multiplicity of congregational needs. A few precautions are adjoined here as we seek to make use of the plethora of instruments available. Biblically, culturally (speaking of African culture in particular), and historically, the singing of words and the verbal forms and the meaning of faith that they suggest take precedence over instruments. The extended discussion in this chapter on the African use of voice affirms this for a people who are reaching back into the African heritage for models of worship. While instruments are omnipresent in the various African cultures, even African musicologists and scholars in other areas observe that singing and movement happen often without the use of instruments. A few examples are cited here:

- Vocal music is truly the essence of African musical art. This fact in no way diminishes the value of musical instruments. On the contrary, since the prime motive of instruments is to reconstitute spoken or sung language, they have a significance which is unparalleled in the music of other continents.[50]
- "Although the cultivation of music performed on instruments receives attention in African musical traditions, instrumental music is not regarded everywhere as something that should be developed in its own right. Many traditions have a tendency to combine instrumental musical performance with some singing."[51]
- "One of the problems facing modern African states is how to integrate the societies politically and culturally within their stated framework. . . . As the economy grew, Western instruments originally introduced through the church and the military became available. . . . [The use of Western instruments was] encouraged by the activities of the church which preached against African cultural practices while promoting Western cultural values. . . . The fact that drums and other percussion instruments were used in the Ethiopian church, which had been established in the fourth century A.D. did not affect the evangelistic prejudices. In some areas, the converts were not only prohibited from performing traditional African music, but even from watching it."[52]
- Like worshipers in African American congregations, Africans, from whom much of African American culture has been reclaimed, are confronted with new sounds almost weekly as a result of the practice of adapting from other places. The initial intent is that the use of borrowed sounds can alter theological and practical reasons for the use of instruments in worship. As musicians borrow church music practices, even from within Western culture, someone in the local church should keep a finger on the pulse of the way that spiritual renewal happens. This concern is in the domain of both the church musician or ministers of music and the pastor. The theological question that remains to be answered is: What is taking place when some of the liturgical symbols that enhance the communion table are required to be moved to accommodate three levels of MIDI keyboards, and a Hammond B-3?[53]

Clearly there is no one instrument that is more sacred than another for offering praise to God. The concern, however, should be for the enhancement of the sung word in worship. African traditions suggest that instruments are not intended to submerge the voice. This one-voice ideology is universal across cultures and need not be posited only in Western culture. For African people at home and in the Diaspora, there was a deliberate effort to find the "one voice" even in slavery. Out of one voice, spirituals were born, carried forward, and survived, even when new harmonies and rhythms were supplied. Let this one voice not be lost into the twenty-first century for lack of knowledge of African and Christian intentions.

Electronic keyboards and organs are ingrained in the worshiping culture of many black churches and congregations. Aesthetic tastes and what is in vogue most often determine the choice of instruments. Many congregations require and encourage the use of at least two large electronic instruments: a Hammond organ and a Rodgers, Allen, or other organ. The term *keyboard* has taken on a new meaning since the mid-1980s, breaking out of its usual definition as a piano or organ to describe a perplexing variety of instruments.

Many musicians deliberately attempt to create sounds that embody the cosmic harmony of the universe. Some musicians strive for sounds that they hear in nonchurch gatherings or on top-selling recordings. For the purpose of worship liturgical questions should be asked as instrumental music is being prepared. Will these sounds in and beyond worship encourage faithfulness to the Almighty God in and through the resurrected Jesus Christ?

These concerns should extend to all instruments used in worship—and there are none available that cannot be used to the glory of God. With an accent on praising God as called for in Psalm 150, worship music should demonstrate spontaneity, flexibility, and change. In addition to bands and small, large, and mixed ensembles, the orchestra is among the commonly used instrumental groups for worship. A special kind of orchestra called the "worship orchestra" is used for congregational and choral accompaniment and provides opportunities for musical interludes. Below are some suggestions for leading an orchestra in worship (these are applicable to other instrumental groups as well):

- Accompaniment should be flexible so that the members of the orchestra can remain open to sudden changes in tempo.
- The director should constantly watch and listen to the choral director and the pastor.
- Arrangements should include words in the score so that musicians can find their place according to what is being sung. This also keeps the instrumentalists aware of the faith message.[54]

With nearly every reform and revival movement in church history there has been a musical movement related to it that reflects its concern for "the people in the pews." In fact, the musical movement has often instigated the movement toward church reform. The general use of a band in worship can be traced to the late 1960s in an attempt to make worship relevant to youth and the unchurched. Small instrumental ensembles with a strong percussion section continue to carry on this task across denominations and cultures and among nondenominational religious groups. Musicians in such groups range from those who cannot read music and who are total improvisers, to those who read musical scores, and to those who simply read charts.

Guitars have been used variously in worship, especially in informal worship settings. The focus in the 1960s on folk music created a revival of interest in the use of the guitar, which led to the incorporation of guitar instruction in public and private schools. Amplification of acoustic guitars further enhances their usefulness in worship.

The most common hand-held percussion instrument for African Americans is the tambourine, which is used for rhythmic accentuation. Tambourines have a historical connection to and are fervently used by worshipers in Holiness and Pentecostal congregations. Gifted musicians attuned to the spiritual dynamics in the worshiping environment have developed a particular art and skill in accompanying the musical dynamics in the service with instruments such as the tambourine.

The use of bells in worship can be traced to the instructions given for the vesting of Aaron, the priest, so that he could enter the holiest portion of the tabernacle:

> You shall make the robe of the ephod[55] all of blue. It shall have an opening for the head in the middle of it. . . . On its lower hem you shall make pomegranates of blue, purple, and crimson yarns, all around the lower hem, with bells of gold between them all around—a golden bell and a pomegranate alternating all around the lower hem of the robe. Aaron shall wear it when he ministers, and its sound shall be heard when he goes into the holy place before the LORD, and when he comes out, so that he may not die. (Exod. 28:31–35)

In addition, a sign reading "Holy to the LORD" is commanded to be fastened to the turban worn by Aaron. For the Israelites, bells signified the sacred in formal worship as well as in ordinary life. For many Christians, the pealing of the church bell calls people to worship or announces that a person is dying. Bells are also sometimes used to call attention to certain high points in the liturgy. A recently reclaimed ringing of the bells is the moment in the Great Easter Vigil. This occurs when the "Alleluia" in the liturgy returns to the lips and hearts of the congregation, as the minister proclaims, "Alleluia, Christ is risen!" and the people respond with a shout: "The Lord is risen indeed!" Another sacred moment occurs when "sacring bells" are sounded at the Sanctus (Holy, Holy,

Holy) and at the elevation of the host during the celebration of the Eucharist. The ringing at the elevation was a twelfth-century innovation in France, where it signaled the completion of the consecration of the elements, and the congregation was encouraged to look at the altar. During this time this was as close as the people got to the bread. After Vatican II the use of sacring bells diminished somewhat. However, the use of bells continues in many black Roman Catholic and Episcopal parishes. Eastern Orthodox churches sometimes attach small bells to the chains of the thurible, which jingles each time an object or a person is censed.

Handbell ringing is an artistic innovation from England that was introduced in America in 1923.[56] Like the playing together in other instrumental groups, this art demands discipline and team cooperation. Although bell ringing is appropriate during congregational singing, care should be taken so that it does not distract the congregation.

Drumming is the most popular instrumental accompaniment used in African American worship. As one pastor states, "This is a way to show that we are truly Afrocentric." Again, it is urged that care be taken so that the music offered is praise to God, and that it facilitates rather than inhibits faith formation.

There are other instruments, such as Orff instruments, that encourage the involvement of youth and children in worship. Orff instruments are uniquely designed percussion instruments created by the German musician Carl Orff to help children learn to improvise rhythms during musical performances. Orff developed a special music education method that has been used to create worship music for children.

Chapter 6

Music as a Liturgical Element in African American Worship

*M*usic is an essential element in African American Christian worship because of its ubiquitous presence in worship practices throughout the centuries. Even in historical periods when singing was curtailed because of the clandestine nature of the gatherings, worship was filled with "silent songs" expressed in kinesthetic movements and rhythms that sang praises to the Almighty as if they were a part of one loud unified voice. Perhaps using the terms *liturgy* and *liturgical* in this context might disturb some readers who have in mind a definition that *liturgy* implies those forms of corporate worship that follow a set of prescribed and usually unchangeable structures as a means of responding to the gift of God's love, presence, and power. Throughout this book, however, *liturgical* denotes worship that follows customary patterns of structure and allows expressions of the shared faith of the community through the use of meaningful cultural symbols. This definition affirms the freedom allowed within structure and acknowledges that the structure of some traditional black denominations is more rigidly fixed than church leaders are willing to admit.

The underlying assumption about Christian worship throughout this book is closely aligned with the meaning of liturgy described: the corporate acknowledgment and public response of particular communities of faith to the presence and power of God as revealed in Jesus the Christ through the work of the Holy Spirit.[1] The fact that the entire volume is related to a particular people—Africans in America—indicates the belief that worship or liturgy is by nature reflective of culture, beliefs, symbols, and the sum total of a particular people during particular times and at particular places. The culture of African American worship and its music is dynamic and reflective of everything that is received and passed on by the community. Culture involves information received through formal education, exposure and experience, lifestyle, mobility and travel, as well as the use of past and current technology. When all of this is combined with individual and corporate stories, attitudes, experiences of singing and dancing, social interaction and aesthetic choices, it can be understood why culture and worship practices are dynamic. God's divine call for corporate gatherings allows the community to claim and affirm unity with Christ and kinship with each other in sacred liturgical spaces where both social and spiritual hospitality are evident.

As communities of faith have created and provided music as part of worship throughout the centuries, some within these communities have raised the concern about the function of music in corporate worship. Is music in its many forms and dimensions used as a means of praising and glorifying God, or is music offered to the glory of the singers and/or instrumentalists? Should music in worship be deliberately composed and performed to offer pleasure and entertainment for worshipers to "enjoy"? Is it possible to glorify God and entertain in a service of worship and to maintain the integrity of worship? Is there a difference between "music in church" and "music for worship"? Since there are no universal characteristics that qualify musical sounds to be isolated as "secular" or "sacred," tensions arise between those who understand this and those who want to impose their own religious distinctions on all music for worship.

Although it is impossible to designate any music as absolutely "sacred" or "religious," this chapter seeks to identify musical elements that represent the "work of the people" empowered by the Holy Spirit. Since humankind cannot always say with certainty what is or is not empowered or initiated by the Holy Spirit, this too remains in the realm of subjectivity. Thus, there is no clear-cut ideal of music for worship. The focus then will be on the function that music serves in the context of worship. Joseph Ashton's observations provide a helpful delineation that will be employed here:

> At the heart of church music must be the consciousness of [the] religious nature: the sense of the divine, of goodness and righteousness, of the Almighty, the Eternal; the sense of exaltation of human life to the divine, and accompanying this, the feeling of humility into which such a sense must lead us. . . . There is in all true church music a spirit of adoration, aspiration and reverence, and a sense of assurance.[2]

A matter of certainty in the history of the use of music in African American worshiping communities is that there is often music that "happens in church" that has little if anything to do with the scriptural or sermon themes for the day. There will be no attempt to romanticize or magnify "liturgical" connections, since there are no extant records of the rationale used by African Americans in their choices of musical offerings. Most music was selected extemporaneously as the worship unfolded. This is one reason that the term "selection" continues to prevail, especially in historically black denominations. The preference for this term apparently frees worship leaders and preachers to select a song based on the momentum that has built, the pastor's favorite song, or according to the memory of a song that established a mood in the distant or immediate past. Since worship and music are so intimately related to experiences and memories that are personal, there is the human tendency to take for granted that music which inspires, uplifts, and moves us also acts the same or in similar ways with others.

For the purpose of this chapter, music as a "liturgical element" is used freely to mean music that intentionally serves a religious or ecclesiastical function according to a variety of situations. Rather than attempt to specify precise functions that the music served in the past, this chapter will provide a general overview where data are available. Attention will be given to the liturgical function of music from the 1940s to the current time. Approximate time lines will be provided in each historical period according to major religious and social events.

The Effect of Patterns of Slavery on Music for Worship

Without extant records to verify exact communal reactions of African people in early America, it is necessary to rely upon general historical data. Each geographical location was unique in that settlers varied in their opinion about blacks, whether they should be slaves or free. Communities of Africans differed in their ethnic and cultural roots such as their languages, and their physical and psychological experiences during the voyage, their ability to cope in strange environments, the extent to which they resisted running away, and their perspective on the Euro-American form of slavery. The individual accounts of two African-born slaves, Gustavus Vassa and Venture Smith, provide helpful information from this period.[3] From 1565 when the first Africans were brought to Florida, to 1619, the year that indentured slaves were brought to Virginia, to the arrival of enslaved Africans on the last slave ships, the *Wanderer* in 1858 and the *Clotide* in 1859, many communities of Africans were established in America.

In New England, the Euro-American population was largely English from the Congregational Church. The middle colonies were settled by a variety of ethnic groups, including Dutch, Swedish, German, and English. Among the religious groups who were interested in the predicament of Africans in America were the Quakers, Congregationalists, Anglicans, Moravians, and, to some extent, the Catholics, Presbyterians, and Methodists. Therefore, this portion of the country carried forth a milder form of slavery than the southern colonies.

Nevertheless, the treatment of blacks provoked a number of rebellions. Due to the paternalistic attitude of "liberal" slaveholders, slaves were evangelized, baptized, and given the family names of their owners.[4]

Musical traditions among African peoples assumed close characteristics of the musical patterns of their captors, and those who granted them freedom early in the Americanizing process. As we will see, the free-flowing, loosely structured liturgy of blacks in the South reflects a longer continuation of the "Invisible Institution" across denominational traditions. At the turn of the century, the black gospel tradition was created as an urban music form, as free blacks in cities sought new ways to sing good news in a personal way. To build upon existing black music and snatches of musical forms in the culture was a natural way to do this. So sacred and secular again embraced each other, making it possible to sing the "blues" in the church, in the street, and on stage. This creative musical impetus continues its cyclical form, validating its role as music for liturgy and life.

The oldest settlement of Africans in the New World can be traced to the year 1565, when a Spanish Roman Catholic colony was established in northern Florida. Both slaves and free blacks were part of the population in this settlement, with St. Augustine at its center. Along with the Africans was a garrison of black soldiers from Cuba. Without sufficient evidence of ritual practices during these times, it has not been determined the extent of musical activities that might have taken place during these years, nor the extent to which Africans participated in the musical portion of the rite. The presence of Africans among the Catholics in the New World in the sixteenth century is bound, perhaps, in the reason that foreigners set foot on new lands around the world. Due to their desire to extend the Catholic religion to all parts of the world, explorers and adventurers traveled to places that seemed fertile for establishing communities. From the beginning, northern Florida was primarily a military outpost to protect Spanish possessions in this new land from English and French merchants. Thus, the oldest "home" for Africans in North America was a military outpost that would later become a haven for slaves who were seeking shelter and a place of safety.

We turn, therefore, to slave quarters, where the music of black America was born, nurtured, and utilized to the fullest.

Music in the Invisible Institution: ca. 1619–1776

From the beginning of the process of shaping a communal response to the power and grace of God in the midst of human suffering and oppression,

Earliest African American Communities in a Strange and Alien Land

Year	Events
1565	Blacks included in Roman Catholic community in northeast Florida.
1619	Arrival of Africans in the English colony at Jamestown, Virginia.
1624	First black male child baptized in the Protestant tradition (Anglican).
1626	Founding of New Amsterdam; eleven Africans brought as indentured servants.
1629	Beginning of New England slave trade. Blacks arrived in Boston on a ship named *Desire*.
1640	*Bay Psalm Book* published in Boston—first book published in the colonies.
1641	Earliest record of a slave baptized and received into membership (a woman); implied approval of institution of slavery.
1667	Virginia law declares that the baptism of slaves does not grant them freedom.
1670	Charles Town, South Carolina, founded; the only "city" in the colonial South.
1681	Philadelphia founded.
1688	Quakers protest institution of slavery.
1693	Society of Negroes founded in the Massachusetts colony.
1701	Society for the Propagation of the Gospel in Foreign Parts (SPG) established in England.

Year	Events
1704	Elias Neau establishes an SPG catechism school in New York City.
1707	Isaac Watts publishes *Hymns and Spiritual Songs.*
1712	New York slave insurrection.
1723	Thomas Bray organizes catechism schools in Philadelphia.
1735	Five slaves baptized by Jonathan Edwards during the Great Awakening.
1738	Establishing of free black town in Florida by Roman Catholics. Runaway slaves from Georgia, South Carolina, and North Carolina could remain if they converted to Catholicism.
1739	Slave uprising in Charles Town, South Carolina; known as the Stono Conspiracy.
1742	Black school opened in Charles Town.
1758	African Baptist Church founded in Luneburg (Mecklenburg), Virginia.
1775	Dunmore Proclamation issued, promising freedom to slaves who serve in the British army.
1776	Declaration of Independence signed.

Africans in America continued to assign a major role to music. The early worshipers did not painstakingly lay out a blueprint for ordering elements. No
doubt the Holy Spirit permeated the "work of the people" in the spontaneous
ordering of elements, acts, or components of worship. The early communities
did not express this process as "liturgical," for it is not the mindset of African
peoples that a name should be given to the community's work at the outset.
Perhaps the Swahili word *harambee,* which means "pull together," might be
more appropriate to describe the community's work to make a divine plan that
would last an eternity. Music helped to serve the important function of assembling the people in a place that would become a common "holy ground."

As worshipers gathered, the space would be blessed and sanctified by the
vocal music of the community. The songs that softly pierced the night air to
convoke the gathering were either created during the assemblage or recalled
from the evolving repertoire of slave songs that would later receive the name
"Negro spirituals." Once the community had been called to worship, music
alternated between several functions. It bonded the community so that despite
their earthly troubles they could transcend the present moment and be lifted
into a divine presence that affirmed them as children of God.

No doubt the melodies of the songs during the earliest clandestine gatherings were reminiscent of Africa. Since the slaves were not all from the same
locations in Africa, new words were honed from common tonal languages and
dialects of Africa and from words used by their oppressors. Songs, therefore,
were a means for slaves to communicate with each other and with God. Their
songs and accompanying bodily movements served as communal offerings
of gratitude to God, whose presence had continued with them from their
Motherland. Obviously, emotional release preceded accuracy of words and
profundity of theological content during the earliest periods. No one would
interrupt these musical offerings to suggest words or phrases that were more
aligned with words of Scripture that were more theologically accurate. The
reality of such gatherings is that these were arenas for the free application of
a black hermeneutics and a free shaping of black theology by which an
African people could survive and find freedom to live.

Songs were forms of proclamation and a means for teaching the necessary
skills for maintaining saneness in an insane environment. Songs helped build
community and provided pastoral care that could function beyond the clandestine gathering into the everyday experiences. In this way, persons who
could not attend would receive the *holy fire* from those who attended. More
importantly, the whispered moans, hums, and other forms of musical expressions that accompanied prayers and preaching (when these could occur) provided *pleasure* and *enjoyment* for slaves who lived in bondage.

Inherent in each of these functions are liturgical reminders that music in black worship functions as a means of glorifying God and edifying humankind. More specific terms, although from the Greek, are equally applicable: Music in worship gatherings of black people functions as *leitourgia* (worship), *kerygma* (proclamation of the good news), *didache* (teaching), *diakonia* (pastoral care), and *koinonia* (fellowship).

We must remember at this juncture that there was no intentional or substantial involvement of uprooted and transplanted Africans in American forms of Christianity until the early eighteenth century. It is likely that if any gatherings were held, such as in rice and cotton fields, the music would have been more reflective of religious ritual music from Africa. Indeed, much of the African cultural heritage survived and was adapted to the strange religion that preached one thing and lived another. Adaptation in these instances meant acculturation or reworking religious beliefs and practices so that a new form of Christianity could be born. A study of the singing, praying, and preaching of Africans in America is in sum and substance the "Africanization" of Christianity in America.

Most if not all African American worshipers can claim historical roots in the earliest African American liturgical gatherings that later became known as the "Invisible Institution." The label *invisible* alludes to the secret or clandestine nature of these gatherings, where mutual relationships, worldviews, social behavior patterns, and political actions were officially constituted by slaves, regardless of religious persuasions. Scattered throughout extant writings and oral testimonies of ex-slaves from the seventeenth and eighteenth centuries are helpful data concerning the elements of worship, with singing noted as a very important part. While these practices may not have been universal in scope, there were no doubt comparable stylistic elements, which black Americans can mutually claim.

In keeping with the African freedom to express in song any matter that they felt the desire to express, Africans in bondage sang as they worked or rested from their labors. Many of these songs can be considered a call to worship communicated in coded language. There is no doubt about the origin of such songs as "There's a Meeting Here Tonight," "Hush, Hush, Somebody's Calling My Name," "Old Ship of Zion," and some perhaps less familiar ones such as "Go in the Wilderness," "Gwine Follow," "Pray All de Members," "Join the Angel Band," and "Meet, O Lord."

Thus, worship began with singing long before the meeting began. When secrecy was necessary, black worshipers speculated that the slave owners would assume they were simply engaging in an activity that they enjoyed— the act of singing. Little did the slave owners know that the songs were of a dual nature, and that the words communicated the place and time of gathering, and if slaves did not hear or understand the words, they would know by the melody where and when to meet.

Singing might have continued as an opening prayer or an invocation with the prayer content heavily interspersed with thanksgiving and praise to Almighty God for making it possible "one more time for us to be here, and to arrive without hurt, harm or danger," as black worshipers prayed then and now. This prayer time would later be used as a time of devotion, frequently symbolizing a time of waiting for other worshipers to arrive, often by foot, from long distances. Communal prayers of black folks are most often chanted by the person praying, with interpolations from congregants in keeping with the rhythm and sometimes the melody of the chant. The concept of songs as "sung prayers" had not reached the liturgical vocabulary of black worshipers, but they were a natural outcome of the worshiping environment.

The natural sequence of the worship would dictate where, when, and how the next musical expression would occur. In this spiritually charged environment, a soloist or "musical prompter" would break forth into song, encouraging full congregational support in the process. According to ongoing evidence among black worshipers similarly charged in current situations, the length of time of the singing depends upon the depth and height of the spiritual flow, the congregational dynamics, and the leadership of the preacher or deacon "in charge." A Bible might not have been available, and if available might not have had a reader or sufficient light for a reader to see the text. However, usually someone there would offer biblical expressions or scriptural interpretation of some text—any text—for those who hungered for a "word from the Lord." These clandestine meetings were under careful watch by a sentinel, whose task was to alert the gathering to the presence of an intruder. Singing was closely guarded so that it would not get "out of hand" by someone filled with the Holy Ghost or filled with the thoughts of moving from the bondage of slavery. (There was a clear connection between these two possibilities!) Quilts that were drenched with water and strategically located around the sacred space diminished the sound. Large black iron pots filled with water also served to deaden the sound of singing, preaching, and praying outside of the sacred space. The community of faith would also sing softly with their heads huddled together around an iron pot filled with water.[5]

One can only speculate about the details of verbal elements, the sequencing and alteration of music and verbal elements, and even the extent to which the content of the words and message was truly Christian. One wonders if Christian preaching actually happened initially, or if these gatherings were opportune times to plan for social survival outside the Christian ramifications of saving grace! The preaching moment might have been spiritually based but more in line with the will of God for a people in the dire circumstances of African American slaves. Clandestine gatherings did not originate for blacks on foreign soil, but continued as a means of accomplishing something related to the religion or the politics of African people on the continent of Africa.

One historical document that communicates an "orderly plan" about communal gatherings of Africans introduced to Christianity in seventeenth-century America is *Rules for the Society of Negroes*, penned in 1693 by Cotton Mather, a Puritan minister who demonstrated early interest in evangelizing African American slaves. Mather's first rule is as follows: "It shall be our Endeavor, to Meet in the Evening after the Sabbath; and Pray together by Turns, one to Begin and another to Conclude the Meeting; and between the two Prayers a Psalm shall be Sung, and a Sermon Repeated."[6] Surely such gatherings with rules this strict were obviously not intended to be secret, nor were they intended to be impromptu. This historical reminder is only an example of *one* group of indentured Africans in Massachusetts, where there was some semblance of freedom. Among these records are requests from Africans in America for church membership and for the privilege of marriage. Thus, these practices cannot be generalized beyond their northern circumstances. However, they serve as an example of the desire of an enslaved people to worship, regardless of the circumstances.

Among the nine rules are an established time of meeting and evidence of "controlled" practices of singing only one psalm. While the manner of singing the Psalms might have been *similar* to what Africans in America heard in Euro-American churches, it was certainly not the *same* sound. Also, according to the *Rules*, catechesis and matters of disciplined behavior were also to be a part of each time of worship. This document also provides evidence that the earliest steps in revising the catechism to make the questions specifically appropriate for Africans in the American Diaspora were already underway. As stated in rule 9, "It shall be expected from everyone in the Society, that he [*sic*] learn the Catechism: and therefore, it shall be one of our usual exercises for one of us to ask the Questions, and for all the rest in their Order to say the answers . . . either the New English Catechism, or the Assemblies Catechism, or the Catechism of the *Negro Christianized*."[7]

With such rigid rules, one wonders why participants continued the Christian journey at all. On the other hand, this rigidity might have inspired a form of Christian discipline that sustained African individuals and families. This unfamiliar approach to confront the Creator also propelled worshipers to find their own space and time to worship. With different music traditions evolving almost concurrently, it can be expected that there would have been different traditions of worship, based on musical and liturgical preferences. Over a period of time, new verbal language forms evolved with basic symbols and manners of expression, albeit utilized differently as forms of liturgical communication. Music was one of the most conspicuously continuous symbols of the African heritage, with various expressions reminiscent of the African diversity of styles and uses.

Music genres employed in early African American worship were rooted in African and African American cultural traditions, with some influences from Euro-American traditions. There is sufficient documentation, for instance, to confirm that the spirituals, the first uniquely African American musical genre, were shaped out of the essence and convergence of traditional African world views and European and American religious thought, then fused with contemporary black folk life and existence.

Music in Worship from the Free African Society Forward

The "Invisible Institution" continued, especially in southern localities, even as some African Americans were establishing their own self-governing organizations and denominations. This era is marked by the enactment of laws offering freedom to slaves who serve in the American army for a number of years, laws providing for the gradual abolition of slavery, and walk-outs by brave African protesters who recognized that self-help begins with communal unity. African people in a new land also continued to connect religion with life. Mutual aid societies, Masonic lodges, African Union societies, and other self-help organizations included religious services and various kinds of musical performances during meetings.

Equally significant was the musical tenor of the time, both in northern and southern cities. Blacks were exposed to local and international professional musicians in concerts, operas, and incidental music for plays and in the performance of oratorios, often with orchestral accompaniment. In many places, professional musicians taught black students. Among the "singing-school masters" was an African, Occramer Marycoo, apparently renamed Newport Gardner by the Gardner family who brought him to America. He began to write music in 1764 when he was only eighteen. An advertisement for one of his choral compositions identifies him as "a native of Africa."[8]

According to minutes of the January meeting of the Free African Society, congregational singing as a corporate act was highly advocated. Among the recommended rules was one regarding music: "It was recommended that at the time of singing the congregation shall stand or keep seated as they find freedom, and that the congregations should supply such books as are necessary to read, sing, and praise the Lord in harmony."[9] In the summer of 1794, a majority of the members of the African Society voted in favor of affiliation with the Episcopal Church. Historic St. Thomas African Episcopal Church of Philadelphia was dedicated in July 1794. Absalom Jones accepted the ministry of this newly aligned Episcopal church. He was ordained a deacon in 1795, and in 1804, he became the first black Episcopal priest.

Music was part of the religious instruction of all persons seeking membership in the Episcopal Church. Contrary to the generally espoused opinion that African Americans were not attracted to the formality of the Anglican worship style, those who opted to become part of this tradition did not oppose or regret the work and time involved in learning the liturgy of the church. Of special significance was the fervent desire of some to sing and play music from a score, or "by note." Among the records of the Society for the Propagation of the Gospel in Foreign Parts is the observation that "the singing of a psalm had produced a good effect: It had engaged many of the [blacks] to a closer application in learning to read."[10] African Americans often met for music instructions in psalmody during the evenings on a regular basis.

Summary of Elements in the Liturgy

Since there is carefully documented information about the music of black Episcopalians, which will be detailed later, it is appropriate here to affirm the close alignment with the traditional order and flow of the liturgy from their eighteenth-century roots in this faith tradition. The sequencing of music that has evolved over centuries follows a classical shape[11] that congregations follow according to pastoral leadership and congregational needs. The established liturgical flow follows a theological order that helps identify Episcopalians, and is often the reason why persons are drawn to this tradition. This point will be reiterated throughout as a counterpoint to the assumption that has stigmatized some African Americans as seeking to mimic Euro-Americans. Irene V. Jackson writes that "there was a high performance standard placed on music in black congregations."[12] She also notes that there was musical syncretism within the colonial Church of England, as blacks fused certain African and Afro-American musical practices with Anglo-American musical practices.[13] Such Afro-American practices might have included the "Dr. Watts style" of lined hymns and the creation of new songs by improvising rhythms and interpolating new lines, short phrases, and revised refrains in existing songs. This awareness provides some evidence that black Episcopalians contributed to the growing body of religious music later identified as spirituals. Jackson contends that one spiritual that might have been shaped and framed in black Episcopal environments is "Let Us Break Bread Together." She bases her contention on the fact that the kneeling position is assumed (by those who are able) during Holy Communion. She bases this assumption on research by Episcopal scholar Robert A. Bennett.[14]

Over the centuries, black Episcopalians have demonstrated concern that the music of the liturgy reflect the best that can be offered to Almighty God. Therefore, careful attention is given to the choice of music leaders, both choral and instrumental. Many of the earliest trained musicians in the African American community, performers and composers, were Episcopalians. Another significant characteristic was the clergy's concern about improved congregational singing. This concern encouraged a desire for music literacy among worshipers, so that early in the life of black Episcopal congregations, many members could "sing by note," thus, enhancing the usual practice of rote singing. Black Episcopalians were among other blacks being trained in singing schools, occasionally by musicians of African descent, and there were often negative comments about their "arrogance" and desire to be "uppity."[15]

African American Episcopal liturgy included the appropriate use of psalms, hymns, anthems, spirituals, and occasional newly composed songs that gave the worship a distinct flow. From roots planted in the establishment of separate black Episcopal congregations in 1794, to the close of the Civil War, a foundation for high musical standards was provided. This foundation has given momentum to black Episcopal congregations as well as other African American congregations and denominations to seek the highest quality in musical offerings in worship. With the persistence of congregations, clergy, and musicians, the major focus is on glorifying God and on the edification of congregations.

Since there is data to support this often overlooked aspect of liturgical history from African Americans, additional information from the black Episcopal liturgical heritage will be provided. An order for the Holy Eucharist follows (with musical elements in italics):

> Liturgy of the Word
> *Entrance Chant (A psalm with antiphons or refrains introit)*
> Litany
> *Hymn*
> Greeting and Collect
> Lections
>   Old Testament
>   *Chant*
>   *Psalm*

Gradual
Epistle
Alleluia
Gospel
Sermon
Creed
Hymn
Liturgy of the Upper Room
Offering and Offertory (*psalms may be sung)*
The Great Thanksgiving (*with portions that are sung*)
The Lord's Prayer
Hymn
The Communion
Hymn
Post Communion Prayer
Benediction

Organs and Trained Choirs in Worship

Leadership in providing a model for the use of trained choirs and organists in African American liturgy came largely from African American Episcopalians, who were the first to introduce both into the worship service, as indicated on page 120. St. Thomas Episcopal Church in Philadelphia installed a pipe organ in 1828 and employed a young black woman as its organist. In addition to the economic realities of such an instrument, the hiring of a young woman provoked comments from the local press that the church was "progressive."[16] If "progressive" means seeking to develop high performance standards and practices with the intention of offering to God the best possible musical gift possible in the light of the time, then black Episcopalians are guilty of being progressive since the beginning of their history. A number of churches in the North and as far south as Baltimore and Washington, D.C., demonstrated their progressive natures by adding an organ and a trained choir to their services.

According to a report by a new pastor called to the St. Thomas Church in 1830, the organ and a well-prepared choir had become a tradition at St. Thomas. His words are echoed in documentation by other so-called progressive congregations of this time: "She [St. Thomas] stood alone in favor of education of ministry and people . . . and once spoken of in disparaging terms on account of care for cleanliness, decency in worship house, her carpeted aisles, her pews and organ, now closely imitated in all respects."[17] "Closely imitated" as used here refers to the model that St. Thomas has provided for other

African American congregations. The organ remained a novelty for some congregations, and numerous African Americans denounced churches, such as St. James in Baltimore, where the organ had been introduced. An observation by one researcher is of interest:

> Reproachful and sneering terms were applied to the church because of this introduction into the public services of the church of the "devil's music box." Thus the church was an early witness for musical accessories in divine services, as well as for order and decorum in public worship. The indirect influence of St. James has been very great in this city [Baltimore] as the marvelous changes in the conduct of services in colored churches witnesseth.[18]

According to published records and comments from subsequent pastors, the quality of music and musicianship continued. These records are primary sources of information from Rhode Island; Newark, New Jersey; New York; Chicago; and Philadelphia.

African American Episcopalians demonstrated ease in using "trained" choirs in worship,[19] a process that apparently occurred without much if any fanfare. Historically, the anthem is a musical form directly related to Anglican worship. The preferred accompanying instrument is the organ, so its introduction provided a means of incorporating choral music in worship. The year the organ was introduced, black Episcopalians heard choral music from professional choirs and began sponsoring sacred music concerts in their own sanctuaries. As mentioned earlier, American cities were bustling with musical activities. Recently freed slaves were electrifying audiences with their talent, and black churches welcomed opportunities to hold sacred concerts. Many opportunities existed for local congregations to participate in the singing of a hymn or a familiar anthem with professional groups in concert. The vocal repertoire included choral settings of works by Handel, Chappell, Haydn, and Mozart.

In order to prepare for concert singing, African American choir members attended singing schools, frequently operated by their own congregations. Many black professional musicians traveled between cities in order to appear in concerts. Among these traveling artists were choral directors Morris Brown, Jr., Robert Jones, and Jacob Stans, as well as orchestra directors William Appo, James Hemmenway, Francis Johnson, and Aaron J. R. Conner.

Among the distinguished African American musicians born in Philadelphia were the members of the Bowers family, children of the custodian at St. Thomas Church. Thomas J. Bowers, the second oldest, was a vocalist and organist and was extolled for his magnificent tenor voice, for which he acquired the title "the colored Mario" to compare his unusual talent with the

Italian opera singer Giovanni Mario. John C. Bowers, the elder brother, was a highly skilled organist, and their sister, Sara, was an excellent vocalist who was better known by her professional name, the "Colored Nightingale." In his 1878 work, *Music and Some Highly Musical People,* James Trotter noted the desire of the Bowers's parents to localize the talents of their children in the congregation rather than in secular settings. They were not opposed to hearing their "sweet sacred strains issued from the choir and organ in church services."[20] With such natural talent available to congregations, African Americans would have been remiss not to nurture such talent for the worship of the church.

The Bowerses were among many highly musical persons from the eighteenth and nineteenth centuries who not only sang during worship but also were encouraged in their careers by congregations. Many black churches became "concert halls" where black musicians such as the Bowerses could be displayed, lauded, and encouraged. Unfortunately, the records of how some of this music was used during worship are not available. Episcopalians are also credited with influencing the use of organs in independent African American worship in general and instrumental music in worship in particular. Many blacks denounced the use of instruments, especially the organ, with the accusation that the organ was "the devil's music box." Nevertheless, music in black Episcopal worship services in the North gained the reputation of being a "cultivated" or genteel tradition, which meant that it was distinct from the black "folk" or vernacular tradition or from the music of Euro-Americans. Against those who would argue that this was an example of "striving to be white," one could rebut that it was comparable to Africans who claimed their right to be Americans by seeking good jobs and economic security, and donning attire that was available in American stores.

Music in African Methodist Episcopal Congregations

By 1839, progressive urban black churches in most denominations had trained choirs that were eager to provide music leadership in worship. Amid the published histories of black denominations, few specifics are provided about musical practices. As indicated earlier, African Americans are indebted to Richard Allen for the publication of his hymnal in 1801, thus establishing the importance of recording black history. As the first liturgical document, it also established the validity of printed resources and their ability to assist congregations in recording the history of a people. Clearly, Allen was communicating in this single act that not only is singing important as a liturgical element but that literacy and spirituality are mutually inclusive.

It is significant that a second edition of this hymnal was published later in the same year. The hymnal was so popular among both black and white congregations that more copies were needed. In addition, membership in the African Methodist Episcopal Church had grown substantially, and Allen found a need to revise and enlarge his musical offerings.

In 1816 when the AME Church held its inaugural General Conference, Richard Allen was ordained a bishop, and the way was opened for the most continuous publication of African American hymnals. A committee of four, with Richard Allen as chairman, published the first official hymnbook of the new denomination, *The African Methodist Pocket Hymn Book,* in 1818. In an acknowledgment of the importance of this inaugural hymnbook, Vivienne L. Anderson, member of the 1984 AME hymnal committee, wrote:

> African Methodism produced its first hymn book in 1818 under the leadership of Richard Allen, Daniel Coker, James Chapman and Jacob Tapisco. It contained 314 hymns and spirituals carefully chosen to enhance the church in doctrine and spiritual food. This was the first book of songs published by the Children of Oppression, and the very first to give expression in their own selected language telling of the Christian hope of the race.[21]

With such a long and informative hymnological history, it is clear that the AME Church takes seriously the use of music in the liturgy, as well as carefully planned orders of service. The range of music in the liturgy includes hymns, spirituals, gospel songs, anthems, and songs from the global community. Service music has a long history in the church, including various settings of the Lord's Supper, with a number of settings of the Sanctus, long and short versions of the Decalogue, a variety of arrangements of the Lord's Prayer, a musical setting of the Te Deum and the Apostles' Creed, a variety of settings of the Gloria Patri, and numerous responses for different portions of the liturgy. Jimmie James, Jr., provides the following summary about the music in AME worship:

> At present, the scope of music used in AME churches continues to expand, and in some instances it is selected and performed differently than traditional church music. However, in recent years, many district choirs . . . have shown a resurgence in selecting traditional anthems, hymns, and spirituals. . . . It is hoped that this renaissance will manifest itself within the general church through a mammoth effort to improve the quality of music used in AME worship services.[22]

The flow of the liturgy is suggested in a number of published denominational orders of service. However, each congregation ultimately establishes its own local identity in the overall context of the AME ethos. Local identity naturally changes with technological developments, global exposure, the reclaiming of elements in the African heritage, and the varying musical dynamics determined to a large extent by the tenor of the time and by the pastor. This is influenced largely by theological seminary exposure, which at the Interdenominational Theological Center focuses on the liturgical year and the use of the Common Lectionary.[23] The basic order that follows is from the 1984 *AMEC Bicentennial Hymnal*, a resource that has the format of a service book with a variety of alternate patterns included. Musical elements are in italics.

Prelude
Processional Hymn
Doxology
Call to Worship
Hymn of Praise
Invocation
Choral Response
Anthem
Prayer of Confession
Scripture Lessons (Responsive Reading)
Hymn (to introduce the Decalogue): "From All That Dwell"
   (tune: Woodworth)
Decalogue
  First Commandment
    Chanted Response ("Lord Have Mercy Upon Us and Incline Our
      Hearts to Keep This Law" [music by J. T. Layton])
  Second Commandment
    Chanted Response ("Lord, have Mercy . . .")
  Third Commandment
    Chanted Response
  Fourth Commandment
    Chanted Response
    Hymn: "My Soul Be on Thy Guard" (music by George Frederick
      Handel)
  Fifth–Tenth Commandments
    Chanted Response (after each one)
    Hymn: "Nearer, My God, to Thee" (music by Lowell Mason)
  Or: Summary of the Decalogue
    Gloria Patri (tune: Greatorex)
Benevolent Offering
Announcements and Parish Concerns
Hymn of Preparation ("sermonic" hymn)
Sermon

The Lord's Prayer (chanted)—optional
Invitation to Christian Discipleship
Hymn of Invitation
The Apostles' Creed
The Offertory
   Special Music from the Choir
Choral Response
Doxology (Closing Hymn) [It is not clear whether one or both are to
   be used]
Benediction
Recessional

The printed order does not in any way describe the ethos of AME worship. As with any worship service, it must be experienced. Until the last quarter of the twentieth century, instrumental music was most often provided by some kind of organ.

Music in African American Congregations of Other Denominations

As these congregations and denominations increased in membership, independent congregations were also established, especially in northern cities where there were large numbers of free African Americans. Many of these independent congregations were established by black protestors who separated themselves from Euro-American churches because of racist, unequal, and restrictive treatment early in the nineteenth century.[24] Due to its polity, it is easier for blacks in the Baptist tradition to leave a congregation and organize their own congregation or denomination than it is for those who are a part of denominations that function more tightly, such as Methodists, Presbyterians, and Lutherans.

This brief historical reminder affirms that worship practices from the beginning were diverse and fluid. Africans in the American Diaspora were not always free in terms of *where* worship would take place, but they were free to adapt worship and musical practices according to their own tastes and exposure. Despite the tendency of black sociologists to suggest certain denominational preferences for free and former slaves, one doubts whether a particular denomination really mattered initially, especially in terms of polity, creedal preference, or the desire to be noncreedal. This is especially true where African American congregations with a particular denominational affiliation function to meet the spiritual needs of the community of faith as needed rather than as the denominational body authorizes. The term *ecumenical* was not part of the vocabulary of early Africans in America, but denominational interaction happened naturally due to the concept of kinship, communality, and the need for black unity. The genesis of black congregations in clandestine gatherings transcended ecclesial labels. Therefore, elements of worship easily began in environments where worshipers were least concerned about denominational ownership. Without utilizing the Greek concept of *oik,* blacks functioned ecumenically in the "Invisible Institution." This is especially evidenced in the common repertoire of music for worship, the sharing of hymnals, and the collaborative compilation of the *African American Heritage Hymnal.*[25]

Nevertheless, denominational labels did, in fact, become meaningful from the postbellum era to the last quarter of the twentieth century, when nondenominational and interdenominational affiliations began to soar. Carter G. Woodson's observation lends significant insight into the post–Civil War period: The focus by northern Euro-American denominations on educating rather that proselytizing the newly freed slaves encouraged numerous blacks to attend schools sponsored by Presbyterians, Lutherans, Congregationalists, and others. Very often, however, graduates would not join these denominations but would take their recently acquired education and their membership to black Methodist and Baptist churches.[26] Woodson also observed that with the new cadre of educated ministers after the Civil War, the tone of worship changed as early as 1875 and decidedly so in 1885. The following liturgical differences are cited here, not because they have universal applicability, but because of the historical reminder that not all black preaching was geared to appeal to the emotions of worshipers:

> Preaching became more of an appeal to the intellect than an effort to stir one's emotions. Sermons developed into efforts to minister to a need observed by careful consideration of the circumstances of the persons served, hymns in keeping with the thought of the discourse harmonized therewith, and prayers became the occasion of thanksgiving and blessings which the intelligent pastor could lead his congregations to appreciate and offer a petition for God's help to live more righteously.[27]

A large number of documents attest to some of the religious activities of slaves, including the fact that some during the late eighteenth and early nineteenth centuries were taught the basic rudiments of music. Many were also taught psalmody and took great pride in singing psalms. This illustrates the freedom that existed to expand the liturgy, not that some worshipers were simply attempting to imitate their Euro-American oppressors. Admittedly, not all slaves were privileged to attend these catechetical classes. However, the few who could "raise a psalm" might have been among those who would later "raise a meter hymn tune" and move congregants to glorify God with heart and voice.[28] In a letter to Joseph Bellamy in 1751, the Reverend Samuel Davies noted that several slaves

> lodged all night in my kitchen, and sometimes when I have awaked about two or three o'clock in the morning, a torrent of sacred harmony has poured into my chambers and carried my mind away to heaven. . . . In this seraphic exercise some of them spend almost the whole night. I wish you and other benefactors could hear some of these sacred concerts. . . . It would surprise and please you more than an Oratorio or a St. Cecilia's day.[29]

According to existing records, slaves received regular training in the charity schools operated by the Society for the Propagation of the Gospel in Foreign Parts (SPG) in Philadelphia from 1758 to 1775; in New York from 1760 to 1775; in Newport, Rhode Island, from 1760 to 1775; and in Williamsburg, Virginia, from 1760 to 1775. Regular procedures included instruction in psalmody and in correct approaches to psalm singing. Africans in America might have studied psalmody as part of their religious instruction as early as 1728, according to newspaper advertisements for a school operated by Nathaniel Piggott that was opened for "the instruction of Negroes in reading, catechizing and writing."[30] There are records countering the level of enjoyment that blacks had toward psalmody, especially among enslaved Africans new to the American environment. New arrivals were still struggling to communicate in the language being adapted by earlier Africans. There was yet a strong preference for African musical expressions, movement (dance) rites, and ritual practices, which some Euro-Americans found entertaining and "heathenish." Included among the creative songs of this era were African chants and tunes—such as work songs, field hollers, and jubilees—that were appropriate for times of communal work. Equally significant were the African primal religious forces and occasional attempts at evangelizing slaves that led to the shaping of the spiritual, both outside and inside of worship.

The Antebellum Period

Liturgical Music in the North

Worship in early black congregations and denominations was centered in the desire for African Americans to praise and glorify God freely and truly without restraint and without fear of reprisal. This hunger to encounter God in and through Jesus the Christ has biblical as well as existential precedence. These early worshipers knew that wherever two or three gathered, Jesus would be in their midst. Furthermore, they were assured that their own communal free-dom and togetherness was divinely ordered and was reflective of the religious fervor of the times, especially as it was expressed in the Great Awakening. Little did the slaveholders realize how deeply embedded the faith would become despite the hesitant and reluctant evangelistic efforts of Euro-Americans. From the historical information available, slaves apparently dis-covered or found anew the God who transcends human barriers and delivers people from oppression. Messages of hope and eventual freedom were cele-brated with great vitality and power in the music and movement of an enslaved people. With divine empowerment, this form of African American celebration contributed greatly to the shape and content of worship in the Great Awakening and the Second Great Awakening and in frontier revivals and camp meetings of the early nineteenth century.

The size of these renewal gatherings was so great that there were no build-ings large enough to contain them. Huge crowds would gather outdoors to worship for a number of days. Slaves were allowed to attend camp meetings, and they attended in large numbers. They were permitted to set up their tents in an area behind the preacher's stand. Their own celebrations were often so enthusiastic that they drowned out the preaching and singing of the Euro-American worshipers. Many worshipers joined in the fervent singing of the songs of blacks, some of which were created in the context of the camp meet-ings and some that had been composed in other settings, including the "Invis-ible Institution." This genre of songs was later called spirituals, and it evolved from African chants, field hollers, and shouts. Euro-Americans continued to use the songs and singing styles of slaves, even as they worshiped in their own (segregated) congregations.

Many series of camp meeting worship services concluded with a march around the meeting space accompanied by leaping, shouting, shuffling, and dancing appropriate to the closing of a series of holy encounters. Despite the discomfort that such "borrowing" brought to some Euro-Americans, these joint worship experiences were the first free exchange between whites and blacks, and perhaps the beginning of a long and continuous pattern of mutual borrowing of music forms and styles between these two cultural traditions. It is to Philadelphia and to the Free African Society that we turn initially to determine historical data about music in northern black congregations. Prior to the withdrawal of African American members of the congregation at Old St. George's Methodist Church, Richard Allen had led a movement to orga-nize an independent religious society. Plans were well underway by the mid-dle of the summer of 1791 to build an African church. In 1792, Richard Allen and Absalom Jones left the Methodist Church and heartily attended to the work of the Free African Society. According to minutes of the January meeting of the society, congregational singing as a corporate act was highly advocated. Concerns about singing from notation or singing by rote in the nineteenth century are not far removed from problems in the twenty-first century according to documentation by William Douglas.[31]

The work of evangelists included lessons in psalmody as a part of the initial religious instructions for African Americans, Native Americans, and other catechists. Teaching words of psalms from songbooks facilitated individuals' abilities to read texts and music. Gradually many worshipers learned to sing and play music from a score, or "by note." By 1830, many so-called progressive northern black churches of all denominations had introduced choral singing into their services, but not without some opposition. Just as in all periods of African American church history, a diversity of music styles functioned simultaneously in most if not all congregations. Daniel Payne of the AME Church describes how Bethel Church in Philadelphia struggled with the changeover from the "old" style of singing in the "common way," by rote, to the "new" style of singing by note. The transition began when the congregation, under the leadership of Payne, moved into a new building in December 1841, and a gallery or separate wing was set aside for a choir to use at the dedicatory services by progressive members. Later an uproar was caused when these members attempted to introduce choral singing into the regular service.[32] According to Payne:

> The first introduction to choral singing into the A.M.E. Church . . . gave great offense to the older members, especially those who had professed personal sanctification. Said they: "You have brought the devil into the church, and therefore, we will go out." So suiting to the action for the word, many went out of Bethel, and never returned.[33]

Payne, a relative newcomer to the AME Church, had studied at Gettysburg Theological Seminary in Gettysburg, Pennsylvania, for two years, and considered education important to the newly evolving black churches. Thus, he was able to suppress some of the irritation among the members by using materials written by John Wesley as well as biblical concepts. Dissention over old and new methods continued in other congregations wherever the concept of separate choirs and/or the use of instruments in worship was introduced. In some instances, either a split would occur in the congregation, or pastors would lose their jobs if they were initiators of the idea. The earliest performance of instrumental music in an AME church took place during a concert of sacred music in Baltimore, Maryland, in 1848. But by 1888, AME churches throughout the denomination proudly acknowledged the high quality of their choirs and organs.

The state of music in African American congregations during this period was no doubt affected by camp meetings sponsored by African Americans throughout the nineteenth century, primarily among Methodists and Baptists. As early as 1818, AME congregations had established independent camp meetings in Pennsylvania, with reports of four or five thousand persons in attendance for three or four days. According to Daniel Payne, both urban and rural camp meetings incorporated the ring shout or simply "shouts" and other practices that reflected the African heritage. His reports affirm the diverse practices that existed perhaps in "blended" form even during regular Sunday worship. Terms Payne used to describe the musical sounds include "unequalled vocalists and excellent musicians," "extraordinary skill in entertaining," "harmony of voices and sweet accords of music," "charm and solemnity," and "sweetness and power."[34] In contradistinction to these positive observations were reports from as far north as Boston, west to Cincinnati, and throughout the South of the existence of significant remnants of the powerful African heritage, albeit reported in negative ways. As Eileen Southern observes, Payne might have represented the prevailing attitude among the clergy in his efforts to "modify extravagances indulged in by the people" including his disdain over their use of "corn-field ditties."[35] While Southern's understanding of Payne's attitude may be too much of a generalization, she may be accurate in her assumption that some educated clergypersons might have concurred with Payne.

The AME Church expressed its consternation over some of the musical practices by passing the following resolution: "Resolved that our preachers shall strenuously oppose the singing of fuge tunes and hymns of our own composing in public places and congregations."[36] "Hymns of our own composing" referred to African American spirituals freely created and recreated in worship and in the meter hymn tradition. Fortunately, the resolution did not suppress the ongoing liturgical music, which is recognized as uniquely African American in theology and methodology. Throughout the nineteenth and early twentieth centuries, black worshipers shaped and reshaped songs that provided the foundation for global music. Additionally, the African-inspired "shouts" and possibly the "holy dances" influenced the direction of some forms of liturgical music into the twenty-first century.

Southern Models of Music in Worship

The forms and styles of music used in African American worship in southern communities depended to a large extent on particular geographical locations as well as the periods of time in American history. While the newly formed black congregations among Episcopalians, Methodists, Baptists, Presbyterians, and the nascent black denominations during the early 1800s functioned as the congregation and pastor determined, blacks in some southern locations were still without religious instruction and under strict supervision. There are data from some southern colonies indicating the belief of some slaveholders that religion was harmful to the slaves. Not only would slaves become saucy or sassy, but the missionaries too often imposed restrictions that denied them much needed pleasures after the rigors of slave work. The instances of insurrections following worship services discouraged any form of gathering among blacks without supervision.[37] Supervision of blacks could take place in balconies or in camp meeting settings. On plantations regularly visited by white missionaries, black deacons and class leaders supervised worship until after the Civil War in some places. Charles C. Jones, a missionary, worked diligently to discourage all levels of spontaneity and emotional responses:

> The public worship of God should be conducted with reverence and stillness on the part of the congregations; nor should the minister . . . encourage demonstrations of approbation or disapprobations, or exclamations or responses, or noises, or outcries of any kind during the process of divine worship; nor boisterous singing immediately after the close. These practices prevail over large portions of the southern country, and are not confined to one denomination, but appear to some extent in all. . . . I cannot think them beneficial.[38]

His preference for their choice of music was hymns and psalms so that they would be induced to lay aside their own "nonsensical chants and catches and hallelujah songs of their own composing."[39] This is the kind of supervision that led blacks to develop their own styles and forms of songs in clandestine meeting places. This old tradition continues especially in southern states through a large number of Baptist worship services. As with other denominational traditions, the forms and styles of worship vary widely most often in accordance with the community in which the church is located. Large black academic communities have in some instances incorporated many liturgical elements, especially the music, which reflects the worshiping ethos of the university chapel, especially if the church is in the immediate neighborhood. Another dominant influence is the liturgical and aesthetic preference of the senior pastor. In all instances, the congregation either claims or discards practices with changes of pastors. Invariably, certain liturgical practices remain in new structures to affirm a black Baptist ethos, even if the old occurs during revivals or during a once-a-week service. This is true regardless of the particular religious body or denomination in which the church has membership—

Missionary Baptist, National Baptist Convention, USA, National Baptist Convention of America, and Progressive National Baptist Convention.

Borrowing from the language of Walter F. Pitts, traditional Afro-Baptist services are ordered around two "ritual frames" or events that are technically a bound sequence of activities that transport worshipers along a continuum of spiritual uplifting moments. Pitts contends that these overarching ritual frames were inherited from secret African initiation rites and the ritual public display of possession trance.[40] Building upon Victor Turner's theory of three successive ritual stages—structure, antistructure, and restructure—Pitts pivots his research of "the Afro-Baptist ritual" around ritual stages in the flow of the service. He uses the imagery of a ship sailing on waters that are sometimes rough. He contends that Afro-Baptist worship experiences function to transport worshipers psychically and emotionally from a hostile world to a smaller, more secure place where they can be equipped to return to the world ready and able to face life at a higher level. Functioning within his basic ritual frame, some more specific elements that are more in line with those of the twenty-first century are presented on page 156. Musical elements are in italics.

Sanctified Churches

The Sunday morning service began when brother Elisha sat down at the piano and raised a song. The song might be, *"Down at the cross where my Savior died!"*

Everybody sang with all the strength that was in them, and clapped their hands for joy. Their singing caused them to believe in the presence of the Lord; indeed it was no longer a question of belief, because they made that presence real.[41]

The voice of James Baldwin often breaks through any conversation about music in the churches that are generally classified as "sanctified." This also expresses the experiences of members and participants in any Holiness, Pentecostal, Apostolic, Deliverance, and other sanctified churches. Fortunately, few African Americans have thus far escaped the wonders of the Holy Spirit at work among the worshiping saints, for few communities are without a sanctified church. My own ecumenical experiences lie in a small rural community where ecumenism was created as an extended family for all black congregations. Nothing else was planned in conflict with sanctified services because a large portion of the community was in attendance. In addition to knowing and borrowing the exciting, Spirit-filled music for other religious gatherings, the

Southern Model of Worship:
African American Baptists

Frame I

Devotion(s)
Prayers
Lined hymns
Scriptures
Other hymns and songs

Testimonies

Explanation

Initiated and led by the deacons, who hold on to memories of the early "Invisible Institution" experiences. This frame is a preparation for the descent of the Holy Spirit. Prayers and the kind of music used are predictable. The praying deacon uses traditional (customary) prayer language and musical speech patterns to afr m that the prayer is directed to the Almighty. Prayers unfold in developmental stages of the opening, thanksgiving, appeals, petitions, and discourse, with a view of the end of life leading to "Amen." In some congregations, the devotion is either shortened to include praise services or eliminated totally and replaced by praise services. This totally disconnects with the traditional African initiation ritual, and thus the service begins with antistructure.

Frame II

The Service
Prelude (instrumental)
Call to Worship
Processional Hymn
Scripture
Prayer
Special Choral Music
Pastoral Prayer with
   Altar Call and *Singing*
Announcements
Offering with *Gospel Music*
Sermonic Music (choir, solo,
   or congregation)

Sermon (the focus of this frame;
   often builds to a *musical climax with*
   "chanted celebration")

Altar Call (if not earlier)
   With *congregational singing*
Offering (alternate place)
   With music
Closing Hymn/Song
Benediction
Choral Response
Postlude

Explanation

In the Pitts model, emphasis shifts from familial structure to antistructure where congregations participate in various kinds of music including hymns, anthems, gospel music, occasional spirituals, free prayer forms.

public school teachers knew all of the "young saints" who could be called upon to lead the singing for elementary and high school events.

The Pentecostal movement in the United States dates from the 1906 Azusa Street revivals in Los Angeles, which were initiated and led by a black Holiness minister, William J. Seymour. This movement, unlike other black church movements, began as part of a distinctly interracial movement and not as a separatist movement. Euro-Americans subsequently withdrew and began their own movement to ensure that power could be under their control.[42] Inasmuch as a black Holiness minister and some of the black Pentecostal groups began as Holiness groups, it is important to delve briefly into the chronological and theological history of the Holiness movement.

Seeds of the Holiness movement were planted during the Second Great Awakening during the 1840s and 1850s with the idea of "perfectionism," which prevailed among some of the established Protestant denominations. With the country besieged with turmoil over slavery, segregation, and racism, a concern for "perfection" and "holiness" was literally out of sync with the thinking of most Americans in leadership positions. The Holiness movement was actually initiated in 1867 by a group of Methodists who organized the National Camp Meeting Association for the Promotion of Holiness, later called the National Holiness Association. During the period of interdenominational camp meetings from 1867 to 1887, local Holiness associations were organized by and among Methodists that centered on a "third work of grace" theology. A number of churches were established during the 1880s because of theological issues surrounding Baptism, the Lord's Supper, the outpouring of the Holy Spirit, speaking in tongues, and evidence of "sanctification." In 1890, dissentions that had been brewing because of the concern that a large number of so-called middle-class ideas had seeped in through newly received members who had come from "established denominations" reached a peak, and schisms began to occur. By 1906, a number of persons attended the Azusa Street revivals seeking spiritual renewal. Thus, these revivals became a source of a more radical form of theology manifested in the early Holiness movement. According to findings compiled by black researchers:

> Both Holiness and Pentecostalism gained momentum in reaction to liberal tendencies at the turn of the century expressed in Darwinism, the ecumenical emphasis, and the social gospel movement. The anti-liberal orientation of the Pentecostal movements led also to the termination of its interracial character as separatist white denominations were organized.[43]

Charles Harrison Mason, a Baptist minister, organized a series of successful revival meetings with his colleagues Charles Price Jones and W. S. Pleasant.

Mason and Jones were dismissed from the Baptist Association because they were preaching the doctrine of sanctification. The first group of converts was organized in 1897 into a Holiness "movement," then the Church of God, and finally was incorporated as the Church of God in Christ (COGIC) in Memphis, Tennessee. While in attendance at the Azusa Street revivals, Mason received the baptism of the Holy Ghost and experienced speaking in tongues for himself. The COGIC General Assembly was divided over the doctrines that confirmed these practices, and the denomination subsequently split over these issues. Those in attendance who agreed with Mason remained in communion with the "Pentecostal faction." The first Pentecostal General Assembly was convened by Mason in 1907, which marked the year the COGIC was incorporated as a denomination. Mason was declared general overseer and chief apostle, and later designated senior bishop. From 1907 to 1914, this body was the sole ecclesiastical authority to which independent white Pentecostal churches could appeal to or call on for matters such as ordinations. Accordingly, white ministers were ordained by Mason and officially specified as ministers in the Church of God in Christ. These clergypersons, who were committed to segregationist societal rules, established their own Pentecostal denomination, Assemblies of God.[44]

Music in the Liturgy of Sanctified Churches

African roots of black gospel music, shouts, and holy dancing are characteristic of music in the Holiness and sanctified movements of black churches. This music and worship heritage is clearly an example of unity between the sacred and secular, and between African spirituality and African American liturgy and life. In worship, the effects of spirituality were transmitted through a consciousness of the immanent presence of God. Vestiges of African divination are present during worship as the exuberant, charismatic preacher facilitates an awareness of the presence of the Almighty. In West Africa, the *mediums* are in close working relationship with the *diviners* or the priests, and they are most prone to spirit possession. Under possession during the most intense phase of worship, there are psychic vibrations that incite physical vibrations of the body, such as jerking, shaking, rolling, and dancing more or less in perpetual motion. African American sociologist George Ofori-Atta-Thomas (Ndugu T'fori Atta) traces this process in some worship services in both women and men, most significantly in the presence of Aunt Jane (pronounced Ain't Jane) in most if not all traditional black worship services:

> How often on Sunday morning, when that special dialectic is in motion in the drama of worship, when the prophet-priest-preacher has been preach-

ing under the holy unction of power, there are certain mothers or sisters . . . who time a complement of response to that rhythm of vibrations in the spirit to make appropriate antiphonal responses under the power of the Holy Spirit. In black church worship this was and is the function of the classical "Aunt Jane" . . . Mediums were and are in spiritual readiness and temperament for the appropriate response in the spirit, authentically intended to embellish the quality of emotional tone in the worship experience.[45]

In early Pentecostal and Holiness services, the focus was on a renewing effort to feel the effects of the Holy Spirit exemplified and expressed in the exercise of the charismatic gifts of the Spirit, especially those of singing in tongues and of prophecy. This has continued in various ways among congregations so that basic elements of worship are included, but the order in which these elements occur is dictated by the Spirit and followed by the worship leader and preacher. A certain "musical" manner of speaking and preaching facilitates the congregation's ability to feel the presence and, more importantly, the unity that the Spirit brings between the worshipers. According to persons responsible for worship leadership, music, movement (dance), and preaching are the means by which the Holy Spirit is invoked as portions of one unified celebration. The preacher and musicians help create the drama, the momentum, and excitement, during which time the common flow of words passes through various levels of heightened speech, bursting forth in "ecstatic musicality." To experience this form of communal worship is to reconnect music with its ancient purpose to evoke, exhibit, and express the "rapture of the soul." Understood in its highest form, black preaching is a manifestation of a transformative power (or *kratophany*) that visibly moves the hearer to some form of physical response.[46] Persons empowered may simply nod their head, raise their arms, hum out loud, stand on their feet, or cry. On the other hand, a worshiper may speak in tongues, run around the church, or dance a "holy dance." Spiritual momentum is enhanced by a reiteration of words and phrases by the preacher in dialogue with the worshipers, who are by now on their feet, swaying in the rhythm of the dialogue. As kratophany, the preached Word of God overflows with power that is expressed with drama and musicality, because the Word is like "fire shut up in the bones" (Jer. 20:9).

Descriptions of basic elements in worship have been and are still being gathered and published by members of a variety of Pentecostal and Holiness bodies and other sanctified groups.[47] This information is helpful because in many instances the collectors of data can express something about "what is going on" from the perspective of worshipers who are sensitive to theological and practical matters of liturgical flow. The order in which elements occur vary, from those in the West Angeles Church of God in Christ in West Los

Angeles, to a small storefront church in any city, to a small rural congregation anywhere in the United States or Canada.

It is somewhat contradictory to refer to the sequencing of elements as an "order" of service in a religious body that functions as freely as sanctified churches. Perhaps it would be more appropriate to speak of an improvisatory form of service, because there is a definite form or frame in which a seemingly informal service takes place. Nevertheless, "order of service" is used here to acknowledge that there is order and a consistent flow that is often adhered to in a less controlling manner than in churches with fixed orders.

It is abundantly clear that the pastor and musicians are major determinants of the flow of elements in worship. With an increase in the availability of pastors and musicians who have attended seminary, and with a few musicians entering into music programs at the college level, new elements are being introduced. Some researchers include liturgical language in the order of service that has been adopted in recent years. These terms will be used with caution. Since music permeates the entire worship service, it will be difficult to isolate any element without noting its musical connection. A composite order of service (usually called a "program") follows. Musical elements are in italics.

I.	Devotional, or prayer service, heavily infused with singing. Initially the singing was a cappella. However, keyboard instruments and drums now are used to establish the mood for worship. Singing is alternated with chanted prayer and the reading of Scriptures. This service has been replaced in many congregations with praise and worship services.
II.	*Processional of clergy and choir with singing;* call to worship
III.	Invocation and Lord's Prayer
IV.	*Praise choruses and testimonials.* Testimonials often begin with a song.
V.	Pastoral prayer—Led with the *singing of "Yes, Lord,"* the official anthem of the Church of God in Christ, composed and transmitted orally by Bishop Charles H. Mason. This anthem may be sung anywhere in the service to indicate any of a number of liturgical "moves." This anthem may not be included in non-COGIC services of worship.
VI.	Offering, with *music led by the choir and reinforced by the congregation*
VII.	Announcements and recognition of visitors; acknowledging of the sick and shut-ins
VIII.	Scripture

IX.   *Special music by the choir, with congregational and instrumental participation*

X.   Sermon *frequently chanted* with *congregational call and response dialogue;* closing moments of the sermon may be *accompanied by the organist/keyboardist and occasionally drums*

XI.   Altar call (invitation to discipleship and/or opportunities for prayer as individuals kneel at altar rail or stand together in front of the Communion Table). *Music is played and/or sung as a very important part of this discipleship moment.*

XII.   *Closing song*

XIII.   Benediction (sometimes with charge and commission) and *choral response or sung "Amen" by choir or congregation and choir*

Among the experiences influenced by the music during worship is the "shout," which is often used interchangeably with "holy dance" and is commonly understood to signify one or more of the following kinds of behavior, as described by McIntyre:

(1) Unusually enthusiastic expression of body rhythm during the course of a song;

(2) Dancing, usually in response to the sermon, in which typically the feet leave the [floor], the body is lightened by raising of the chest cavity, and the dancer gives free rein to his/her passing emotional states;

(3) Any behavior that takes place under the trance state, whether the latter is brought on by the healing ceremony or by other musical or spiritual stimuli.[48]

In explaining these physical behaviors, McIntyre notes that number 1 assumes the prior existence of a musical environment. Number 2 is at least in part an expression of faith as a positive response to the message of the sermon. It also takes place in a musical context and is at least to some extent a result of musical stimulation. Behavior described in number 3 may include anything found in the other two categories. It is hardly possible that trance can be induced without the person "passing through" the other stages; thus, the depth of this form of "shouting" or "dancing" cannot be repeated "on cue" at the request of an interested researcher.[49]

African American Seventh-Day Adventists

The Seventh-Day Adventists emerged from an interdenominational movement that started in 1844 and was formally organized in 1863. The denomination stresses the imminence and importance of the Second Coming or Advent of Christ. Its other major point of distinction is its observance of the seventh day as the Sabbath. This denomination is an interracial body with a large African American constituency. The denomination is organized into geographical areas called unions, with seven African American conferences, which focus on the concerns of and foster communication with African Americans.[50]

The worship of Seventh-Day Adventists is very much in the free church tradition. Worship for Adventists is the "natural response of intelligent human beings once they realize they are in the presence of God."[51] The Adventist *Church Manual* includes a suggested order, which is adapted by each local church according to standards established within the limits of the Adventist theology of worship and conditioned by sociological factors. The Lord's Supper is to be celebrated quarterly, with the order changed to include time for the sacrament.

The seriousness with which African American Adventists take music for worship and music in general is evident in the music of local congregations, the extremely talented members on concert circuits, and the tremendous musical tradition of Oakwood College in Huntsville, Alabama. Among the outstanding educators was Eva B. Dykes, the first black woman to earn a doctorate in the United States and founder of the Aeolian Choir, one of two outstanding choirs at Oakwood College.[52]

Alma Montgomery Blackmon provides a picture of church music in black Adventist congregations, noting at the outset that

> black Seventh-Day Adventists are fragmented in their perceptions of music that is appropriate for the worship of God. Cultural differences within families, dissimilar opportunities for musical training and exposure, varying musical traditions within local churches, and wide diversity in the degree to which our clergy, musicians, and members have dedicated themselves to the study of church music all contribute to the fragmentation that we are now experiencing.[53]

Blackmon's research indicates that black worshiping congregations have parallel histories and are experiencing many of the same concerns within the denomination. First of all, like other congregations in Euro-American denominations, the hymnal for the Seventh-Day Adventists, developed in the early 1940s, contained music from around the globe, but no spirituals. The struggle all-inclusive (or so-called inclusive) denominations face is a need to take seriously the faith-related purposes of music in worship, and biblical mandates that serve to determine what is appropriate or inappropriate. Blackmon cautions that care should be taken to distinguish between the authentic gifts of the African musical heritage and those elements that are not African.

Corporate Sabbath services among black Adventist vary greatly. Some congregations conduct services very formally, with lots of singing and a variety of accompanying instruments. Others are more informal with praise music and different amounts of African American cultural music offerings. The examples that follow reflect numerous worship experiences by the writer, Adventist seminarians, and other observers. Musical portions are in italics.

TRADITIONAL FORMAL VERSION	INFORMAL OR CONTEMPORARY VERSION
Organ Prelude	*Prelude* (Organ or Other Keyboard)
Announcements	*Processional* (optional)
Introit	*Choral Praise* (Led by a Team of Musicians)
Processional (Choir and Clergy)	Prayer
Invocation	Welcome
Doxology	Announcements
Welcome by Worship Leader	Congregational Response
Reading of Scripture	Greeting and Communal Fellowship
Hymn of Praise	with Embraces and Handshakes
Pastoral Prayer	*Congregational Song of Praise*
Choral Response	Reading of Scripture
Congregational Singing	or *Anthem, Spiritual, or Other*
Anthem, Spiritual, or Other	*Special Music by the Choir*
Special Music by Choir	Offertory
Offertory	*Offertory Music*
Offertory Music	*Doxology*
Choral Response	*Congregation Singing*
Baptism (*with Singing*)	Sermon
Hymn of Consecration	Occasionally Replaced by Drama
Sermon	*or Special Music Offering*
Seasonal Oratorio	*or Other Art Form*
Often Replaces Sermon	*Closing Song*
Closing Hymn	Benediction
Benediction	*Recessional* (occasionally)
Choral Response	
Recessional	

The longstanding tradition among Adventists of emphasizing music is reflected in the amount of music used in worship, especially in the singing of hymns.

Churches that are attempting to become "contemporary" or "renewal" churches extend the time devoted for singing.

Conclusion

African Americans did not hesitate to sing songs from other cultures and traditions even in a strange and weary land as long as they could "fix" the songs to meet their African specifications. The new sounds, melodies, and harmonies upon which words of faith could be expressed were shaped for worship in and out of doors. The songs began with simple African chants and expanded to other genres, from religious folk songs—spirituals, psalms, hymns, and gospel songs—to anthems, all of which helped carry the good news of hope from the church to the world.

Chapter 7

Western Roots of Theology as Reflected in African American Music for Worship

*T*he published records of African American music and worship history reveal constant comparison with Western roots. Even among worshipers in the twenty-first century, Western church theological and musical biases often permeate the measure by which all church music is evaluated. It is appropriate, then, to include a brief theological review of the Western roots of the theology of church music. This review will identify several major figures including some African theologians who helped shaped Western music and liturgy.

The Western musical tradition is fraught with "musical puritanism." The early church began to censure the use of music in worship during the latter part of the second century. This stricture lasted through the fourth century for two basic reasons. First, certain forms of music were associated with superstitious, irrational, and sensual worship in so-called pagan religions. Music was used throughout the acts of worship, and often led to sexual excitement and orgiastic frenzies. The flute (*aulos*) was one of the instruments associated with the frenzies, and so it was declared immoral. During this era, choirs of females who performed during the rituals were called "harems of the gods," and their moral behavior was questionable. For this reason, male choirs were preferred in Christian worship, with the soprano parts sung by young boys with unchanged voices. This was a step backward for women, who had served as participants in congregational and choral singing for two centuries. There were organized choirs of women separate from the congregation who performed at the liturgy.[1]

A second critique of music in Christian worship through the fourth century was a belief that music possessed moral qualities that could affect human behavior and character. In Greek thought, the human soul was viewed as a composite that was kept in harmony by numerical relationships. Music reflected this orderly system and also penetrated the soul, subsequently affecting one's entire life. The Platonic philosophical idea is that "music is in itself a heavenly reality. 'Real' music is celestial, spiritual, and therefore inaudible.

Even 'earthly music' is not simply a matter of sound—which can also be mere chaotic—but depends on the proper proportion and order being present in the sound."[2] Augustine put music in the Platonic context of the struggle between spirit and flesh. Whereas he recognized and affirmed the usefulness of song for "raising the soul to God," he expressed fear that its pleasures would entrap the soul in a lower order of beauty and prevent its ascent to the true Good.[3] The idea of music as fundamentally and wholly spiritual, thus entirely within the soul, was the determining factor for the Greek classification of music as one of the "liberal arts." Other liberal arts were mathematics and logic, while painting and sculpture were considered servile arts because they require an effect on matter. This distinction persisted in the curriculum of the universities throughout the Middle Ages. It was believed that the essence of music is separable from sound, so the medieval mind could regard all proportions and dimensions of structure as "musical." An example of this principle is in the conception and construction of Gothic cathedrals, designed to echo the higher "music" of the mathematical proportions of the universe itself.

Shapers and Movements

The most influential scholars in the early church, known as the church fathers, interpreted Scripture and then set forth principles of guidance. Some, such as Clement of Alexander, Origen, Basil, and John Chrysostom, wrote in Greek; others, such as Ambrose, Augustine, and Jerome, wrote in Latin. In general, they believed the value of music was in its power to inspire divine thoughts and also influence the character of the listeners. Music was considered the servant of religion. Only music that opened the mind to Christian teachings and inclined it to "holy thought" was deemed worthy of hearing in church. Certain music was, therefore, forbidden in worship.

Augustine of Hippo

The relationship between music and words concerned the African church father Augustine of Hippo (345–430). While Augustine struggled over the use of music in the church (ultimately affirming its appropriateness), his struggle was compounded by his concern for which was of greatest importance: words or music. One of his confessions concludes:

> [W]hen I recall the tears which I shed at the song of the Church in the first days of my recovered faith, and even now as I am moved not by the song

but by the things that are sung, when sung with fluent voice and music that is most appropriate, I acknowledge again the great benefit of this practice. Thus I vacillate between the peril of pleasure and the value of the experience, and I am led more—while advocating no irrevocable position—to endorse the custom of singing in church so that by the pleasure of hearing, the weaker soul might be elevated to an attitude of devotion. Yet when it happens to me that the song moves me more than the thing that is sung, I confess that I have sinned blamefully and then prefer not to hear the singer.[4]

Singing for the sake of the text needs to be emphasized continually and emphatically. Nevertheless, Augustine's point of view also challenges the current reality that much attention is given to the beauty of performance. Persons who are guilty of this are likely to "fall into the power of sensuality and abandon true spiritual interiority."[5] In modern terms, this simply means that the true intent of spiritual worship has been overtaken by physical concerns.

Augustine also states his approval of a kind of nonverbal "sung praise," a process that he called the *jubilus,* a spontaneous wordless, musical outpouring of the heart's joy before the Lord. He praises the spiritual value of music without words in this observation:

The *jubilus* is a melody which conveys that the heart is in travail over something it cannot bring forth in words. And to whom does that jubilation rightly ascend, if not to God the ineffable? Truly is He ineffable whom you cannot tell forth in speech; and if you cannot tell Him forth in speech, you ought not to remain silent, what else can you do but jubilate? In this way the heart rejoices without words and the boundless expanse of rapture is not circumscribed by syllables. Sing well unto Him in jubilation.[6]

The depth of Augustine's concern about music is further attested in his treatise on music, *De musica.* The first book of this six-book work includes a brief introduction, which is a definition of music, followed by four books on the principles of meter and rhythm. The sixth book is a discussion of psychology, ethics, and the aesthetics of music and rhythm. Augustine originally projected six more books on melody. [7]

Anicius Manlius Severinus Boethius

The most influential authority on music in the Middle Ages was Anicius Manlius Severinus Boethius (ca. 480–524/26). His *De institutione musica* (*The Fundamentals of Music*) is a digest of music written in the first years of the sixth century. Boethius divides music into (1) *musica mundana* (cosmic music), the orderly numerical relations seen in the movement of the planets, the changing of the seasons, and the elements; (2) *musica humana* (human music), which controls the union of the body and soul; and (3) *musica instrumentalis* (the art of music), audible music produced by instruments, including the human voice, which exemplifies the same principles of order, especially in the numerical ratios of musical intervals. He emphasized the influence of music on character and morals, and the discipline of examining the diversity of high and low sounds by means of reason and the senses. For him, the "true musician" is not the singer or someone who makes up songs by instinct without understanding the nature of the medium, but the philosopher, the critic, "who exhibits the faculty of forming judgement according to speculation or reason relative and appropriate to music."[8] Boethius and Martianus Capella are credited with compiling and transmitting the music theory and philosophy of the ancient world to the West during the early centuries of the Christian era.[9]

Thomas Aquinas

Thomas Aquinas (1225–74) provides excellent reflections on his own perceptions of music from a theological perspective in his *Summa Theologica*. He raises a question about the use of song in prayers, and answers by saying that songs should *not* be so used. He bases this on Augustine's notion that mental praise is a high form of praise and that it would be impeded by singing since singing requires concentration and the sung word is less understandable to others than the spoken word. Nevertheless, Aquinas concludes by saying that singing has a valid place in worship even if the words cannot be understood. In contrast to Augustine, Aquinas contended that the intention, or movement toward God, can be present without special attention to the words.

Chants

From the fourth century through the Middle Ages, music in the Western church centered on the singing or chanting of texts. The compilation of existing chants by St. Gregory and his organizing or reorganizing of the schola cantorum (school of singers) in 600 no doubt provided a strong impetus for the propagation of Roman chant and the later development of intensive training for church music ministry.[10]

Chanting is a basic primal form of musical expression that is prevalent in African cultures as well as in other cultures around the world. In a definition directly applied to music in Christian churches, *chant* is a general term for liturgical music that is monophonic and in free rhythm, and it falls into two main divisions: Eastern chant and Western chant. Eastern chant includes Armenian,

Byzantine, Coptic, and Syrian. Western chant includes Ambrosian, Gallican, Mozarabic, Gregorian, Old Roman, and Anglican.[11]

In each tradition, chants are important to the life and history of the church in that their use in worship helps to embody a sense of community. Any number of African American congregations continually utilize the chant form, especially when singing or chanting the Lord's Prayer. The use of traditional liturgical chants among African American Roman Catholics and Episcopalians continues to the extent that priests determine that it facilitates the flow of the order of service. Presbyterians, Lutherans, and Methodists have encouraged chanting of the Psalms by including psalm tones and procedures for chanting in their more recent hymnals. There has also been a resurgence of interest in Gregorian chants, along with interest in recordings of other sacred music from non-Western traditions as a form of meditation.

The Protestant Reformation

Concerns about the music of the church have emerged in virtually every era of the church's history. The need to reform the music of the church in this age is a constant topic in conversations and in religious journals and newspapers. Since a universal religious system has never existed in sub-Saharan Africa, any concerns that have been raised have been handled locally. Since many of the institutional religions established by Africans in America and those in which a large number of African Americans are currently members have Western origins and traditions, a brief review of theological trends related to and following the Protestant Reformation is important.

Foundational rumblings of the sixteenth-century Reformation were heard in voices of protest across Europe during the Middle Ages. The concerns were related to the abuses of theology and practices of medieval Catholicism. In the mid-to-late fourteenth century, John Wycliffe attacked some of the doctrines of the church on the grounds that Scripture was the supreme authority; Wycliffe believed the church had moved from this stance. His writings influenced John Hus, a religious reformer in Bohemia. After Hus's death, his followers in Moravia continued their struggle, and by the eighteenth century began to regain their strength. The Hussites, especially the Moravians, are known for their hymns and fervent singing. The Moravian Church maintained a rich program of church music both in Europe and in America. Their rich musical life, hymnody, and congregational singing influenced the music of John and Charles Wesley.

The Reformation occurred just as the Renaissance was approaching its peak and humanist thought was emerging. With the emergence of movable type printing, opinions could be shared in printed form, thus encouraging the desire for personal freedom in various areas of life, including religion. The need for reform included the way that music was used in the liturgy. In addition to the three reformers often highlighted (Luther, Calvin, and Zwingli), there were others with more radical views. Among them were Anabaptists and Nonconformists who produced their own hymns and musical forms that continue in the heritage of Mennonites, Hutterites, and Amish groups. Space does not permit an investigation of African Americans in other religious groups, such as Black Moravians, Mennonites, and Church of the Brethren.

Martin Luther

Martin Luther (1483–1546), the Augustinian monk of Wittenberg and theological architect of the Reformation, was familiar with traditional Gregorian chants and was also a gifted composer who understood the power of music for good and evil: "Next to the Word of God, music deserves the highest praise . . . whether you wish to comfort the sad, to subdue frivolity, to encourage the despairing, to humble the proud, to calm the passionate, or to appease those full of hate . . . what more effective means than music."[12] Luther also said that "music is next to theology," a concept that can be interpreted in a variety of ways. First, it can be taken to mean that music, as a discipline of study, is next in importance to theology. It can also mean that music has a theological reason for being: It is a gift of God. In Luther's judgment, music in the church served as a resounding sermon. As such, it is to be valued not only as a vehicle for sacred texts but also as a mirror of God's beauty and thus a means for reaching the soul directly with a message about God that is inexpressible in words.[13] With the assistance of his collaborator, Johann Walter, Luther established congregational singing in the vernacular as an integral part of the liturgy, and introduced the role of the cantor as a ministry in the evangelical church.

Black Lutherans

During the last quarter of the twentieth century, African Americans within the Lutheran Church—Missouri Synod set in motion a project that took shape in 1993 and was finalized in the publication of *This Far by Faith: An African American Resource for Worship* in 1999.[14] More importantly, the initiative allowed a new "reformation" as the black members of two Lutheran denominations worked together on a liturgical project. (The other denomination was the Evangelical Lutheran Church in America [ELCA].) This excellent resource demonstrates what can happen when "the interplay between worship and culture in which practices that seemed right in one era and within one culture may be judged odd or quaint in another."[15] Surely Martin Luther would have no objection to this observation, since he understood the need for music and words to be in the vernacular of the people.

However, before the publication of *This Far by Faith,* the ELCA published a resource for worshipers, "to assist them to sing their faith with a better awareness of Paul's charge to the church in Rome" to "live in harmony with one another . . . that together you may with one voice glorify . . . God" (Rom. 15:5–6). The title of this resource, *With One Voice,* communicates this aim so that one voice of the church represents an amazingly diverse fabric, of many songs of many cultures in many styles, woven together by the one Spirit.[16] A representative collection of songs from black communities around the world is included in this ecumenical collection.

The Lutheran Book of Worship, published in 1978, was a joint effort of four Lutheran denominations. The committee was deliberate in its attempt to embody the Lutheran tradition of worship, which received its characteristic shape during the early centuries of the church's existence and was reaffirmed during the Reformation. The desire to provide an equitable balance among hymns of the various Lutheran traditions and to follow closely the Christian church year resulted in a book of worship, with one significant shocker: James Weldon Johnson and J. Rosamond Johnson's "Lift Every Voice and Sing."

John Calvin

French-Swiss Reformation theologian John Calvin (1509–64) is considered the guiding influence in the shaping of metrical psalmody. His entry into religious life occurred following a conversion experience and a subsequent encounter with a psalm-singing evangelical community in 1535. Calvin opposed the music traditions of the Roman Catholic Church, especially the use of choirs, organs, and songs composed by humans. He proposed the singing only of scriptural texts, primarily versified psalms. His philosophy of songs for worship led to the production of a series of Psalters beginning with the Strassburg Psalter published in 1539, continuing with other Psalters published in Geneva, and terminating with the Genevan Psalter in 1562. The latter compilation included the entire book of 150 psalms, the Ten Commandments, the Apostles' Creed, and canticles, including the *Nunc dimitis* (Luke 2:29–32). Calvin was neither a poet, nor a composer or musician. He did, however, receive assistance in versifying and composing music for these texts from Clement Marot (ca. 1497–1544), Theodore de Beze (1519–1608), and Louis Bourgeois (ca. 1510-ca. 1561).

Calvin's theological position on music is articulated in his *Institutes of the Christian Religion* in the section on prayer,[17] the prefaces to the Genevan Psalter in 1542, and the Genevan Psalter in 1543. Calvin is clear that there are two kind of prayers: one with words alone and the other with singing.[18] He resonates with Augustine's concern that music should not get in the way of the meaning of the text:

> And surely, if the singing be tempered to that gravity which is fitting in the sight of God and the angels it both lends dignity and grace to sacred actions and has the greatest value in kindling our hearts to a true zeal and eagerness to pray. Yet we should be very careful that our ears be not more attentive to the melody than our minds to the spiritual meaning of the words. . . . Therefore, when this moderation is maintained, it is without any doubt a most holy and salutary practice. On the other hand, such songs as have been composed only for sweetness and delight of the ear are unbecoming to the majesty of the church and cannot but displease God in the highest degree.[19]

Calvin did not recommend the silencing of music totally, but he was clear that music should be congregation friendly. His basic conception was that it should be written in a simple melodic line, with one note to a syllable, and sung in unison and preferably a cappella. In this manner, Calvin was close to the early church, in that he wanted music for worship to be distinct from music of the world. He differed from the early church in his desire to move away from inherited practices as did the early church which continued and built upon music practices of the synagogue.

African Americans in Reformed Traditions

The Calvinist tradition continued in a number of churches in North America. Reformed denominations with the largest numbers of African Americans are the Presbyterian Church (U.S.A.), the Cumberland Presbyterian Church of America (formerly Second Cumberland Presbyterian), the Reformed Church in America, the Reformed Presbyterian Church of North America, and the Christian Reformed Church in North America. The one African American denomination is the Cumberland Presbyterian Church in America, which was founded in 1869 following the withdrawal of blacks from the Cumberland Presbyterian Church. The authorized hymnal of this denomination, adopted in 1999, is the *Worship and Service Hymnal* (Carol Stream, Ill.: Hope Publishing Co., 1957), a conservative evangelical hymnal with no African or African American songs. The number of blacks in the Christian Reformed

Church is minimal, and is not listed in the *Directory of African American Religious Bodies*.[20] The Christian Reformed Church's *Psalter Hymnal*[21] includes songs from Africa and the African American tradition, as well as songs from around the globe. According to a 1995 report, approximately 2.5 percent of the membership of the Reformed Church in America is African American.[22]

African American Presbyterians

African American membership in the Presbyterian Church (U.S.A.) ranges between 2 and 2.5 percent. One of the factors that led pioneer members to this denomination was its emphasis on the value of education. Gayraud Wilmore notes that African American Presbyterians, with respect to attitude, ambition, lifestyle, and the vision of a future for themselves and their children or grandchildren, are solidly middle class.[23] Like other African Americans, whether they opted to pull away from or remain part of a Euro-American denominational tradition, black Presbyterians know the meaning of oppression and the need to develop survival skills.

Although the theology of Calvin undergirds Presbyterianism, the term *Presbyterian* actually refers to a system of church government with power vested in bodies of individuals rather than in a bishop. Presbyterians initiated the evangelization of Africans enslaved in America in 1747. Questions about the unchristian nature of slavery were raised by the Presbyterian Church first in 1774 and continued until the Civil War, at which time the church divided into North and South. Separate congregations were initiated and organized by pioneering black preachers, with educational institutions developed in relation to these congregations. In many instances, the education of African Americans took place only in churches and meeting houses related to local congregations. Thus, singing traditions started in the context of worship and parochial education. From all indications, metrical psalmody was not included in the repertoire. If used, this never became a tradition. Like other African American worshipers, black Presbyterians counted spirituals and the hymns of Isaac Watts among their favorites.

Prior to the publication of *The Presbyterian Hymnal* in 1990, few songs by African Americans appeared in Presbyterian publications.[24] Planning for the 1990 hymnal was deliberate in its "conscious effort to recognize various racial and ethnic musical traditions in the church and to express them, taking into account their influence on past, present, and future hymnody."[25] A publication of service music in 2002, titled *Holy Is the Lord,* includes a setting of the Eucharistic prayer by several African American composers, including Isaiah Jones, an African American clergyperson and musician.[26]

Ulrich Zwingli

Ulrich Zwingli's thoughts about music represent a combination of factors. Zwingli (1484–1531) was a naturally gifted vocalist and musician, who combined this with academic training in music and Greek, and he was considered the best musician among the Reformers. He was at first a humanist, a Swiss patriot, and, with the insistence of the Dominicans in Bern, he entered the monastery to share his beautiful voice. During a period of time in Vienna he studied music and became grounded in the use of a variety of instruments as well as composition. Too often his exclusion of music from worship is announced without explaining that this has to do with his theology as well as his approach to music. His theology was shaped as he prepared for the priesthood and for service as chaplain and preacher of the Word of God for the pilgrims at the shrine of the Black Virgin at Einsiedeln. In his second post as priest at Great Minster in Zurich, Zwingli cast aside the lectionary and began preaching *lectio continua* ("continuous readings") first from the New Testament, except from Revelation, and then from the Hebrew Bible, Genesis through Malachi.

Matters that helped shape his theology include his understanding of worship and prayer as being synonymous, in that both required literal obedience to Christ's command in Matthew 6:6 to "go into your room and shut the door and pray to your Father who is in secret." In devotion, a person should be alone, so the individual was foremost in his mind. Singing or any form of music in public arenas was for him like shouting while people were in the middle of their meditations. However, he was in theological agreement that visible public gatherings of the community for worship were important for the ongoing life of the church. He therefore required silence in public worship, except for the reading and interpretation of the Word of God for the community to hear. His focus was on the need of the people to be educated in the Word of God. In addition to music, Zwingli also eliminated vestments, relics, images, and organs. Zwingli denied both the Roman Catholic position on transubstantiation and Luther's understanding of the real presence, and he changed the frequency of the Lord's Supper to a quarterly celebration. His preference for silence during worship created a change that had existed since the time of Justin Martyr. Another concern that supported his elimination of music was God's silence on this subject. Instances of the use of vocal and instrumental music abound in Scripture, but without evidence that God commanded it. Still, despite Zwingli's attempts to expunge music from worship, in Zurich, where Zwingli had been most powerful and persuasive, the church began to sing again in 1598.

The Council of Trent

The Protestant Reformation provided the impetus for the Roman Catholic Church to seek change within its own structure. Worship and music were included in this renewal movement, which was referred to as the Counter-Reformation and was organized at the Council of Trent, a series of twenty-five meetings from 1545 to 1563. Although music was not a major concern of this special council, complaints about the music of the Church were taken seriously. Some contended, according to Grout and Palisca, that

> [B]asing the music on secular *cantus firmi* [plain chants] such as chansons, profaned the Mass. Complicated polyphony made it impossible to understand the words, even when pronounced correctly. Musicians were accused of using inappropriate instruments, being careless, and having irreverent attitudes.[27]

Polyphony was perhaps the most serious musical concern. Some of the cardinals at the council suggested that all music should be eliminated or at least should be strictly monophonic. Efforts to reform music in the liturgy were effective in some parishes in general. However, musical diversity existed in parishes throughout Europe following the council and lasting well into the seventeenth century. Nevertheless, this council set the course for liturgical music for four centuries until the Second Vatican Council.

A draft of the recommendations from the Council of Trent follows:

> All things should be so ordered that the Masses, whether they be celebrated with or without singing, may reach tranquilly into the ears and hearts of those who hear them, when everything is executed clearly and at the right speed. In the case of those Masses which are celebrated with singing and with organ, let nothing profane be intermingled, but only hymns and divine praises. The whole plan of singing in musical modes should be constituted not to give empty pleasure to the ear, but in such a way that the words be clearly understood by all, and thus the hearts of the listeners be drawn to desire of heavenly harmonies, in the contemplation of the joys of the blessed.[28]

Vatican II and Twentieth-Century Reforms

As a part of his desire to update the policies of the Church and renew the life of the church, Pope John XXIII called the Second Vatican Council, which lasted from 1962 to 1965. Its first decree provided the foundation for future reforms in liturgy and music. The value of Gregorian chant was stressed, but a way was opened to encourage active participation of the people, thus permitting vernacular languages in worship. Of special note was the acknowledgment that people in mission lands have their own musical traditions, which are important to their religious and social lives and should be held in proper esteem. Local instruments were allowed on the condition that their use contribute to the edification of the faithful. In an effort to involve the congregation, some churches abandoned Latin immediately, although Vatican II did not require this. Gradually, the heritage of chant and polyphony was eliminated. The affirmation that music belonged to the people created a desire for the congregation to sing together rather than to rely upon the choir to sing on its behalf. One of the outcomes of Vatican II was the acceptance and incorporation of the musical gifts of Africans, African Americans, and other cultures of the world.

Black Catholics in the Twenty-First Century

Vatican II spawned a resurgence of interest in the music from African and African American traditions. In the 1960s, Father Clarence Joseph Rivers, the renowned African American liturgist, scholar, and musician, revitalized Catholic worship and "stirred international interest in the indigenization of Catholic liturgy."[29] Rivers also inspired black Catholics to bring their artistic abilities to Roman Catholic worship through consultations and through the National Office for Black Catholics, the first such office in a predominately Euro-American religious body. Rivers coordinated numerous black Catholic liturgical conferences and led the way in publishing documents on African American worship and music.[30]

With *Lead Me, Guide Me: The African American Catholic Hymnal,*[31] black Roman Catholics provided their first published documentation of music in the liturgy. The music reflects the commitment of the black constituency to wed the Roman liturgy and the black tradition, according to the depth of knowledge of both traditions, and in keeping with the documents of Vatican II. Apparently J-Glenn Murray, S.J., is acknowledging here the twofold process of *acculturation* (the process of incorporating cultural substitutes for or illustrations of ritual elements of the Roman rite) and *inculturation* (the process whereby a pre-Christian rite is permanently given a Christian meaning), which is a further task of the black constituency.

Anglicans

The Reformation in England is associated with a series of incidents: (1) England removed itself from Roman Catholic control, (2) Henry VIII divorced, and (3) Henry VIII destroyed the monasteries to gain wealth, power, and control. One of the legacies of the Anglican Reformation was Thomas Cranmer's *Book of Common Prayer,* which in its language and structure influenced Christian worship wherever English was spoken.[32] Since there were no theologians among the Anglicans who responded to musical issues of the day, Thomas Cranmer, archbishop of Canterbury, is the name that is remembered in relation to the liturgy, and due to his leadership of the Protestant party in England. Cranmer had relics and images destroyed and old rituals and rites cast aside. The *Book of Common Prayer* was the source of the structure and content of the Communion service, which was essentially the same as that of the Roman Catholic Church.[33]

John Merbecke (1510–83), organist at St. George's Chapel in Windsor, is remembered for his musical setting of the Ordinary portion of the Communion service in the *Book of Common Prayer.* His concern for the inclusion of the congregation in the service was not shared by other composers of the day, who preferred to compose music for choirs. The new form of music composed was called the *anthem,* which replaced the *motet* in the Roman Church. Other choral settings used in the Ordinary mass and canticles for morning and evening prayer were gradually called *services.* With the rise to power of the Puritans, the Anglican services and chants desisted. By 1660 monophonic chants were restored, and harmony was added to the performance practices. The singing of metrical psalmody, modeling the settings of John Calvin, became popular. Over sixty editions of the Sternhold and Hopkins setting of the Psalms, published in 1562 and considered "Old Versions," appeared over a period of thirty-nine years. The new version of Tate and Brady settings was published in 1696. However the foundation for metrical psalmody and, subsequently, hymnody was the "Old Version" by Sternhold and Hopkins. Congregations were singing and enjoying the freedom to sing without assistance from instruments or choirs. Gradually congregational songs included chorales. Other publishers joined in efforts to publish psalms, some of which found their way into the New World, where African Americans were introduced to a musical form that could be taught in a manner that was familiar to the African call-and-response method of singing.

African American Episcopalians

The Episcopal Church is the American branch of the Anglican communion. Its roots in what is now the United States extend to the land (now California) where Sir Francis Drake came ashore in 1578. Church of England colonists came to Virginia under Sir Humphrey Gilbert, Sir Walter Raleigh, and others.

In 1783 at a conference in Annapolis, Maryland, the Church of England in America formally adopted the name Protestant Episcopal Church ("Protestant" to distinguish it from Roman Catholic; "Episcopal" to distinguish it from Presbyterian and Congregational).[34] The first African American Episcopal parish was founded in 1794 under the leadership of Absalom Jones. Like their Euro-American counterparts, black Episcopalians inherited the tradition of the *Book of Common Prayer.* While continuing the tradition of psalmody, hymns, and anthems, many congregations incorporated the black folk tradition, using music as a means of providing group solidarity and identity.[35] Without apology, black Episcopalians affirmed their reputation of excellence in church music. They appreciated the flow of the liturgy and yet continued the use of black folk music, and no doubt helped in the creation of spirituals.

The Wesleyan Tradition

The first hymnal published in North America for use in Anglican worship was *A Collection of Psalms and Hymns* by John Wesley, published in 1737.[36] Carlton Young identifies this publication as a prototype of the modern English hymnal. It includes in one format a variety of selections: translations, metrical psalms, and English devotional poetry.[37] Charles Wesley was the most prolific hymnist of the eighteenth century, composing over 6,500 hymns. The Wesleys were influenced by the devout singing of the Moravians during their journey to Georgia in 1735. In an effort to learn more about the Moravians, John Wesley spent several weeks in fellowship and prayer with them.

Wesleyan hymns are filled with Arminian theology (which, in contrast to Calvinism, emphasizes human freedom in responding to God) and the Wesleys' actual conversion experiences. Although the following characteristics offered by Harry Eskew and Hugh McElrath are not designated as reasons for the fervency and enthusiasm that accompany the singing or hearing of Wesleyan hymns, they are nevertheless helpful: (1) a rich variety of poetic meters, (2) the coinciding of sound and sense, (3) bold and free scriptural paraphrasing.[38]

African American United Methodists

African American congregations in the United Methodist Church began with the organization of the African Zoar congregation in Philadelphia in 1794. Worship and music in all separate black congregations reflected a synthesis of Methodism with the black folk tradition. A separate structure was institutionalized in 1939 when the delegates of the three merging bodies—the Methodist Episcopal Church, the Methodist Episcopal Church, South, and the

Methodist Protestant Church—voted to segregate the new church's African American membership into one unit. This decision gave birth to the Central Jurisdiction, which included the Negro Annual Conferences, the Negro Mission Conferences and Missions in the United States of America.[39] With this configuration and, to a large extent, liturgical privacy, a distinct black Methodism was able to develop and survive.

In 1968, the United Methodist Church came into existence with the merger of the Methodist Church and the Evangelical United Brethren Church. This merger abolished the Central Jurisdiction and provided theoretical support for racial inclusivity. With the fervor that had been created during the civil rights movement, and the subsequent establishment of the caucus Black Methodists for Church Renewal (BMCR), a more satisfactory pronouncement against racial exclusion became part of United Methodist doctrine in 1972: "We rejoice in the gifts which particular ethnic histories and cultures bring to our total life. . . . We commend and encourage the self-awareness of all ethnic minorities and oppressed people."[40]

One year later, the Board of Discipleship sponsored a consultation on the black church, during which a proposal was approved for the publication of a songbook from the black religious tradition. William (Bobby) McClain brought attention to the sparse number of hymns by racial minorities in previously published hymnals. The 1964 *Book of Hymns* included one hymn by a black composer and five spirituals, which was a denial of the gifts of black history to the total life of the church. In the preface to *Songs of Zion,* the hymnal that was developed and published following the consultation; McClain notes the importance of the unique liturgical gifts that are available to the church through its African American members:

> The Black religious traditions in America, while unique to Black Americans, can contribute much and have made a vast difference in the Christian Church in this nation. For it has been Black people's understanding of God in the context of their own experiences . . . i.e., the Black experience in which they have groped for meaning, relevance, worth, assurance, reconciliation, and their proper response to the God revealed in nature and in Jesus Christ.[41]

This supplemental hymnal is considered by musicologist Eileen Southern to be a "landmark publication," following sixty years after an earlier published "landmark"—*Gospel Pearls.* Both resources provide in a single source a variety of religious songs belonging to the black tradition. Like Richard Allen's hymnal and *Gospel Pearls, Songs of Zion* was and is widely used across denominational lines.

Chapter 8

Music Ministry
in Theological Perspective

*T*he combination of the words *music* and *ministry* signifies that music can render a service to Almighty God and to people. This combination has been used over the years, often without careful thought about what it means. There is value in utilizing this term because of its biblical roots and ecclesial function of service, which is the work of the gospel in general. For African Americans who question the use of foreign terminology to describe what is or should be going on in black worship, we must begin with where we are. African Americans have taken the term *music ministry* to refer to an approach to doing what God has called one to do through an art that has universal appeal. In this chapter we will explore in more detail what African American musicians mean when they use this term. If the Greek origin is offensive, then we should seek new terminology and initiate ways to assure its acceptance in the African American religious community. This confirms Robert Hood's belief that Afro-cultural God-talk does not have to remain Greek.[1] This concern is also foundational to this book. As has been indicated throughout, gifted African people have always improvised, adapted, reworked, and recreated in a manner that ultimately reflects a new environment. It is good, then, to explore the origin of the term *ministry.*

The concept of ministry as service used in Scripture is found in the translation of several words: *diakoneō* ("to serve") and the corresponding noun *diakonia,* which signifies service, serving, administration, and office; *douleuō,* which means "to wait upon," as a servant; and *leitourgeō* ("to give service to God, as a priest") and *leitourgia,* the noun that signifies such service. Ministries in Scripture include the service of priests and Levites in the Hebrew Bible, of apostles, prophets, evangelists, and pastor-teachers in the New Testament, and the general ministry of elders and the individual and mutual ministries of all believers. The term *ministry* refers, therefore, both to the work of those commissioned for leadership and of the whole body of believers.[2]

Music is one of the ministries or services of the faith community that can involve many persons.

The last two words in the title of this chapter, *theological* and *perspective,* declare as if in conclusion that the service that music renders in the community is for the glory and praise of God and for the edification of the people of God. It is appropriate then to begin the discussion of music ministry with the theological perspective of its rendering a service to Almighty God.

Music Ministry in Theological Perspective

Theology is also a term from Greek. *Theos* means "god" and *logos* means "word" or "rational thought." *Theology,* therefore, is not simply a Christian term. This term is used, for instance, in African societies in conversations about "primal" gods, which may or may not relate to God in and through Jesus the Christ. *Theology* as used here refers to beliefs, assumptions, and suppositions enlightened by the Christian faith. Theological concerns about music ministry are often projected in the form of questions that can be answered according to Scripture, and as experienced in cultural contexts. Answers are simply theological presuppositions that must take into consideration the tensions that must exist in what we think (albeit rational) and the truth that we must constantly seek. As Calvin M. Johansson observes, "God is immanent yet transparent, sovereign yet permissive. Our finite minds understand God in dynamic paradoxes—in musical terms, a counterpoint."[3] Johansson skillfully uses the concept of counterpoint as understood musically as note-against-note and melody-against-melody to establish a "dialogical" theology of church music. In contrapuntal music, independent melodic lines are combined in order to affirm both their independence and also their dependence on one another. Dialogue is established texturally between the horizontal (melodic) lines and the resulting vertical (harmonic) chords. The chordal structure that occurs from combining independent melodies must ensure that certain theoretical principles are followed and that the melodies maintain their independence. It is the interplay between musical agreement and disagreement in counterpoint that makes it useful in music ministry.[4] Musicians need to be in constant dialogue with God through Scripture in light of different cultural contexts and emerging musical trends.

Nowhere in Scripture is there a specific statement of theology of music or music ministry. Many approaches to music ministry based on biblical statements are typical ways of proof-texting to provide biblical sanction for an interpretation that may be totally inaccurate or inappropriate for particular contexts. The plethora of pamphlets and tracts built upon other pamphlets and tracts and sold at exorbitant prices at national and local music workshops is embarrassing and scandalous! But sales are up and prices continue to soar. Tidbits of information sold in this manner reflect the hunger of those who have labeled or classified themselves "ministers of music" or who have been boxed in by a term given to them for which they seek definition. Serious servants of God would not purchase yet another list of twenty to thirty scriptural instances (proof texts) to find an answer to justify what they are doing or not doing. A scant plunge into isolated portions of the Bible for answers should be replaced with an understanding of the conditions surrounding the use of music within given contexts. One should also develop a sensibility to the basic principles of God's Word so that the good news can be made applicable and take new roots in local contexts. This is, of course, a lifelong process and a challenge that can be facilitated under the power of the Holy Spirit. What follows are basic assumptions that should be understood by all persons involved in music ministry. Hopefully, these will lead to some clarity about how one renders this kind of service to Almighty God.

The Divine Origin of Music

Music is a gift given by the Creator that engages humankind and all creation in artistic explorations of the mystery and holiness of God. It is God's gift of creative power unleashed in a continuously creative world for artistic expression. As a universal means of expression, music has been imbued by God with the power to communicate on different levels and to transcend cultures and religious traditions. The unlimited range of sounds, rhythms, melodies, and harmonies in music portrays an Almighty Creator filled with love for audible beauty. The mysterious power of music makes it one of the best means of communication between the creative God of mystery and all of creation.

Throughout the ages, humans have been fascinated and mystified by the persuasive powers of music to affect both the performer and the listener. Some scholars have grouped these persuasive powers into families. The first family includes such objective foundations as the elements of rhythm, pitch, timbre, and form. Although all music contains these four elements, these elements help distinguish one kind of music from another. For example, a person well versed in musical style can determine the date and geographical location of a composition by the manner in which these elements are presented.

The second of the persuasive families in music includes the subjective, aesthetic qualities that can also distinguish one kind of music from another. The abstract qualities of this family of music give music its aesthetic powers and allow music to communicate, gratify, and motivate large numbers of people. This power is more difficult to define than the elements of music because it involves emotional responses to particular kinds of music. Individuals are uniquely and personally gratified, and motivated in ways that often transcend universality. Ordinarily, the emotions, images, and feelings that are stimulated by music are correlated with the experiences of the listener. This is why the expression "Music is a universal language accepted and understood by all" is not accurate. Music *is* a universal means through which meaning can be accepted and understood by all. Music has the power to evoke from listeners' subconscious a variety of associations with concrete images in the life of the listener. Therefore, music can activate an unfolding of a person's thoughts and unlock one's mind to a deeper understanding and to creativity.

In many cultures, the persuasive power of music as a medium of communication between God and humans affirms that music is a door opening into the Infinite. Music, like other arts, is a response to and a continuation of the pattern and order of God's creation. In this way, according to the Hebrew tradition, music is a means by which humans reflect the image of God, the *imago Dei,* in a continuing creative process. Theological interpretations of *imago Dei* over the centuries run the gamut of perspectives, including the following:

- Humans are formed in God's bodily likeness;
- The potential for knowing, reasoning, and accepting responsibility is a reflection of the divine;
- Humans "image" God as they follow the divine mandate to have dominion over the world, a mandate that is inseparably bound with God's ongoing creation through humans;
- The creative nature of God continues in the natural gift of divine creativity;
- Humans cannot create exactly as God created, but we can be alert to God's creation as the ultimate example of the importance of purpose and meaning in the creation process.

Humans are given a divine requisite to be creative. In fulfilling this command, we are to begin with the creative subconscious (the idea or imagination) in order to bring into existence, give birth to, or to produce something. Although some humans are more creatively endowed than others, the seed of creativity is planted in all humans and can potentially burst forth in the imagination. Therefore, the designated musicians in each congregation should remain humble as they share their musical talents in the context of worship. Johansson observes that "Christians face the prospect that through their actions (including their music) *God is made known.* Church music is testimony, and in worship believers use cultural expressions, such as music, to offer testimony as to what God has done in their lives."[5]

Music is often connected with the creation process in relation to Job 38:4–7, where Yahweh answered Job out of the whirlwind. The questions asked of Job presume that the vocal sound of music accompanied the divine acts of the Creator:

> Where were you when I laid the foundation of the earth?
>   Tell me, if you have understanding.
> Who determined its measurement—surely you know!
>   Or who stretched the line upon it?
> On what were its bases sunk,
> or who laid its cornerstone
> when the morning stars sang together
>   and all the heavenly beings shouted for joy?

There are some that have linked music with worship because "they both spring from a God-implanted desire to search for truth and order."[6] Wilson-Dickson continues in this connection:

> Music, like other arts, is in and of itself a response to the patterns of God's creation order. Music is a manifestation of that search in the mental and physical realms; worship is its expression in the cosmic. What is more, God has ordered creation in such a way that the unfolding of its truths is profoundly satisfying.[7]

To affirm that God established orderliness onto a formless world so that the world would have purpose and meaning also affirms that the created world is basically good and that the artist-musician should mirror reality. Humans hunger for wholeness; music deals with authenticity in a holistic manner, utilizing the ingredient of form and structure, which actually makes music an art form. Church music that is well crafted, whether by the natural creative gifts of musicians or by carefully structured theoretical procedures, is the ultimate expression in song with words or by instruments that reflect coherence. This doctrine of creation includes the awareness of God's ongoing creation, for the divine work of creation is never finished. To understand the creation process is to understand that God is ever creating. Within this concept lies our human responsibility as cocreators.

The perspective that the foundation of music and other arts was established at the time of creation supports the divine artistic enterprise set forth "in the beginning." The basic physical and mental raw material provided in the formation of the world, including humankind, provides the impetus of personal creative ability and the desire to produce. Human artists, unlike the Divine Creator, are not creating *ex nihilo* but are relying upon God's creative order and God's gifts of raw materials, senses, and abilities. Robert McLaren observes that whatever an artist creates is dependent upon preexistent materials; the artist merely reorganizes those God-given elements into some meaningful reality: "In the truest sense artists do not 'create,' they can only represent, symbolize, or translate what is given. At best they can take materials such as pigment, stone, words, or musical symbols, and rearrange them in such a way as to give communicable impressions of their ideas."[8]

The close association between theology and music is deeply rooted in God's interaction in God's ordered world through people and nature. In many cultures, music is connected with the beginning of all of life, health, wholeness, power, and all that mysteriously springs from the divine. Music in some cultures is one of the symbols of God's presence in the world as evidenced in its power to facilitate the growth of plants and adjust the generative stamina of animals so that they can produce to their highest capacities. The mysterious ability of music to tame savage beasts, quell the evil in humans, penetrate the mind of humans in order to ease pain, induce healing, and facilitate the carrying out of difficult labors is attributed to the presence of the divine in music.

The association of music with religion, worship, theology, and the sacred is often taken for granted by Christians. This is especially true when persons are born into a tradition where music permeates the liturgy. In African American traditions, even infants and young children respond to the intensity of congregational singing of the various styles of hymns, Christmas carols, spirituals, and black gospel songs, and they are fascinated by the choral performance of anthems, cantatas, and oratorios. From such early exposure, music becomes one of the means by which a worshiping consciousness is shaped and framed. Over the years some musicians and worshipers in pews have not always given thought to why music and worship are intricately related. Some simply associate certain kinds of music with church, and establish their likes and dislikes according to what is familiar, what makes them feel good, or what "turns them on or off." This is compounded by the reality that throughout the centuries large numbers of persons have converted to the Christian faith either with little or no exposure to the Christian music tradition, often because they are attracted by the music. Unfortunately, in many instances the emphasis on the number of members as the determining factor for "effective" ministry has minimized the emphasis on the reason for worship.

Recent studies of music in Africa reveal that music is a means of expressing life in all of its aspects through the medium of sound. Francis Bebey, an African musicologist, observes:

[M]usic is an integral part of African life from the cradle to the grave and . . . African music covers the widest possible range of expression, including spoken language and all manner of natural sounds. . . . Nevertheless, it would be a mistake to assume that all Africans are necessarily musicians in the full sense of the word. Africans themselves are fully conscious of this fact.[9]

Another human impulse is order, which is related to the natural life process: the beat of the heart, rhythmical breathing, and the rhythm of sleeping and being awake. This relates to the divine order in the universe: alternation of day and night, light and darkness, weeks and seasons. Humans yield quite early and naturally to this impulse by making rhythmical movements and expressions outside of themselves. This develops into rhythmical expressions as ordered sound, notable among African people for whom the heartbeat continues to be foundational for drumming rhythms. Music is created through sustained tones, which can express individual or communal personality in action and life. This unique characteristic of the source of music helps determine the nature of music for worship and the theology of music ministry.

Music as a Way of Approaching God

Studies of African music remind us of the relationship between music and the sacred, with roots deeper than those of the debates about the subordination of music to words and vice versa. An assumption persists among Africans that music is one way of approaching God. The tensions that have existed since antiquity between music and the sacred are beyond the bounds of a detailed discussion in this book. However, a number of authors have adequately pursued this subject, and a summary of their findings will be incorporated here.[10] A renewed interest in theology and the arts in some theological seminaries is encouraging this research in many instances.[11]

African Americans have always recognized the interrelationship between aesthetics and religion, and the articulation of this connection has continued in the oral tradition of the people. Stated succinctly, it is a matter of feelings and emotions connected with experiencing and knowing that the mystical presence of God permeates the beauty of God's holiness. For many African Americans that which is "beautiful" has a "black cultural bias," meaning that it is measured by experiential existence and not by superimposed standards. The beauty of music for worship in black American culture is the process and accomplishment of creating, and not the end product. Jimmy Stewart suggests that "what results therefrom is merely the momentary residue of that operation."[12] Without apologies, African Americans affirm that beauty resides in the process of creating, the procedure of becoming rather than in the "thing" that is finished. This explains why this writer often refers to spirituals as "always in process of becoming"! Each time the same spiritual is sung it is shaped anew by the singers, and each ending is a momentary residue of what is yet to become in the voices of another community of faith.

Such statements as "We had church today!" and "Wasn't God present in a mighty way!" and "The preaching and music today took me out of here!" are expressions of the experience of the sacred that would get lost in traditional ways of Western theologizing. The African heritage of feelings and emotions permeating all of life continues undeniably in the black church.

The question we must ask now is: What is it in the music that makes it possible for sacred meaning to be conveyed? Music is a kind of symbolic language that voices unspeakable reality. It is a voice that communicates natural symbols in the sound itself. It is a tonal analogue of emotive life that can directly symbolize certain feelings.[13] When we hear certain sounds, we grieve, we rejoice, we love, or we have the urge to fight. A complicated series of associations or reminders of sounds and rhythms in our bodies apparently control this symbolism. Added to this natural symbolic language are certain cultural determinants in our experience. Musical sounds are related to certain basic human feelings that are conditioned by factors that often lie in our subconscious memories. Music has the capacity to allure the sense with pleasurable or religious experiences, but it can also engage the mind and heart by likewise representing emotional states. As sound engages the mind, meaning is evoked in association with those particular states of the mind.

The feelings evoked by an encounter with the Holy Other are analogous to human-related feelings of goodness and beauty. The presence of one set of feelings (as described by theological students who have a disciplined life of meditation) can stimulate the appearance of the other set of feelings. For example, some of the fugal passages and "riffs" in jazz have invoked an analogy of logic that is related to mathematics, whereas the listener or performer or both can transcend time and reach conclusions. While this is related to logic, there are some who contend that this, too, is an approach to a holy encounter.

In his *Idea of the Holy*, Rudolf Otto describes his interpretation of the numinous (the holy, religious, spiritual, or ethereal), which is best described in emptiness, darkness, and vastness of space. For instance, the wide expanse and emptiness of the desert, according to Otto, "sets vibrating chords of the numinous along with the note of the sublime," according to the principle of the association of feelings.[14] Void is, like darkness and silence, a negation that does away with every "this" and "here" in order that the "wholly other" may become actual. The experience that grounds religion is the *mysterium tremendum et fascinans* ("the awesome attractive mystery") that defies definition. Otto is help-ful in his observation that whereas the numinous cannot be "uttered" in music, in some sense the awesome mystery can be described: "The weird cadences . . . the pauses and syncopations, and the rise and fall in astonishing semitones, which render so well the sense of awe-struck wonder—all of this serves to express the *mysterium* by way of imitation rather than by forthright utterance."[15]

However, Viladesau raises questions in light of Otto's theory that are often asked of persons involved with the music of the church. For example: Is musi-cal experience merely the emotional analogue of sacred experience so that it works exclusively by association, or can music and art in themselves be an experience of the sacred?[16] His proposal is based on the conviction that there is also an underlying or transcendental dimension of religious experience. He contends, unlike Otto, that the *numinous* is identical with intellectual experi-ence. The sacred is experienced as the dimension of mystery implicit in all human knowing and loving. Music can lead the mind to the sacred, following his analysis, in three different but interconnected ways:

- By being the bearer of accompaniment to sacred words, gestures, or motions;
- By association with emotions characteristic of religious psychological states;
- By the manifestation of beauty as the sign of the transcendental goal of the human spirit.[17]

This has validity in African American communities of faith as long as the definition of beauty is defined by black aesthetics. The African American community, by virtue of its diversity, remains free to provide a music ministry that is in counterpoint with biblical and theological truths that are screened through an African American theological lens. In other words, music alone is a "sound" bearer of transcendental meaning. When combined with words, there are two different levels of communication going on simultaneously in any song. The musical sounds are in and of themselves communicating one thing and the text another. Texts are verbal pronouncements of the faith. The words in the song should express the Word of God in grassroots language. The musical sound is also communicating, and the musical meaning may contra-dict the meaning of the text. In other words, there must be a "marriage" of text and tune, which is not always an easy task. For this reason, anyone interested in truly understanding the role of a church musician must become a student of music in all of its dimensions. Musical sounds—melodic lines, pitches, and rhythms—create musical meanings that many black clergypersons under-stand because of their special concern for the text.

Musical compositions without texts cannot, in essence, justify or authorize specific statements regarding God's love, grace, power, and purpose for humanity, nor can they explain salvation or the mission of the church. They are, however, capable of providing a foundation for critical thought about theological matters. Certain combinations of sounds with no words will carry the mind in numerous directions. This is why music has undergone various periods of control by some churches, and in many instances been totally omitted as an accompaniment for the sung word. S. Paul Schilling observes that "people of faith may find in music support for some beliefs. . . . Faith is not inevitably produced—but it may be enhanced—by musical sensitivity. . . . Though hymn tunes do not in themselves convey definite theological ideas, when they are joined with texts they may strengthen or undermine the meanings expressed."[18]

Music as Congregational Faith Expression

The current focus in African American congregations on the performance of the choir requires that congregations reconsider the earliest role of music in African American worship practices, which included the edification of the congregation. Songs can serve the gathered community in common prayer, praise, and adoration to God. Although the people may read together, responsively or in unison, a different level of mutual involvement takes place when the community sings the faith together.

The use of technology, which allows words to be projected onto screens for congregational use, is most convenient. This process has nearly replaced the use of hymn books in some congregations, although this is not recommended. Nevertheless, the current reality in a local congregation should always be the starting point for persons involved in planning the music of the church. If hymn books are available, this should be the starting point. The best option is to use the denominational hymnal, with a careful plan for cooperation between the pastoral staff and musicians in the choice of hymns, psalms, and spiritual songs. Sufficient time is needed to plan ahead so that unfamiliar songs can be appropriately taught.

Persons responsible for coordinating music with the pastor or preacher would find it helpful to function with an overall plan for the year, a particular season, or a theme set by the pastor or a worship and music committee. Unfortunately, worship planning resources on the market will not provide equal help for all congregations. Thus, a local planning team is extremely important. Keep in mind that God calls the community together in the name of the risen Christ. The congregation is one of the most communal symbols of the body of Christ, and they should be reminded of their mutual ministry with the leaders of music, worship, and pastoral shepherding. The Word proclaimed, heard, shared, and carried forth into the world nourishes mutual service and mutual ministries.

A Word about Words

"Is there a word from the Lord?" This question commonly used in African American worship carries a meaning that is foundational for all that happens in worship. While its focus is on the preached Word, the assumption is that the people have gathered for worship to be fed by the real Word of God, with much of the spiritual overflow emanating from the words in the songs. A "word from the Lord" was from the beginning considered good news in bad times—the voice of the gospel, statements of faith, beliefs, convictions, and bread of life—filled with mystical power and spiritual sustenance that kept individuals and communities grounded in hope.

In his classic study *The Negro's God as Reflected in His Literature,* Benjamin E. Mays recognizes the spiritual as the pinnacle literary source of ideas of God, because it is a corporate theological reflection that grew out of corporate experiences and helped sustain communities of faith. According to Mays, the ideas of God in the spirituals adhere to the traditional compensatory (rewarding), redeeming patterns because they are ideas that enable the creators of these songs to endure hardship, suffer pain, and withstand maladjustment. Mays concurs with other black scholars in his observation that the spirituals appropriated the ideas of God found in the Bible, particularly the magical, spectacular, and miraculous ideas of the Old Testament.[19] The spirituals as "mass" literature also reflect the response of the people to ideas about God as they seek physical and emotional security, especially through turbulent times. Mays recalls such texts as:

> Sometimes de fork-ed light-nin' an' muttering thunder too,
> Of trials an' temptation make it hard for me and you,
> But Jesus is our friend; He'll keep us to the end.
>
> I'm troubled in mind.
> I got a home in-a-dat Rock, don't you see.
> My Soul's been anchored in de Lord.[20]

Based on his interpretation of spirituals, Mays was one of the earliest proponents of the otherworldly idea of God, which finds fertile ground among oppressed people. However, he is quite clear that this is not true of all spirituals. Many are protests of social ills that African Americans suffered, such as "Go Down, Moses," "Oh Freedom," and "No More Auction Block for Me," which are illustrative of spirituals that revolt against earthly conditions without seeking relief in heaven.[21] Such protests grow dimmer as social and economic conditions improve.

In addition to the oral song tradition, which permeates black congregations, the hymnals serve as a sourcebook of practical theology for the community of faith. As indicated in chapter 3, from 1801 to the present, the table of contents and theological indices of hymnals provide only *one* indication of a congregation's articulation of "a word from the Lord" in song. As an oral people, there is still the important tendency to rely upon "the Spirit's leading" in the choice of music used in worship, rather than simply being guided by the theological organization of the hymnal. In some congregations, a hymnal serves little if any purpose as a resource for congregational singing. If there is a printed bulletin, rarely are song titles given either for the congregation or the choir.

In conclusion, persons involved in all aspects of the ministry of the church should take seriously what is communicated in the words of songs. This is an opportunity for the pastor and musicians to share together mutually and realistically in worship planning. This also helps musicians to understand and appreciate the role of the pastor—the one who will "bring a word from the Lord." The preached word is based on Scripture passages, which the preacher chooses. Not only should the chosen texts be shared with leaders of the music ministry, but the trend of thought that will flow from these passages should be shared with musicians, along with suggestions about musical choices, especially those in which the congregation will participate.

The major theological themes that can be enhanced by the choices of music include God, Jesus the Christ, the Holy Spirit, the Trinity, the church and its mission, the Christian life, service, salvation, redemption, stewardship, prayer, peace, worship, and so on. As these are organized as the foundation of spontaneous musical responses, both the pastor and the musician should consider these facts:

- Words of songs carry meanings and are therefore the central means of communicating the beliefs of the congregation.
- Words embody theological beliefs that can be good, bad, or totally extraneous to the gospel message; therefore, words must be carefully chosen.
- Words are fundamental teaching tools, and *all* songs used in worship provide opportunities to teach the faith.
- Words and music together connect thoughts with emotions and can be retained in the memory for reflection more so than words delivered as an oratory.
- Words and music together are powerful tools for evangelizing.

Rendering Service as a Minister

This chapter began with the explanation that *music* and *ministry* signifies the reality that music, in its broadest understanding, can render a service to Almighty God and to people. Rather than use scriptural reminders only, we have centered on what happens in the context of worship in the twenty-first century. Each era included overlapping change. Those called to the task of ministering or rendering a service to God, as well as the entire community of faith, continue to respond to the musical sounds created—not for pure auditory pleasures but for the glory and honor of God.

The terms *minister* and *music* have been used over the years often without careful thought given to what they truly mean. Music ministry is uniquely difficult. Calvin M. Johansson says it very simply and well:

> Music ministry at its best is a cooperative venture among congregation, pastor, and musician. Though each has its own particular role to play, a concerted effort toward a common goal not only makes its actual achievement more likely, but produces an *esprit de corps* absolutely essential to healthy corporate life.[22]

If all are aware that the concerted effort is based on the "word from the Lord," a word that keeps the local community of faith listening and feeling the dynamic of spiritual growth, then there is indeed cooperation between music and ministry.

Chapter 9

African American Music in the Twenty-First Century

Church music practices generally flow from one century to another without abrupt changes or signals to mark the arrival of a new century. This is made clearer as one is able to stand astride two centuries, review the written histories of previous centuries, and attempt to isolate music factors that are totally unique to the new century.

One overriding concept connecting church music practices between centuries is embodied in the word *diversity*. This includes diversity of theological viewpoints of the purpose of music in worship, diversity of forms and styles of music offered, diversity of perceptions over the respective roles of clergy and musicians as worship planners, diversity of localities and differences in congregational needs and experiences, and diversity of understanding of the role of the congregation and "auxiliary" choir(s). In other words, people are free to choose theological perspectives as well as to create modes and practices of their own.

The term *pluralism* found special meaning during the twentieth century following the pronouncements of Vatican II in 1969. Although defined and interpreted in a variety of ways, *pluralism* further endorsed the coexistence and *equality* of racial ethnic traditions within a dominant society. This term received mixed reviews in cultures and congregations that relied strongly upon Western cultures as models for church music. For some African Americans, an affirmation of musical equality was never a question. Therefore, the concept of pluralism was barely noticed, except among Roman Catholics and white Protestant denominations worldwide. For some, an affirmation of the equality of the cultural traditions of Africans, Asians, Hispanics, Native Americans, and other racial ethnic minorities around the globe provided newfound freedom to reclaim traditional aspects of their heritages.

The timing of the Vatican II pronouncements that affirmed a pluralistic society at the height of the civil rights movement found African Americans already reclaiming elements of African and early African American traditional music, worship, dress, and lifestyles. The movement was, of course, evoked by the lack of equality between diverse people. Thus, the desire for change transcended the liturgical environment of the Roman Catholic Church. In like manner, reverberations from the civil rights movement were heard and felt around the world. A reminder of the continuities between worship and life and protest and praise was expressed as worshipers, led by African Americans, "pounded the pavement," protesting human inequality.

The timing and level of entry by African Americans into freedom efforts varied and advanced aggressively most often according to corporate commitment by the people and geographical localities. As a newfound freedom, the movement to Afrocentrism took place more rapidly among African Americans in Euro-American denominations, which were more closely tied to "fixed" liturgies. The freedom to utilize African and African American traditions as the starting center for theological thinking and music making continues to strengthen and empower a people once relegated to the margins of society.

African Americans and Global Music

The church universal is continually affected by the outpouring of fresh and old musical ideas. Perhaps the most amazing transformation taking place is the cross-cultural sharing of congregational songs in worship all over the world. The use of music that has sustained other people in other lands in places far removed from the faith experiences of the original creators is no doubt evidence of the ongoing work of the Creator. Congregations find it difficult to voice the creative outpourings of a people without breathing, walking, and talking symbolically with them. Only by the power of the Spirit can African American worship and music life transcend time and space and affect other people of faith.

Spirituals have been identified as the earliest liturgical offering created by African Americans. They have endured for generations and appear in many denominational hymnals. Translations of these heritage songs are published and sung around the world.[1]

Traditional hymns, meter hymns, and gospel songs are also available in published forms. The publication of these traditional oral expressions will assure continuance for several generations.

African American songs and liturgical expressions continue into the new millennium in numerous published editions of global community worship resources. These publications encourage cross-cultural appreciation and provide suggestions for incorporating formerly neglected liturgical elements into other worship traditions.

Of course, the inclusion of songs in published resources by no means ensures that congregations will ever use them. Nor does it ensure that the people from whose culture the songs emerged will ever be loved equally as members of the family of God. Nevertheless, the history of a people is now in a form that is available for sharing.

The struggle of honest acceptance of the traditions of so-called racial ethnic cultures continues into a new century embedded in the theoretical language of multiculturalism and multilingualism, with brief worship experiences allowing moments of a taste of God's kingdom. The co-opted language of *multicultural-ism* by some who misuse this term has been challenged and remains unacceptable in relation to *cultural diversity*. The latter concept denotes a natural process of the ordering of creation: Humankind is indeed diverse. Some have argued quite effectively that the multicultural image of society assumes an existing reality or, more specifically, a dominant group into which others outside of the group are now welcomed. Newcomers can participate, but not as equals with the dominant group. Although the lines of distinction between these concepts when verbalized may not always be clear, the *feelings* that are evoked among newcomers in deliberately organized multicultural gatherings bespeak a "them" and "us" attitude. Knowledge of the history of one's own culture as unique continually affirms the importance of the diversity of humankind. Whether or not others in the human family accept the gifts that African Americans offer is not really the problem. Maintaining and building upon the God-given creativity is the gift of light that shines so that others may see. God may then be glorified forever.

The exposure to music from the diverse cultures around the globe began centuries ago when human travel was basically nomadic. The church is indebted to the work of ethnomusicologists around the world who approach the study of ethnic music in relation to the cultural context out of which it emerges rather than in comparison to music of other cultures and traditions.[2] Prior studies by scholars who used Western traditions as the starting point from which other traditions were evaluated created the confusion of what was good or bad in aesthetic tastes. Academic programs of study for ethnomusicologists include training in basic musicianship that utilizes non-Western music traditions. Ethnomusicologists understand that research methods based on Western historical musicology are inadequate for studies of non-Western music traditions. Qualitative decisions must use aesthetic criteria from within each particular culture.

Exposure to music that is unfamiliar is often uncomfortable, especially if the learner assumes that only music of his or her culture, or music that is already known by the learner, is sufficient for a well-rounded repertoire. The desire to "write off" new music because it does not entertain or bring pleasure can cause a blockage in receptivity. It is natural for this to occur because most if not all people start with a basic cultural music center from which all other music is measured. Even from a central point of reference, however, one must assume that there is value in music forms and styles that are not part of one's center. To do otherwise is to establish a musical bias that will prevent an effective understanding of the value of other music traditions. Harold M. Best suggests that the pattern of the Golden Rule should be followed so that if persons genuinely love themselves, culturally and ethnically, then loving the ways of others will come naturally. According to Best, "To love our own musical ways brings us the resilience, assurance, and freedom to look lovingly into the musical ways of others and even be nurtured by them."[3]

The words of Best can be a call to encourage African American congregations especially to use the musical gifts of others, especially other people of color, in worship. This admonition is made while recognizing the important role of musicians and pastors in choosing music for worship. This word should be passed on to all persons responsible for planning and carrying worship forward. Exposure to a variety of cultures will help broaden the liturgical repertoire and expand the appreciation of other people of the world.

To encourage the use of songs from other cultures without reminding African Americans of the need to keep them spiritually alive would be a travesty. This is of vital historical importance now that arrangements of spirituals for choirs and congregations are widely circulated and used too often by those other than African American congregations.

Range of Church Music Genres and Styles

A wide range of church music genres and styles created by African Americans is currently being used around the world. A plethora of data has been gathered to ensure that this history will continue into the future. The list of black authors of nineteenth- and twentieth-century hymn texts as well as black composers of music to accompany texts continues to grow, thanks to the scholarly work of researchers. The texts and musical arrangements of gospel musicians continue to move from performance to published manuscript so that copyrights can be attached and these works made available for use by congregations in this country and around the world. Despite this trend, authors and composers of hymn texts and music for hymns have not yet come forth with zeal to make their creative gifts widely known in this arena. This is due, perhaps, to the relative infrequency with which African American congregations use hymns and hymnals in worship. The current preference for praise choruses and songs that can be electronically projected onto screens has diminished the desire for congregational hymn singing. This is an area of study that should be pursued more vigorously whenever church music is studied. This includes denominational and ecumenical workshops, annual church music conferences, and festivals.

With the assistance of clinicians and leaders at national and local church music workshops, new anthems, arrangements of spirituals, and organ compositions are available in published form. All of these are signs of the time and provide hope for the future use of music by African Americans. A continuation of the oral tradition among African Americans has perhaps led to the preference for music forms and styles that can be learned by choirs (partially, at least) from recordings. This practice has historical and ethnical value, but may soon be discouraged because of copyright laws.[4] Musicians should secure copyright protection for their own creative publications using existing and future copyright laws.

With such extensive repertoires, one can recognize the broad horizons of church music available, which includes publications in most categories by African Americans. Each of the various Afrocentric interpretations of liturgy and music assumes that the center from which other aspects of life are interpreted is Africa and/or the African American community. The reclaiming of the African heritage in this manner is a positive sign of continuity from the past and the ongoing shaping of self-respect of African people in the future.

One of the missing aspects of Afrocentric identity is familiarity with the current repertoire of songs from the African continent, especially songs that can be used in worship. The use of African songs is, of course, not required for persons to prove their blackness. However, an awareness of and interest in these songs will help to broaden and increase understanding of the spiritual and musical roots embedded in the African culture.

Songs from Africa, like other aspects of African culture, gained in popularity with the onset of pluralism and the subsequent affirmation by European and Euro-American denominations in the 1980s. African songs were published in hymnals along with other global songs as denominations attempted to affirm the wholeness of the body of Christ as reflected in their membership. One such example is "Prayer for Africa" (*Nkosi Sikelel'I Afrika*), composed in 1897 by Enoch Sontonga, a Zulu musician. The song's words and text appeared in a collection of world songs in 1958. This song was published in several Euro-American denominational hymnal supplements compiled and edited by African Americans in the 1980s.

African Americans involved in the ordering of worship services in local congregations should be aware of African songs that are published in their own denominational hymnals. This may require a careful scrutiny of a hymnal, especially if it was published since the 1980s. If a companion to the hymnal is not available, planners of worship should examine hymnals of other denominations, ecumenical hymnals, and collections of African songs that are available for worship. With the infrequency of the use of African liturgical resources, it is important for pastors, musicians, and other planners of worship to develop an interest in affirming African music and other liturgical acts in worship. This might require special sessions with consultants learning how to introduce the materials. Some musicians and pastors are adept at introducing new materials during times of gathering for worship. Whatever the situation, care should be taken when introducing new forms of worship so that the congregation will learn to expand its liturgical tastes effectively.

The inclusion of African songs in African American denominational hymnals is a recent phenomenon. The African Methodist Episcopal Church has taken the largest step in this direction in its comprehensive collection and publication of songs from South Africa in its 1984 *Bicentennial Hymnal.* This was facilitated by Edith Ming, the wife of one of the bishops assigned to South Africa. Another step forward is the inclusion of a number of African songs in the 2001 publication of the ecumenical *African American Heritage Hymnal.*[5] A representative number of songs from various African countries is also included in African American supplementary hymnals published by the Lutherans and Episcopalians. Nevertheless, the incorporation of African songs into African American worship on a regular basis is only slowly beginning to occur. The songs that emerged in the twentieth century and those continuing to emerge reflect diverse perspectives of life and spirituality but are never far removed from the original foundation of spirituality that gave birth to African American songs.

Experiencing Music in African American Worship

No two worship settings or experiences of the divine will be exactly the same. Diversity persists even where people affirm that they are of one blood and are in accord with each other. Diversity in worship and music exists as an indication of the ongoing creation process of the Creator. Diverse ways of expressing musical thoughts will always exist. However, there is much to be done in this century to stretch individuals and congregations into an awareness that God's gift of diversity to humankind is yet another opportunity for God's people to grow. Although many African Americans avoid the use of the term *liturgy,* we should consider the fact that because God initiates the "work of the people," it is therefore not confined to printed documents.

On the whole, African American congregations agree that Christian worship is a corporate response to the presence and power of God as revealed in Jesus the Christ under the enabling power of the Holy Spirit. Published denominational polity sources and/or the pastor of a local congregation determine the structures, forms, and styles that these corporate gatherings take. In general, the empowerment granted early worshipers to be free in spirit and in truth continues in various forms into the twenty-first century. Congregations connected to traditionally liturgical churches maintain close ties to the ritual structure and liturgical forms with which they are familiar.

Readers are reminded to follow the basic pattern and flow for worship suggested by their denomination. Most, and I dare say all, denominations have a desired ritual ordering or shape that expresses some aspect of "what's going on" or what the leader expects is "going on." Ritual structure need not feel "empty" or too full, for worshipers who understand the importance of relational movement may be led to an encounter with the risen Christ, under the guidance of the Holy Spirit. Ritual is very important in gatherings of African people. What often appears to be random movement often leads to familiar structure, even in Holiness and Pentecostal worship. The time between movements varies: Sometimes it is quite short, and at other times extremely long.

In freely structured churches, the freedom occurs because limits or boundaries are not "fixed" according to Western watches. In earlier African American traditions, it was considered impossible and a sacrilege to "fix time" around a person's opportunity to "come through," or receive the divine power of conversion. Prolonging time is not exactly a "black phenomenon." It is a primal phenomenon that has worked its way into the twenty-first century. It might be helpful to conduct research to determine how many persons actually missed flights or ocean cruises because they were in church waiting for the Holy Spirit to come and set them free!

Some African Americans balk at establishing specific blocks of time for worship because they connect this practice with Eurocentric thinking. One way of looking at this is to return biblically to the understanding that God reveals God's self in time: In the beginning God created . . . and God caused things to happen in time . . . on the first day . . . the second day . . . for six days God labored, and then God rested. In time, day becomes night, and seasons come and go.

African Americans adopted a faith and a worship life that is posited in recurring rhythms. Life happens in God's time through persistent rhythms. Therefore, meaning is established through structure and patterns. And so, Christian worship is the pattern of the *ordo,* the ritual ordering that prevents acts from being haphazardly thrown together. The adoption of the faith by African Americans and the comparable recurring rhythms, circumstances, and conditions of their lives necessitated the establishment of certain patterns unique to their own situations. Patterns of worship were established out of their own marginal experiences. Times and places were necessarily irregular, so that praising and thanking God were often juxtaposed with everyday work life. Thus, the songs of the people at work helped to create the space and time for worship. As indicated earlier, songs bonded and unified them so that they could be receptive to the movement and power of the Holy Spirit. Under the power of the Spirit, the people were sent out, empowered to do the will of God.

In the following list of suggested planning ideas, utilize with care and creativity each of the genres and styles of African American music, as well as hymns, anthems, and instrumental music. Take the introduction of this music to your congregation seriously. You may be introducing music and the sequencing of Scriptures that might be totally new to the congregation as well as to the pastors. Involve others in the planning process, and trust them to be of help.

- Make use of resources provided by your denomination in the planning and ordering of services of worship. Allow the resources to serve as your guide rather than as demands.
- Utilize materials from other sources, especially those that are based on the church year. With frequent and consistent use of the church year, the congregation will be able to experience movement in time around the life of Christ.
- Use sources that highlight time, special days, and seasons in the African American community. Use these sources frequently and consistently so that the community of faith will develop respect for order guided by the biblical *ordo.*
- Become committed to constantly expanding your own knowledge of key factors in African American music history and practice. Keep helpful resources in the church library or in your office.
- Seek to understand "what's going on" before adopting any new trend just because it makes one "feel good."

The Praise and Worship Movement

"Praise and worship" is an approach to corporate worship that has become quite popular in North American churches in general and in black congregations in particular. This approach is rooted in the Protestant branch of the charismatic movement but also includes the Roman Catholic Church. The major thrust of worship leadership is the use of contemporary religious songs from the "pop" idiom. The songs used are closely aligned with Eurocentric "seeker friendly" contemporary worship music.

"Praise and worship" has gained momentum and maintained its popularity because of the ability of leaders to engage a corporate body of worshipers for a lengthy period of time. After studying the approach in a number of sources, a composite description incorporating a variety of themes provides clarity. The order of worship[6] is sequenced so that music provides a means through which worshipers are transported through a succession of spiritual or emotional states until they experience a strong sense of the presence of God. This form of worship is based on a Hebrew progression into the tabernacle. A praise team that is often accompanied by a praise band leads a time of singing of contemporary music at the beginning of the service. The leaders remain closely in touch with the congregation so that they can sense the congregation's progressive states, offer prayers, and change the songs and content of the music, accordingly.

The service begins with songs of thanksgiving. These songs are rendered in an upbeat tempo, usually in major keys, to proclaim the goodness of God's character and activity. The next phase is an extended time of sung praise to represent the outer courts of the worship area. The next threshold incorporates songs of repentance or supplication to prepare worshipers to enter the "inner sanctum" of God's presence. At this entrance, worshipers sing songs of intimate worship with the Almighty. Songs are rendered much softer as congregants commune with God. In some settings, the intimate fellowship with God concludes with some members of the congregation "singing in tongues," under the power of the Holy Spirit. It is appropriate in settings where preaching before the Lord's Supper is not required that the elements of Communion are administered at this time.

Preaching and other acts of worship follow this time of praise and worship. Spontaneous prayers are offered by the leader throughout this time, which can be quite extended. An outline of this fourfold approach follows:

The initial threshold
   Songs of thanksgiving
Outer courts of the worship area
   Songs of praise
Entrance into the inner sanctum
   Songs of repentance or supplication

The inner sanctum of God's presence
> Singing, which culminates in tongues under the power of the Holy
> Spirit.
> Some churches incorporate the Lord's Supper (Eucharist) at this point
> as well.
> Prayer is used intermittently.
> The singing is often extensive, from thirty minutes to an hour or more.
> Preaching and other acts follow this time of praise and worship.

Advocates of "praise and worship" define *praise* as an act of extolling God by remembering or proclaiming God's character and activity. *Worship* is defined in more relational terms of direct communion with God. It is not clear whether the meaning of the topology is shared with congregations so that they are able to follow this sequence. There is general confusion about how this title is used when the entire service is called "worship."

Although I am not an advocate for this approach to worship, I find the explanations quite interesting and wonder if leaders of worship understand this process and if they ever share the progressive sequence with the congregation for their own edification.

African American Devotional Services

In the oral tradition of African Americans, such a carefully thought-through liturgical structure proposed by the shapers of the "praise and worship" approach would have been unheard of. An excellent example is found in the devotional ritual that precedes the worship of African American Baptists in rural settings. This ritual began in the "Invisible Institution" and has continued for more than two hundred years in its oral form. Walter F. Pitts, Jr., who carefully researched and published an excellent resource on African American worship as ritual action,[7] suggests that the devotion can be considered the first "frame" of the worship service. This frame consists of lined hymns and prayers and is designed to bond the community of faith and help prepare it to be open to receive the Word of God, to encounter the living Christ. Such leadership can only be carried out by deacons. Their duty is to set the spiritual momentum for worship as they help shape and mold the community of faith for worship. The structure, which remains very much intact and has been transmitted orally, is a preliminary act. This time of preparation was also traditionally a sacred time of waiting, as the members who lived a great distance walked to church.

This is a similar form to that used by the praise and worship movement. It is quite clear in the handling of the tradition of the devotions that this is a ritual act, but it is clearly *not* worship. Worship begins when the preacher comes forward and begins the call to worship. Amid the many acts of worship are lots and lots of songs, sung by the congregation.

Rather than a call to return to devotions, this is a call to review the musical moments throughout African American history and find ways to continue the creative music process with a focus on what this new thing has to do with keeping the ship afloat as it travels over smooth and troubled waters.

Conclusion

From 1536, when Africans set foot on this continent, to the twenty-first century, some have sought to create music to the glory of God. As evidenced through the history that has unfolded in these pages, the most important music making is communal. African people, at home on the continent and in the Diaspora, feel the constant presence of the Creator seeking and yearning for humans to respond personally and corporately, in spirit and in truth. It could be that there is a divine connection between the spirit of the Holy One and humanity—in its diversity—that urges the "seeking spirit" with constancy. This is not to suggest that the people of African blood are the only seekers of the spirit of God, nor the carriers of the divine breath from the beginning who yearned desperately for the truth. But it could be that they have been used by the divine Instigator, Creator, Spirit to tap into the truth and express it in one voice to bring humanity back to its spiritual senses.

This is not to imply that the sound of the Spirit was founded upon American soil, for there is sufficient evidence that the taproot of all existence is in the nurturing soil of Africa. This volume is simply a reclaiming of an inheritance that would allow examples of ways that humanity is in constant search of the one voice that will allow the world to sing of God's love. It is a reminder that the world should be constant in its search for truth. Maybe the sounds created by a people who are oppressed by other "sound makers" draw attention to the God of love, justice, and freedom.

Many changes have occurred in the songs, sounds, texts, rhythms, and forms of music. Throughout this process, there has been a constant overlapping of genres, styles, forms, and manner of performances. The old is used to create something new, and yet nothing is ever completely tossed out, whether in worshiping communities, on streets, or in concert halls. Debates about "sacred and secular" emerge and receive endorsement, followed by criticism and complaints. Yet the beat, sound, and styles of performance continue. Generations of artists emerge in worshiping communities, move out into other arenas, and return to the sanctuary, admitting the necessity and the importance of being connected to worshiping communities.

Over the years there have been attempts to utilize the "offerings" of musical gifts as a means of manipulating worship so that music, rather than worship, becomes an end in itself. African American music has suffered from efforts to negate its history and usefulness. But it has survived and remains a vehicle through which God shapes and reshapes the people. There have been internal and outside attempts to set the various genres, forms, and styles in competition with each other: black gospels in opposition to spirituals; hymns preserved in printed forms in books and on paper in opposition to folk-style singing where tonal memory prevails; and so-called black classical music in opposition to "down home, improvisatory" folk music.

History will one day record evidence that tension existed between proponents of traditional gospel, modern gospel, and so-called contemporary gospel, and that each survived turbulent storms. Without the music of hip-hop and pop culture of the late twentieth and early twenty-first centuries, which struggle to gain a place in the worshiping congregation, there would be little concern about such challenges.

The clamor of voices over the centuries attests to the concern of humanity to seek truth in ways of worshiping. Along the way, we have adapted the terms *spirit* and *truth* to suit our own localized interpretations, so that we can place parameters around their initial meanings and sit in judgment of others. At one time parameters were placed ecclesiastically, so that differences in denominations could be identified according to the musical tastes of some persons within denominations. But this is no longer universally true. The experience of "thinking outside of the box" has created communities of nondenominations for whom different freedoms prevail. It has also freed communities of faith, whether as denominations or ecumenical groups, to acknowledge the global context in which each generation will live.

We are at the cutting edge of taking seriously the fact that music for worship in spirit and in truth must also help prepare an aging population that is living longer and experiencing the variety of problems that occur with age. We must seek and acknowledge the truth about adequate worship preparations for moments when *spirit* no longer means activity and *truth* cannot be measured by an alert mind. The freedom of God—the Spirit that we constantly seek—allows the kind of recall as one approaches the silent halls of death that allows one to sing the faith freely. The amazement of all of this is that God's

Spirit and *truth* prevail even as one experiences the loss of mental acuity and physical prowess. If worship has demonstrated both spirit and truth, we as the body of Christ have experienced life at its fullest.

Therefore, planning for such life-fulfilling worship must be done by worship leaders, preachers, musicians, teachers, the young, and the aging, who all understand that the true meaning of *spirit* and *truth* remains as always as God in action among seekers.

Appendix A: Chronological List of African American Hymnals

Year	Denomination/Other Source	Title	Compilers/Editors	Comments
1801	African Methodist Episcopal Church	*A Collection of Spiritual Songs and Hymns Selected From Various Authors, by Richard Allen, African Minister*	Richard Allen	54 texts only (no music like other hymnals of this period; the authors of text were not included).
1801	African Methodist Episcopal Church	*A Collection of Hymns and Spiritual Songs from Various Authors, by Richard Allen, Minister of the African Methodist Episcopal Church*	Richard Allen	Second edition, 64 texts (10 added to 54 in the first edition).
1818	African Methodist Episcopal Church	*The African Methodist Pocket Hymn Book*	Richard Allen Daniel Coker James Champion	314 texts; first official AME Church hymnal
1820	Thomas Cooper	*The African Pilgrim's Hymnal*	Thomas Cooper	372 texts
1822	Ezion Union African Methodist Church	*The African Union Hymn Book*	Peter Spencer	132 texts
1837	African Methodist Episcopal Church	*The African Methodist Episcopal Church Hymnal*	George Hogarth	Similar subject headings as other Methodist hymnals.
1839	African Methodist Episcopal Zion Church	*Hymns for the Use of the African Methodist Episcopal Zion Church*	Samuel Giles Christopher Rush Joseph Thompson	Abridged edition of the 1831 Methodist Church hymn book.
1858	African Methodist Episcopal Zion Church	*Hymns for the Use of the African Methodist Episcopal Zion Church*	(Same committee)	Adopted by the church at the 1860 conference; 596 hymns.

(continued)

Appendix A: Chronological List of African American Hymnals (*continued*)

Year	Denomination/Other Source	Title	Compilers/Editors	Comments
1869	African Methodist Episcopal Zion Church	*Hymns for the Use of the African Methodist Episcopal Zion Church*	(Same committee)	Short-lived reprint of 1858 hymnal.
1872	African Methodist Episcopal Zion Church	*A Collection of Hymns for Use of the AME Zion Church*		Exact replica of the 1849 Methodist hymnal, stamped with the AMEZ insignia.
1876	African Methodist Episcopal Church	*The Hymn Book of the African Methodist Episcopal Church*	Henry McNeal Turner	Compilation of 1,115 texts from hymn books available, largely from the Wesleyan tradition. Substantial evidence of Emancipation with the inclusion of the category "Anniversary of Freedom." Songs include "Freedom's Morn," "Freedom's Jubilee," and others by African Americans.
1882 1883	Methodist Episcopal Church (African American members) (Revised and Enlarged edition)	*A Collection of Revival Hymns and Plantation Melodies*	Marshall W. Taylor	First new hymnal published for African American congregations after Emancipation, with 150 songs plus 7 with text only. Includes a large number of spirituals.
1891	Colored Methodist Episcopal Church ("Colored" later changed to "Christian")	*Hymnbook of the Colored Methodist Church*	Lucius Holsey	Adaptation of the 1889 Methodist Episcopal Church, South, hymn book.

1892	African Methodist Episcopal Church	*Hymnal Adapted to the Doctrines and Usages of the African Methodist Church*	James C. Embry	Deliberately designed so that a hymnal with music could follow; fewer texts than the 1876 hymnal, with texts arranged metrically in order to accommodate the printing of texts and tune in close proximity for subsequent hymnal.
1892	African Methodist Episcopal Zion Church	*New Hymn and Tune Book: An Offering of Praise for the Use of the African Methodist Episcopal Zion Church*	Phillip Phillips	Included 1,216 "words only" gospel songs and hymns. Includes hymns by Zion composer William Howard Day, the first African American graduate of Oberlin College (in 1847).
1893	William Henry Sherwood (Baptist)	*Harp of Zion*	William Henry Sherwood	A collection of gospel hymns, many of his own composing. Sherwood was first to publish songs that were cast in the "pre-black gospel mode." Also in 1893, the National Baptist Convention Publishing Board was granted permission by Sherwood to publish *Harp of Zion*, with some revisions, under the title *Baptist Young People's Union National Harp of Zion*.
1897	National Baptist Convention, USA	Hymn and Tune Books Series: 1. *Gospel Voices and Choice Songs* 2. *The National Gospel Voices* 3. *National Tidings of Joy* (with rudiments of music) 4. *Celestial Showers* Book 1 5. *Harp of Zion* (BYPU hymnal) 6. *Choice Songs*		Prior to first official hymnal, a series of hymn and tune books was compiled, by committees selected and appointed by the National Baptist Convention Publishing Board before their adoption by Sunday School and Young People's Society

(continued)

Appendix A: Chronological List of African American Hymnals (*continued*)

Year	Denomination/Other Source	Title	Compilers/Editors	Comments
1898	National Baptist Convention, USA	*Pearls of Paradise* *Celestial Showers*, Book 2		Continuation of songbook series
1898	African Methodist Episcopal Church	*The African Methodist Episcopal Hymn and Tune Book*	James C. Emory	The first AME hymnal with music.
1899	Church of Christ (Holiness), USA	*Jesus Only*	Charles Price Jones	First of numerous songbooks in which Jones published over 1,000 hymns, songs, and anthems.
1901	Church of Christ (Holiness), USA	*Jesus Only* (nos. 1 and 2)	Charles Price Jones	Contains essays on the fundamentals of music as well as historical and theological information about church music and musicianship.
1903	National Baptist Convention, USA	*The National Baptist Hymnal*	R. H. Boyd William Rosborough	Adapted from the 1883 American Baptist publication including index of authors. Contains 632 hymns and chants. Text only pocket edition followed.
1904	Colored (Christian) Methodist Episcopal Church	*Songs of Love and Mercy*	F. M. Hamilton Lucius Holsey	198 hymns, many composed by members of the CME Church, including Holsey's "O Rapturous Scenes," set to music by Hamilton. Reprinted in 1968 for the 1970 CME centennial.

1905	National Baptist Convention, USA	*The National Baptist Hymn Book*	R. H. Boyd	Similar to the 1903 edition; 632 songs, no chants; hymn numbers were retained wherever hymns were placed, so that numbers were out of sequence.
1906	Church of Christ (Holiness), USA	*His Fullness*	Charles P. Jones	Hymns examined are similar to other gospel hymns of this period.
1906	National Baptist Convention, USA	*National Anthem Series*	National Publishing Board	A collection of anthems by Rosborough, J. H. Carter, and W. J. Tobias, for use with growing numbers of church choirs, and to increase choral music by black composers.
1909	Charles A. Tindley	*Soul Echoes: A Collection of Songs for Religious Meetings*	Charles A. Tindley	Compositions by Tindley for use in his congregation. His gospel style influenced the black gospel composition style.
1909	Black American ecumenical (Charles A. Tindley)	*Soul Echoes: A Collection of Songs for Religious Meetings*, rev. ed.	J. S. Caldwell (AMEZ) Charles Tindley (ME) G. L. Blackwell (AMEZ) L. J. Coppin (AME)	Includes 51 hymn texts, most of which are set to music. A facsimile reprint by AMEZ Bishop Walls in 1964 includes 5 additional songs, one of which is a hymn, entitled "Freedom," by Bishop Walls.
1909	African Methodist Episcopal Zion Church	*New Hymn and Tune Book for the Use of the African ME Zion Church*		Duplication of the 1882 ME hymnal, the first hymnal printed at the AMEZ Publishing House in Charlotte.
1916	National Baptist Convention, USA (R. H. Boyd)	*The National Jubilee Melodies*	K. D. Reddick Phil Lindsley	Historical collection of spirituals (slave songs) with footnotes indicating how the spirituals were corporately composed, maintained, and transmitted orally. Dedicated to the memory of black ancestors.

(continued)

Appendix A: Chronological List of African American Hymnals (*continued*)

Year	Denomination/Other Source	Title	Compilers/Editors	Comments
1916	Charles A. Tindley (Methodist Episcopal Church)	*New Songs of Paradise*	Charles A. Tindley	This collection is the second of six editions of *Soul Echoes*.
1921	National Baptist Convention USA (Willa A. Townsend)	*Gospel Pearls*	Willa A. M. Townsend John Work Frederick Work Lucie E. Campbell	Popular book of 164 songs grouped in three categories: worship, revival, and spirituals. An anthology of sacred songs for African American worship into the early 20th century.
1924	National Baptist Convention USA (A. M. Townsend)	*The Baptist Standard Hymnal*	Willa A. M. Townsend J. D. Bushnell Emma Haynes J. H. Skipwith	The first official standard hymnal produced by the incorporated "Townsend Convention." Modeled after the Euro-American Baptist Hymnal, 1883, with a limited black repertoire. Sixteen women served on the hymnal committee.
1927	National Baptist Convention USA (A. M. Townsend)	*Spirituals Triumphant, Old and New*	Edward Boatner A. M. Townsend	Comparable to the 1916 Baptist *National Jubilee* and the Johnson and Johnson collections, *The Book of American Negro Spirituals* (1925) and *The Second Book of Negro Spirituals* (1927); largely Boatner arrangements.
1927	R. Nathaniel Dett	*Religious Folks-Songs of the Negro as Sung at Hampton Institute*	R. Nathaniel Dett	The fifth edition of Hampton's songs (1874, 1891, 1909, 1926), with a note that these are traditional settings since 1868. Dett uses the title "hymns" to categorize these songs theologically.

Year	Denomination	Title	Compiler/Author	Description
1928	Church of Christ (Holiness), USA	*His Fullness*	Charles P. Jones	Enlarged edition with 144 hymns, 88 composed by Jones, plus spiritual arrangements, and other compositions by black composers, gospel hymnists, and Watts, Wesley, etc.
1934	African American ecumenical	*The Colored Sacred Harp*	J. Jackson	Compiled and published under the auspices of Dade County (Florida) Colored Musical Institute and the Alabama and Florida Union State; old familiar texts set to new melodies.
1940	Church of Christ (Holiness), USA	*Jesus Only Songs and Hymns Standard Hymnal*	Charles P. Jones	First official hymnal of the denomination; nine editions published between 1940 and 1966.
1941	African Methodist Episcopal Church	*The Richard Allen AME Hymnal*	John A. Gregg W. A. Fountain, Sr. D. Ward Nichols Edward C. Deas F. A. Clark Frederick Hall	This hymnal was published as a result of the slow-moving process in a joint hymnal to be developed by the AME and AMEZ denominations.
1942	Member of the Church of God in Christ (Pentecostal)	*The Jackson Bible Universal Selected Gospel Songs*	H. C. Jackson	Collection of 35 songs, possible forecast of *Yes, Lord!* Church of God in Christ, 1982 official hymnal.
1944	House of God, which is the Church of the Living God, The Pillar and Ground of the Truth, Without Controversy, Inc.	*Spiritual Songs and Hymns*	Mary L. Tate Mary F. L. Keith	A documentation of 254 hymns and songs utilized by the denomination through the life and ministry of Bishop Mary Tate, edited by Bishop Mary Keith. Includes standard gospel hymns by blacks and Euro Americans.

(continued)

Appendix A: Chronological List of African American Hymnals (*continued*)

Year	Denomination/Other Source	Title	Compilers/Editors	Comments
1954	African Methodist Episcopal Church	*AMEC Hymnal*	Henry Belin	Revision of 1941 Allen hymnal; 184 hymns added (totaling 645) with 4 spirituals for the first time in an AME official hymnal; 7 hymns arranged by Edward C. Deas, and 4 Tindley hymns.
1957	African Methodist Episcopal Zion Church	*The New African Methodist Episcopal Zion Hymnal*	Stephen Spottswood William J. Walls	Large number of Wesley hymns; clear effort to ensure that the hymnal was doctrinally and theologically sound; 9 spirituals included (first time!); all 29 hymns by Zion ministers, each paired with familiar tunes.
1966	Fire Baptized Holiness Church	*Hymnal of the F.B.H. Church*		A total of 79 texts incorporated as the second part of the denomination's *Book of Discipline.* Meter indications are provided for these traditional hymn texts. No indication of the spirit-filled singing traditionally heard in worship.
1976	Progressive National Baptist Convention	*The Progressive Baptist Hymnal*	D. E. King	Special edition of the outdated 1940 Broadman hymnal; only 41 of the old hymns were replaced with songs by African American arrangers and composers.
1977	National Baptist Publishing Board (Boyd Convention)	*The New National Baptist Hymnal*	Ruth Lomax Davis W. Elmo Mercer Virgie DeWitty A. Charles Bowie	A popular hymnal used by a large number of African American congregations. Highly evangelical in nature. Among the 545 songs are spirituals, and patriotic and gospel songs for a variety of age groups.

Year	Denomination	Title	Compilers/Editors	Description
1977	Church of Christ (Holiness), USA	*His Fullness Songs*, rev. ed.	Herbert L. Wilson Andrea May Gladys Moore Rayford W. Lee	Compilation of 512 songs from previous hymnals by Charles P. Jones.
1981	United Methodist Church (Afircan American members)	*Songs of Zion*	J. Jefferson Cleveland Verolga Nix	Supplemental resource of African American songs; three sections: hymns/songs from traditional black worship, spirituals, and black gospel songs.
1981	Episcopal Church (African American members)	*Lift Every Voice and Sing*	Irene Jackson Brown	One of several twentieth-century examples of African Americans in Euro-American denominations reclaiming their heritage. The 151 songs represent a well-balanced sacred repertoire. Although limited in number of musical inclusions, the arrangements of spirituals and musical settings of traditional liturgical texts are quite good. Few of these songs appear in other denominational sources.
1982	Church of God in Christ	*Yes, Lord!*	Iris Stevenson J. O. Patterson Norman N. Quick	First official hymnal of the COGIC. The title of the praise chant by the founder, Charles H. Mason, as the title of the hymnal helps establish the ethos of the denomination. The 525 musical entries document other aspects of COGIC liturgy. Many composers are represented and musical phrases (in a variety of keys) are highly reflective of the improvisatory musical gifts of black Pentecostals. Includes a number of anthems from European traditions as well.

(continued)

215

Appendix A: Chronological List of African American Hymnals (*continued*)

Year	Denomination/Other Source	Title	Compilers/Editors	Comments
1984	African Methodist Episcopal Church	*AMEC Bicentennial Hymnal*	Henry A. Belin, Jr.	Vast improvements are noted in this volume of 670 music entries, two liturgical settings of the Eucharist, plus liturgical settings for baptism and other rituals of the denomination. Clearly evident is the expanded number of black composers, the inclusion of African music, and a celebration of the rich AME heritage of music for worship.
1987	Christian Methodist Episcopal Church	*The Hymnal of the Christian Methodist Episcopal Church*	Lawrence L. Reddick Othal Lakey	The committee chose to place a new cover on *The New National Baptist Hymnal* and to include one Holsey song, a CME order of service, and changes in liturgical readings.
1987	Roman Catholic Church	*Lead Me, Guide Me: The African American Catholic Hymnal*	James P. Lyke Arthur Anderson J-Glenn Murray	This hymnal was born out of the need to incorporate African American liturgical history into the total life of Roman Catholic congregations.
1993	Episcopal Church	*Lift Every Voice and Sing II*	Horace C. Boyer Deborah H. Hines Richard C. Martin Robert L. Simpson Arthur B. Williams	Music from the following genres is included in this volume of 234 musical entries: African American spirituals, traditional and contemporary gospel music, Protestant hymns, evangelical and missionary hymns, and service music using traditional and gospel settings.

Year	Denomination	Title	Editors	Description
1996	African Methodist Episcopal Zion Church	*The African Methodist Episcopal Zion Bicentennial Hymnal*	George W. Walker, Charlotte Alston, Permilla R. Dunston	This hymnal consists of 734 musical entries, with many of the hymnists members of the AMEZ Church. This edition celebrates the founding of the denomination; thus, the AMEZ ethos permeates this volume.
1999	Evangelical Lutheran Church in America and African American congregations of the Lutheran Church—Missouri Synod	*This Far by Faith: An African American Resource for Worship*	Karen Ward, Bryant Clancy	This liturgical resource is an excellent historical journey into biblical, African, African American, and Caribbean rituals. The 301 musical entries affirm the global nature of the body of Christ.
2001	African American ecumenical	*African American Heritage Hymnal*	Delores Carpenter, Nolan E. Williams, Jr.	This volume of essays, responsive readings celebrating black history, and 581 music entries is to date the most ecumenical liturgical resource available to African American congregations and others seeking to learn more of the black heritage.
2001	National Baptist Publishing Board	*The New National Baptist Hymnal: 21st Century Edition*	T. B. Boyd III	Continuing the singing tradition of African Americans in general and Baptists in particular, this volume of 561 musical entries holds faithfully to the familiar repertoire while entering cautiously into the twenty-first century. There are thirty-five new music entries from the current repertoire of contemporary songs, as well as a glossary of musical terms.

Appendix B: Historical Evolution of African American Congregations and Denominations

(Asterisks indicate founding dates of denominations.)

Date	Congregation/Denomination	Location
1758	African Baptist Church (Bluestone)	Luneburg (Mecklenburg), Va.
1773/75?	African Baptist Church	Silver Bluff, S.C.
1784	Oldest black Catholic parish	St. Augustine, Florida Territory
1794	African American Episcopal congregation	Philadelphia, Pa.
1794	African Zoar Methodist congregation First African American congregation in the Methodist Episcopal Church.	Philadelphia, Pa.
1794	Bethel AME Church. This congregation later joined with other churches to become the AME denomination in 1816.	Philadelphia, Pa.
1796	AME Zion Chapel	New York, N.Y.
1805	Ezion Methodist Episcopal Church	Wilmington, Del.
*1805	Union American Methodist Episcopal Church, Inc. Traces its origin to the Ezion Methodist Episcopal Church, which severed its ties with the Methodist Episcopal Church in 1813.	Wilmington, Del.
1807	First African American congregation of the Presbyterian Church	Philadelphia, Pa.
1813	Union Church of African Members	Wilmington, Del.
*1816	African Methodist Episcopal Church	Philadelphia, Pa.
*1820	African Methodist Episcopal Zion Church	New York, N.Y.
1829	First African American congregation among Congregationalists	New Haven, Conn.
1834	First African American congregation in the Christian Church (Disciples of Christ)	Midway, Ky.

*1863	Seventh-Day Adventist African American Seventh-Day Adventists claim membership from the founding date.	Battle Creek, Mich.
*1865	Colored Primitive Baptists of America	Columbia, Tenn.
*1867	United American Free Will Baptist Denomination, Inc.	Green County, N.C.
1869	Colored Cumberland Presbyterian Church	Huntsville, Ala.
*1870	Christian Methodist Episcopal Church (formerly Colored Methodist Episcopal Church)	Jackson, Tenn.
1871	Church of Christ (Disciples of Christ) An African American body that is autonomous from the majority Euro-American Christian Church (Disciples of Christ).	Lenoir County, N.C.
*1874	Second Cumberland Presbyterian Church (current name: Cumberland Presbyterian Church in America)	Huntsville, Ala.
1876	First African American congrega- tion of the Dutch Reformed Church	Orangeburg, S.C.
*1885	National Baptist Convention of America, Inc.	Shreveport, La.
*1889	Church of the Living God (Christian Workers for Fellowship) This denomination believes that Jesus was black, based on the lineage of Abraham and David.	Oklahoma City, Okla.
*1894	Church of God in Christ, Inc. (Pentecostal) Was founded in 1894 and incorporated in 1907.	Memphis, Tenn.
*1894/98	Church of Christ (Holiness), USA	Jackson, Miss.
*1895	National Baptist Convention, USA, Inc.	Nashville, Tenn.
*1897	Church of God in Christ (Holiness)	Lexington, Miss.
*1897/1901	Church of God (Apostolic), Inc.	Danville, Ky.
*1901	Church of God (Sanctified)	Columbia, Tenn.
*1903	House of God, which is the Church of the Living God, The Pillar and Ground of the Truth, Without Controversy, Inc.	Dickson, Tenn.

*1905	Free Christian Zion of Christ Church	Redemption, Ark.
1907	Church of God in Christ (Pentecostal) First incorporated body of Pentecostals.	Memphis, Tenn.
*1908	Fire Baptized Holiness Church of the Americas	Anderson, S.C.
*1961	Progressive National Baptist Convention, Inc.	Akron, Ohio
1969	Reformed Church in America Related to the Dutch Reformed Church.	New York, N.Y.
*1988	National Missionary Baptist Convention of America	Los Angeles, Calif.
*1989	African American Catholic Congregation This denomination declared independence from the Roman Catholic Church in 1990.	Washington, D.C.

Notes

PREFACE

1. Antonin Dvorak, "Dvorak on Negro Melodies," *Musical Record* (Boston) 378 (July 1893): 13. Reprinted from the *New York Herald,* May 25, 1893.

2. Wardell J. Payne, ed., *Directory of African American Religious Bodies,* 2d ed. (Washington, D.C.: Howard University Press, 1995), 197. Specific connections cited are the American Baptist Churches in the USA and the Southern Baptist Convention, the latter group with more than 1,500 churches as of 1993.

3. See Elmer Towns, *Putting an End to Worship Wars* (Nashville: Broadman & Holman Publishers, 1997).

4. One example is William D. Romanowski, *Pop Culture Wars: Religion and the Role of Entertainment in American Life* (Downers Grove, Ill.: InterVarsity Press, 1996).

5. See Marva Dawn, *Reaching Out without Dumbing Down* (Grand Rapids: Wm. B. Eerdmans Publishing Co., 1998), for her treatment of a theology of worship for contemporary culture.

6. See Robert Webber, *Planning Blended Worship: The Creative Mixture of Old and New* (Nashville: Abingdon Press, 1998).

7. R. Nathaniel Dett, ed., *Religious Folk Songs of the Negro as Sung at Hampton Institute* (Hampton, Va.: Hampton Institute Press, 1927), 7.

CHAPTER 1: AFRICAN FOUNDATIONS
OF AFRICAN AMERICAN LITURGICAL MUSIC

1. John S. Mbiti, *African Religions and Philosophy* (New York: Doubleday, 1969), 1.

2. Howard Thurman, *The Luminous Darkness* (New York: Harper & Row, 1965), 59–60.

3. I initiated the approach to seeking theological foundations in African primal religions at the Interdenominational Theological Center in my inaugural lecture for the Helmar Nielsen chair, "Afro-American Liturgical Experiences: Discovery, Recovery, and Renewal" (inaugural address given at the Interdenominational Theological Center, October 18, 1986).

4. See Elias S. Hardge, Jr., "The Role of Music in the Vitalization of the Worship in Black Congregations," D.Min. diss., Columbia Theological Seminary, 1987; and Denzil D. Holness, "Renewal of Worship through the Discovery and Recovery of the African American Liturgical Tradition," D.Min. diss., Interdenominational Theological Center, 1991.

5. Molefi Kete Asante, *Afrocentricity: The Theory of Social Change,* rev. and exp. (Chicago: African American Images, 2003), 2.

6. See Yaya Diallo and Mitchell Hall, *The Healing Drum: African Wisdom Teachings* (Rochester: Destiny Books, 1989), 141–71.

7. See Diallo and Hall, *Healing Drum,"* 141–71.

8. Ibid., 131. The healing drum is an instrument for transmitting traditional knowledge among the Minianka of Mali, West Africa. This particular drum is a hand drum, known as the *djembe* and the *balafon,* which is found among Africans whose ancestors were transported to the West Indies.

9. Geoffrey Hindley, et. al., *Larousse Encyclopedia of Music,* 1st American ed. (New York: World Publishing Co., 1971), 17.

10. *Universe* and *cosmos* will be used interchangeably throughout this book.

11. See Michael C. Kirwen, *The Missionary and the Diviner* (New York: Orbis Books, 1987).

12. See esp. Mbiti, *African Religions and Philosophy,* 1–36; John S. Mbiti, *Concepts of God in Africa* (New York: Praeger Publishers, 1970); J. Omosade Awolalu, *Yoruba Beliefs and Sacrificial Rites* (London: Longman, 1979); and Peter Paris, *The Spirituality of African Peoples* (Minneapolis: Fortress Press, 1995).

13. See Melva Wilson Costen, *African American Christian Worship* (Nashville: Abingdon Press, 1993), 19, for a discussion of previous misuses of this term.

14. John B. Taylor, ed., *Primal World Views: Christian Dialogue with Traditional Thought Forms* (Ibadan, Nigeria: Daystar Press, 1976), 3.

15. See esp. Albert Raboteau, *Slave Religion* (New York: Oxford University Press, 1980), 43–92. Raboteau differentiates between various forms of African spiritual possession and the spiritual shouting traditions of African Americans. See also Robert Hall, "African Religious Retentions in Florida," in *Africanisms in American Culture,* ed. Joseph Holloway (Bloomington: Indiana University Press, 1990); and Mechal Sobel, *Trabelin' On: The Slave Journey to an Afro Baptist Faith* (Princeton, N.J.: Princeton University Press, 1988). Sobel skillfully builds the Afro-Baptist faith upon the foundation of the African sacred cosmos, which ultimately becomes a new Afro-Baptist sacred cosmos.

16. Mbiti, *Concepts of God in Africa,* 178.

17. Ibid., 178.

18. Ibid., 218.

19. Olaudah Equiano, *The Interesting Narrative of the Life of Olaudah Equiano, or Gustavas Vassa, the African, Written by Himself* (1791; reprint, New York: W. Durrell, 1989), 1:8.

20. J. H. Kwabena Nketia, *The Music of Africa* (New York: W. W. Norton & Co., 1974), 4.

21. Ibid. Nketia provides an excellent study on historical migrations among Africans that have helped to create unique cultural identities and practices.

22. Francis Bebey, "The Vibrant Intensity of Traditional African Music," *The Black Perspective in Music,* ed. Eileen Southern (Fall 1974), 117.

23. Francis Bebey, *African Music: A People's Art* (New York: Lawrence Hill, 1975), 115.

24. Bantu languages are a family of Niger-Congo languages spoken in central and southern Africa characterized by a musical quality.

25. For a more detailed explanation of the importance of intonation, see Bebey, *African Music,* 119–45.

26. Nketia, *Music of Africa,* 177–78. This excellent study and documentation of structures in African music, organization of vocal music, melody, polyphony, and rhythmic structures in vocal music is based on Nketia's experience and research as director of the Institute of African Studies at the University of Ghana in Legon.

27. Bebey, *African Music,* 115.

28. Ibid., 40.

29. Curt Sachs, *The History of Musical Instruments* (New York: W. W. Norton & Co., 1940), 455ff.

30. For more details, see Bebey, *African Music,* 91–92.

31. Jacqueline Roumeguere-Eberhardt, *African Thought and Society* (Paris: Mouton & Co., 1963).

32. Bebey, *African Music,* 82–84.

33. Nketia, *Music of Africa,* 125.

34. Dominique Zahan, *The Religion, Spirituality, and Thought of Traditional Africa* (Chicago: University of Chicago Press, 1979), 114 and 154.

35. Other churches that broke away were the Nestorian Church (the Church of East Syria), and the Monophysite churches, consisting of the Jacobite Church of Antioch and the Armenian Church.

36. It is believed that the Falasha tribe of northern Ethiopia, which practices a form of Judaism, is descended from the Israelites.

37. Andrew Wilson-Dickson, *The Story of Christian Music: From Gregorian Chant to Black Gospel* (Minneapolis: Fortress Press, 1996), 163.

38. Father J. Lobo, *A Voyage to Abyssinia,* trans. Samuel Johnson (London, 1735); cited in Wilson-Dickson, *Story of Christian Music,* 162–63.

39. Michael Powne, *Ethiopian Music, an Introduction* (New York: Oxford University Press, 1968), 91.

40. Ibid., 98–99.

41. Robert E. Webber, ed., *The Complete Library of Christian Worship,* vol. 4, *Music and the Arts in Christian Worship,* book 1 (Nashville: Star Song, 1994), 208–216, includes the same articles by Wilson-Dickson from *Story of Christian Music* cited above.

42. Asante, *Afrocentricity.* Asante makes very clear that his argument is essentially a "congruence position." He maintains that African Americans can never achieve their full psychological potential until they find congruence between who they are and what their environment says they ought to be. To be Afrocentric is to place Africans and the interest of Africans at the center of our approach to problem solving.

43. See Melva W. Costen, "African American Liturgical Music in a Global Context," in *The Journal of the Interdenominational Theological Center: African American Worship: Faith Looking Forward* 27, nos. 1–2 (Fall 1999–Spring 2000): 63–106.

44. Molefi Kete Asante, *The Afrocentric Idea* (Philadelphia: Temple University Press, 1987), 5.

CHAPTER 2: AFRICANS IN AMERICA

1. Lerone Bennett Jr., *Before the Mayflower: A History of Black America* (Chicago: Johnson Publishing Co., 1982), 31.

2. Charles Johnson and Patricia Smith, *Africans in America: America's Journey through Slavery* (New York: Harcourt Brace & Co., 1998), 5.

3. Ibid., 12.

4. Louis Jadin and Mireille Dicorato, eds., *Correspondance de Dom Afonso, roi du Congo 1506–1543* (Brussels, 1974). Cited in Cyprian Davis, O.S.B., *The History of Black Catholics in the United States* (New York: Crossroad, 1993), 16.

5. Cited in Davis, *History of Black Catholics,* 17.

6. Davis, *History of Black Catholics,* 18. This is an excellent source of history in general and of Roman Catholic history in particular, with documentation of Africans who rose to high positions in the church.

7. Ibid.

8. Ibid., 28.

9. Ibid., 30.

10. Cited by Davis from John Jay TePaske, *The Governorship of Spanish Florida, 1700–1763* (Durham, N.C.: Duke University Press, 1964), 140–44.

11. Davis, *History of Black Catholics,* 31. According to Davis, these are the oldest ecclesiastical documents for the United States.

12. Ibid., 31.

13. Ibid., 38. The second chapter of this book is titled, "Catholic Settlers and Catholic Slaves: A Church in Chains." This is appropriately descriptive of the church of Jesus Christ seeking freedom in a land made strange and alien by explorers.

14. For details, see Helen Tunnicliff Catterall, ed., *Judicial Cases Concerning American Slavery and the Negro,* 4 vols. (Washington, D.C.: Carnegie Institution, 1926).

15. Quoted in Edgar Pennington, "Thomas Bray's Associates and Their Work among the Negroes," in *Proceedings of the American Antiquarian Society,* new series, 48 (1938): 333.

16. Henry Edward Krehbiel, *Afro-American Folksongs: A Study in Racial and National Music* (New York: Frederick Ungar Publishing Co., 1962), 3.

17. John Lovell, Jr., *Black Song: The Forge and the Flame: The Story of How the Afro-American Spiritual Was Hammered Out* (New York: Macmillan, 1972), 17.

18. There are no records to indicate when a common American language actually began.

19. For further details, see Benjamin Brawley, *A Social History of the American Negro* (New York: Macmillan, 1921), 4–7; and Davis, *History of Black Catholics,* passim.

20. Bennett, *Before the Mayflower,* 29.

21. Ibid., 35.

22. Cited in Eileen Southern, *The Music of Black Americans: A History,* 3d ed. (New York: W. W. Norton & Co., 1997), 36. The statement appears in John Winthrop's *Journal* and is reprinted in Lorenzo Johnston Greene, *The Negro in Colonial New England 1607–1781* (Port Washington, N.Y.: Kennikat Press, 1966), 257.

23. Cited in Southern, *Music of Black Americans,* 37.

24. Samuel Davies' letter of June 28, 1751, to a Mr. Bellamy of Bethlehem, England, in the appendix to Benjamin Fawcett, *Compassionate Address to the Christian Negroes in Virginia,* 2d ed. (London: Salop, 1755), 37.

25. Lawrence W. Levine, *Black Culture and Black Consciousness* (New York: Oxford University Press, 1977), 33.

26. See esp. John Lovell, *Black Song;* Jon Michael Spencer, *Protest and Praise: Sacred Music of Black Religion* (Minneapolis: Fortress Press, 1990); Wyatt T. Walker, *"Somebody's Calling My Name": Black Sacred Music and Social Change* (Valley Forge, Pa.: Judson Press, 1979); and Cheryl A. Kirk-Duggan, *Exorcizing Evil: A Womanist Perspective on the Spirituals* (Maryknoll, N.Y.: Orbis Books, 1997).

27. See Melva Wilson Costen, *African American Christian Worship* (Nashville: Abingdon Press, 1993), 36–54, for further details.

28. Albert J. Raboteau, *Slave Religion: The "Invisible Institution" in the Antebellum South* (New York: Oxford University Press, 1978), 212–13.

29. For a more detailed interpretation, see Melva Wilson Costen, "African American Spirituals," in *Journal of Religious and Theological Information* 4, no. 3 (2001): 59–82.

30. Costen, *African American Christian Worship,* 52–54.

31. Ibid., 54.

32. Samuel A. Floyd, Jr., *The Power of Black Music* (New York: Oxford University Press, 1993), 6.

33. Lovell, *Black Song,* 19.

34. William Francis Allen, Charles Pickard Ware, and Lucy McKim Garrison, *Slave Songs of the United States* (New York: A. Simpson & Co., 1867).

35. Ibid., xliii.

36. J. B. T. Marsh, *The Story of the Jubilee Singers and Their Songs* (Boston: Houghton, Mifflin & Co., 1881).

37. R. Nathaniel Dett, *Religious Folk Songs of the Negro as Sung at Hampton Institute* (Hampton, Va.: Hampton Institute Press, 1927).

38. Nicholas Ballanta, *St. Helena Island Spirituals* (New York: G. Schirmer, 1925); James Weldon Johnson and J. Rosamond Johnson, *The Books of American Negro Spirituals* (New York: Viking Press, 1969); and John W. Work, *American Negro Songs and Spirituals* (New York: Bonanza Books, 1940).

39. For an excellent discussion of both sides of the argument, see Lovell, *Black Song,* pp. 3–117.

40. Robert William Fogel and Stanley L. Engerman, *Time on the Cross: The Economics of American Negro Slavery* (Boston: Little, Brown & Co., 1974), 4–6.

41. W. E. B. Du Bois, *The Souls of Black Folks,* rev. ed. (New York: Avon Books, 1965).

CHAPTER 3: AFRICAN AMERICAN HYMNODY

1. See Bernhard W. Anderson, *Out of the Depths: The Psalms Speak for Us Today,* rev. and expanded ed. (Philadelphia: Westminster Press, 1983), 44–45.

2. Quoted in James McKinnon, *Music in Early Christian Literature* (New York: Cambridge University Press, 1987), 158.

3. Samuel Davies, *Letters from the Rev. Samuel Davies and Others: Shewing [sic] the State of Religion in Virginia, South Carolina, Particularly among the Negroes* (London: Printed by J. & W. Oliver, 1761). Quoted in Eileen Southern, ed., *Readings in Black American Music,* 2d ed. (New York: W. W. Norton & Co., 1983), 28–29.

4. A line of poetry with four iambic feet is called *iambic tetrameter* (*tetra* meaning "four"); a three-foot line of poetry is called *trimeter,* etc.

5. The first line of nine "Rules for the Society of Negroes" in 1693 was that a psalm shall be sung between the prayers at the beginning of the meeting. This society was formed "for the welfare of [those] that were servants." See reprint of "Rules for the Society of Negroes, 1693" in Melva Wilson Costen, *African American Christian Worship* (Abingdon Press, 1993), 142.

6. Thomas Walter, *The Grounds and Rules of Music Explained* . . . (Boston, 1721). Quoted in Edward Bailey Birge, *History of Public School Music in the United States,* new and augmented ed. (Washington, D.C.: Music Educators National Conference, 1966), 4–6.

7. Wyatt Tee Walker, *"Somebody's Calling My Name": Black Sacred Music and Social Change* (Valley Forge, Pa.: Judson Press, 1979), 77.

8. Wendell Phillips Whalum, "Black Hymnody," in *Review and Expositor: The Black Experience and the Church,* LXX, no. 3 (Summer 1973): 342.

9. See esp. Melva Wilson Costen, "Published Hymnals in the Afro-American Tradition," *The Hymn: A Journal of Congregational Song* 40 (January 1989): 13–14; and Jon Michael Spencer, *Black Hymnody: A Hymnological History of the African-American Church* (Knoxville: University of Tennessee Press, 1992).

10. See Costen, "Published Hymnals in the Afro-American Tradition," 83–86, for a list of dates of the establishment of separate denominations and congregations.

11. A facsimile of this hymnal is contained in *A Collection of Hymns and Spiritual Songs* (Philadelphia: Mother Bethel African Methodist Episcopal Church, 1987). A note on the front page indicates that this is a facsimile reproduction of the original 1801 edition.

12. Ibid., p. xxiv.

13. Ibid., xi.

14. See the 1987 facsimile of Richard Allen's hymnal cited in note 11, or Southern, ed., *Readings in Black American Music*, 52–61; see also Eileen Southern, "Hymnals of the Black Church," in *The Black Christian Worship Experience*, rev. and enlarged ed., ed. Melva Wilson Costen and Darius Leander Swann (Atlanta: Interdenominational Theological Center, 1992), 128–34.

15. Eileen Southern, *The Music of Black Americans: A History*, 3d ed. (New York: W. W. Norton, 1997), 79.

16. Ibid.

17. This resource is available from Mother Bethel African Methodist Episcopal Church in Philadelphia. The Reverend Richard Allen, *A Collection of Hymns and Spiritual Songs* (Philadelphia: T. L. Plowman, Carters Alley, 1801; reprint, Philadelphia: Mother Bethel African Methodist Episcopal Church, 1987).

18. Southern, *Music of Black Americans*, 75.

19. The preface of the 1818 edition is reprinted in Southern, *Readings in Black American Music*, 86.

20. Charles E. Stewart, "Our Church Music," *AME Review* 36, no. 2 (October 1919): 339–40.

21. William J. Walls, *The African Methodist Episcopal Zion Church: Reality of the Black Church* (Charlotte, N.C.: AME Zion Publishing House, 1974), 33 and 34.

22. Ibid., 48.

23. J. W. Hood, *One Hundred Years of the African Methodist Episcopal Zion Church* (New York: AME Zion Book Concerns, 1895), 524; cited in Walls, *African Methodist Episcopal Zion Church*, 50.

24. Walls, *African Methodist Episcopal Zion Church*, 90.

25. Quoted in Walls, *African Methodist Episcopal Zion Church*, 139.

26. Ibid., 89. Walls notes that Absalom Jones, who was in Philadelphia, was the other African to preach on behalf of African people.

27. *The Doctrines and Disciplines of the Wesleyan Methodist Episcopal Zion Church in America* (New York: AMEZ Church, 1920), 56–58.

28. Ibid., 67–68.

29. Walls, *African Methodist Episcopal Zion Church*, 117.

30. *A Collection of Hymns for the Use of the Methodist Episcopal Church* (New York: J. Emory and B. Waugh, for the Methodist Episcopal Church, 1831).

31. Spencer, *Black Hymnody*, 27.

32. Walls, *African Methodist Episcopal Zion Church*, 118–19.

33. Lawrence L. Reddick III, "The Newly Published C.M.E. Hymnal," *Christian Index* 120, no. 20 (1987): 2.

34. C. Eric Lincoln and Lawrence H. Mamiya, *The Black Church in the American Experience* (Durham, N.C.: Duke University Press, 1990), 28.

35. Southern, "Hymnals of the Black Church," 136.

36. William B. McClain, Preface to *Songs of Zion* (Nashville: Abingdon Press, 1981), xi.

37. Charles Price Jones, "Autobiographical Sketch of Charles Price Jones," in *History of Church of Christ (Holiness) U.S.A., 1895–1965,* ed. Ortho B. Cobbins (Chicago: National Publishing Board, Church of Christ [Holiness], USA, 1966), 21–32. The quotation appears in *Journal of Black Sacred Music* 2, no. 2 (Fall 1988): 54.

38. Charles P. Jones, "Dedication," in *His Fullness Songs* (Jackson, Miss.: National Publishing Board of the Church of Christ [Holiness], USA, 1977).

39. From lectures by Iris Stevenson in three music classes.

40. *Lift Every Voice and Sing II: An African American Hymnal* (New York: The Church Hymnal Corp., 1993).

41. See Clarence Joseph Rivers, *The Spirit in Worship* (Cincinnati: Stimuli, Inc. 1978) and *Soulful Worship* (Washington, D.C.: National Office for Black Catholics and the Liturgical Conference, 1977). See also *This Far By Faith: American Worship and its African Roots* (Washington, D.C.: National Office for Black Catholics, 1978), an anthology of major papers presented during a conference on "Worship and Spirituality in the Black Community."

42. J-Glenn Murray, S.J., "The Liturgy of the Roman Rite and African American Worship," in *Lead Me, Guide Me,* xi.

43. Ibid., xiii.

44. *Genre,* as used in this book, means "category," "classification," or "form," in contrast to *style,* which is used in relation to manner of performance or the technique by which something is performed.

45. Obery M. Hendricks, Jr., "I Am the Holy Dope Dealer: The Problem with Gospel Music Today," *African American Worship: Faith Looking Forward: The Journal of the Interdenominational Theological Center*, 27, nos. 1–2 (Fall 1999–Spring 2000): 9–10.

CHAPTER 4: THE EVOLUTION OF GOSPEL MUSIC

1. For historical details of the reception of the message of freedom by blacks in different states, see William A. Wiggins, Jr., *O Freedom! African American Emancipation Celebrations* (Knoxville: University of Tennessee Press, 1987).

2. Portia K. Maultsby, "The Impact of Gospel Music on the Secular Music Industry," in *We'll Understand It Better By and By,* ed. Bernice Johnson Reagon (Washington, D.C.: Smithsonian Institution Press, 1992), 19.

3. Eileen Southern, *The Music of Black Americans: A History*, 3d ed. (New York: W. W. Norton, 1997), 333.

4. James Cone, *The Spirituals and the Blues: An Interpretation* (New York: Seabury Press, 1972).

5. Nat Shapiro and Nat Hentoff, eds., *Hear Me Talkin' to Ya: The Story of Jazz by the Men Who Made It* (New York: Rinehart, 1955), 7.

6. John W. Work, *American Negro Songs: 230 Folk Songs and Spirituals, Religious, and Secular* (1940; reprint, Mineola, N.Y.: Dover Publications, 1998), 32–33

7. Michael W. Harris, *The Rise of Gospel Blues: The Music of Thomas Andrew Dorsey in the Urban Church* (New York: Oxford University Press, 1992), 69.

8. Unfortunately, vestiges of this discontinuity continue among some members of Pentecostal churches, while non-Pentecostals research and write vigorously about the connection.

9. Pearl Williams-Jones, "Afro-American Gospel Music: A Crystallation of the Black Aesthetic," *Ethnomusicology* 19, no. 3 (1975): 373.

10. Pearl Williams-Jones, "Performance Style in Black Gospel Music," in *Black People and Their Culture: Selected Writings from the African Diaspora* (Washington, D.C.: Smithsonian Institution Press, 1976), 115–16.

11. The late Pearl Williams-Jones was minister of music at the Bible Way Church in Washington, D.C., and was a graduate of Howard University. She had degrees in music, and she pursued additional post-graduate studies at Temple University. She received an honorary doctoral degree from Lycoming College, was a concert pianist and vocalist throughout the United States and Europe, held teaching positions at Howard University and the University of the District of Columbia, and served on the advisory committee at the Smithsonian Institution.

12. Ira D. Sankey, *My Life and the Story of Gospel Hymns and Sacred Songs and Solos* (Philadelphia: Sunday School Times, 1907), 50.

13. See esp. Horace Clarence Boyer, *How Sweet the Sound: The Golden Age of Gospel* (Washington, D.C.: Elliott & Clark Publishing, 1995); and Reagon, ed., *We'll Understand It Better By and By.*

14. Reagon, ed., "Pioneering African American Gospel Music Composers," in Reagon, ed. *We'll Understand It Better By and By*, 15.

15. Boyer, *How Sweet the Sound,* 26.

16. Ibid.

17. Willa A. Townsend, preface to *Gospel Pearls* (Nashville: Sunday School Publishing Board, National Baptist Convention, USA, 1921).

18. Charles A. Tindley, *New Songs of Paradise* (Philadelphia: Paradise Publishing Co., 1916).

19. For a detailed account of this style, see Harris, *Rise of Gospel Blues,* 47–90.

20. Southern, *Music of Black Americans,* 461.

21. Mellonee Victoria Burnim, "The Black Gospel Music Tradition: Symbol of Ethnicity" (Ph.D. diss., Indiana University, 1982).

22. See Boyer, *How Sweet the Sound,* 49–109.

23. Ibid., 43.

24. Ibid., 50.

25. See Southern, *Music of Black Americans,* 311–12.

26. Wyatt Tee Walker, *"Somebody's Calling My Name": Black Sacred Music and Social Change* (Valley Forge, Pa.: Judson Press, 1979), 128.

27. Southern, *Music of Black Americans,* 464.

28. Boyer, *How Sweet the Sound,* 187.

29. Ibid., 53–54.

30. Southern, *Music of Black Americans,* 607.

31. Ibid., 598.

32. K. Maurice Jones, *The Story of Rap Music* (Brookfield, Conn.: Millbrook Press, 1994), 46.

33. Ronald Jemal Stephens, "The Three Ways of Contemporary Rap Music," in "The Emergency of Black and the Emergence of Rap," ed. Jon Michael Spencer, special issue, *Black Sacred Music: A Journal of Theomusicology* 5, no. 1 (Spring 1991): 25–26.

34. See Sonja Peterson-Lewis, "A Feminist Analysis of the Defenses of Obscene Rap Lyrics," in "The Emergency of Black and the Emergence of Rap," 68–79; see also, Angela Spence Nelson, "Theology in the Hip Hop of Public Enemy and Kool Moe Dee," ibid., 51–59.

35. Southern, *Music of Black Americans*, 464.

36. Ibid., 465.

37. Clara Ward, "How a Visit to the Holy Land Changed My Life," *Color,* May 1956, 15–17.

38. Quoted in Viv Broughton, *Black Gospel: An Illustrated History of the Gospel Sound* (New York: Poole, 1985), 37.

39. Della Reese, "Gospel to Pop to Gospel," *Ebony,* July 1962, 107–12.

40. See Paul Oliver, *Songsters and Saints: Vocal Traditions on Race Records* (New York: Cambridge University Press, 1984).

41. Boyer, *How Sweet the Sound,* 190.

42. Maultsby, "Impact of Gospel Music," 20.

43. Ibid., 27.

44. Ibid., 28.

45. Burnim, "Black Gospel Music Tradition," 192.

46. Ibid., 193.

47. Ibid.

48. Ibid., 194–95.

49. Obery M. Hendricks, Jr., "'I Am the Holy Dope Dealer': The Problem with Gospel Music Today," *Journal of the Interdenominational Theological Center* 27, nos. 1–2 (Fall 1999/Winter 2000): 9–10.

50. Langston Hughes, "Church, Theatre, and Gospel Songs," *Chicago Defender,* July 26, 1942. The entire article is reprinted in *Black Sacred Music: A Journal of Theomusicology* 7, no. 1 (Spring 1993): 30.

51. Ibid., 30–31.

52. Wendell Whalum, "Music in the Churches of Black Americans: A Critical Statement," *The Black Perspective in Music* 14, no. 1, special issue (Winter 1986): 17.

53. Ibid., 19.

CHAPTER 5: INSTRUMENTS IN WORSHIP

1. See Dena J. Epstein, *Sinful Tunes and Spirituals: Black Folk Music to the Civil War* (Chicago: University of Illinois Press, 1977), 47–62. Epstein's excellent research remains one of the most helpful descriptions of African cultural retentions in North America mainland and the islands. Conditions in the islands were more conducive to the preservation of African cultural patterns.

2. Quoted in Russell R. Menard, "The Maryland Slave Population, 1658–1730," *William and Mary Quarterly,* 3d series, January 1975, 37.

3. *The Colonial Records of the State of Georgia,* 22, part 2 (1739), compiled by Allen D. Chandler (Atlanta: C. P. Byrd, 1913), 234–35.

4. George Whitefield, Letter 3, *Three Letters from the Rev. Mr. Whitefield* (Philadelphia: Printed by Benjamin Franklin, 1740), 14.

5. Epstein, *Sinful Tunes and Spirituals,* 49.

6. Ibid., 49 and 55.

7. People of African descent are careful about what facilitates "having church" and what movements should be avoided. The snapping or "popping" of fingers is not for church. In the "ring shout" tradition, feet could shuffle but not lift from the floor.

8. J. H. Kwabena Nketia, *The Music of Africa* (New York: W. W. Norton & Co., 1974), 69. See other African instrumental categories on pp. 25–27.

9. Ibid., 67.

10. Curt Sachs, *The History of Musical Instruments* (New York: W. W. Norton & Co., 1940), 455ff. Although non-European instruments outnumber by far those of European art music, consideration was not given to new classifications until this period of time.

11. Francis Bebey, *African Music: A People's Art* (New York: Lawrence Hill, 1975), 17.

12. Ibid., 17.

13. This concept, a part of my own tradition, is referenced by Donald P. Hustad, *Jubilate II: Church Music in Worship and Renewal* (Carol Stream, Ill.: Hope Publishing Co., 1993), 131.

14. Johannes Quasten, *Music and Worship in Pagan and Christian Antiquity* (Washington, D.C.: National Association of Pastoral Musicians, 1983), 67.

15. Willi Apel, *Harvard Dictionary of Music* (Cambridge, Mass.: Harvard University Press, 1944), 445.

16. Jeremy Montagu, "Kinnor," in *The New Grove Dictionary of Musical Instruments* (New York: Macmillan, 1984): 2:432.

17. Joseph Gelineau, SJ, *Voices and Instruments in Christian Worship* (Collegeville, Minn.: Liturgical Press, 1964), 149.

18. *First Clement* 34, quoted in James McKinnon, *Music in Early Christian Literature* (Cambridge: Cambridge University Press, 1987), 18.

19. Clement of Alexandria, *Paedagogus* 2.4 (PG 8:443–444), quoted in McKinnon, *Music in Early Christian Literature,* 33.

20. Ibid., 439–40; trans. McKinnon, p. 32.

21. Quoted in Gustave Reese, *Music in the Middle Ages* (New York: W. W. Norton & Co., 1940), 62.

22. James McKinnon, "The Meaning of the Patristic Polemic against Musical Instruments," *Current Musicology I* (1965), 69.

23. For an introduction to ritual music in non-European traditions, see Geoffrey Hindley, ed., *Larousse Encyclopedia of Music* (New York: Excalibur Books, 1971), 17–40.

24. Quasten, *Music and Worship in Pagan and Christian Antiquity,* 126.

25. Augustine, *De doctrina Christiana* 2, 18:34.

26. Philip Beggrov Peter, "The History of the Organ in the Christian Church," in *The Complete Library of Christian Worship,* ed. Robert Weber, vol. 4, bk. 1, *Music and the Arts in Christian Worship* (Nashville: StarSong, 1994), 400.

27. St. Aldhem, *De Virginitate*; quoted in *The Complete Library of Christian Worship,* vol. 4, bk. 1, 399.

28. Orpha Ochse, *The History of the Organ in the United States* (Bloomington: Indiana University Press, 1975), 4. This book includes broad coverage of information about organs in Euro-American churches, but nothing about organs in African American churches.

29. Ibid., 5.

30. Justus Falckner, letter to Heinrich Muhlen of Germany; quoted in David W. Music, *Instruments in Church: A Collection of Source Documents* (Lanham, Md.: Rowman & Littlefield, 1998), 127.

31. Ibid., 128.

32. Samuel Sewell, *The Diary of Samuel Sewell,* 1674–1729, Collections of the Massachusetts Historical Society, 5th series, vols. 5–7 (Boston, 1878–82). Sewell's entry is in reference to a funeral that he attended in the same room where he had heard the sound of Mr. Battle's organ.

33. William Arms Fisher, *Notes on Music in Old Boston* (Boston: Oliver Dittson, 1918), 8.

34. Ochse, *History of the Organ,* 20–21.

35. Ibid., 265.

36. Ibid., 370.

37. Eileen Southern, *The Music of Black Americans: A History*, 3d ed. (New York: W. W. Norton, 1997), 128.

38. Quoted in Southern, *Music of Black Americans,* 102. See also *A Statistical Inquiry into the Condition of the People of Color of the City and Districts of Philadelphia* (Philadelphia, 1849).

39. Southern, *Music of Black Americans,* 105.

40. Ibid., 105.

41. Ibid., 99.

42. Lathan N. Windley, *Runaway Slave Advertisements: A Documentary History from the 1730s to 1790,* 4 vols. (Westport, Conn.: Greenwood Press, 1983). This work contains a collection of six thousand advertisements from twenty-one newspapers.

43. Jacqueline Delores Cogdell Djedje, "The One String Fiddle in West Africa: A Comparison of Hausa and Dagemba Traditions," vols. I and II (Ph.D. diss., University of California at Los Angeles, 1974). This two-volume work is an excellent resource on the intricate techniques used by two different African societies.

44. Windley, *Runaway Slave Advertisements.*

45. Herbert Aptheker, *A Documentary History of the Negro People in the United States* (New York: Citadel Press, 1941), 4.

46. Ibid., 28.

47. Excerpt from a letter recorded in Edward Turner, *The Negro in Pennsylvania: Slavery, Servitude, and Freedom, 1639–1861* (Washington, D.C.: American Historical Association, 1911), 42.

48. See Southern, *Music of Black Americans,* 41–58, for a well-documented account of slave activities during this period.

49. A. Daniel Frankforter, *Stones for Bread: A Critique of Contemporary Worship* (Louisville, Ky.: Westminster John Knox Press, 2001), 122.

50. Bebey, *African Music,* 115.

51. Nketia, *The Music of Africa,* 139.

52. Ibid., 14–15. This very lengthy reminder is deliberately quoted from the prominent African scholar who served as director of the Institute of African Studies at the University of Ghana in Legion, Ghana. This concern was expressed to the writer while at the University of Ghana during the summer of 1974.

53. MIDI is an international standard acronym for "musical instrument digital interface." This language enables any MIDI-equipped device to communicate with any other MIDI-equipped device. Computers can "talk" to electronic keyboards, a synthesizer can be played from a guitar or organ console, and so on. Musicians should become familiar with this language since it appears to be the wave of the future.

54. These suggestions were adapted from an article by Frank Longina, "The Orchestra in the Praise and Worship Tradition," in *The Complete Library of Christian Worship: Music and the Arts in Christian Worship,* vol. 4, bk. 1, 423–26.

55. This was a vestment worn by the priest.

56. Donald L. Clapper credits Margaret Surcliff with organizing the first band of ringers in 1923. See Clapper, *The Complete Library of Christian Worship,* vol. 4, bk. 1, 433.

CHAPTER 6: MUSIC AS A LITURGICAL ELEMENT
IN AFRICAN AMERICAN WORSHIP

1. Melva Wilson Costen, *African American Christian Worship* (Nashville: Abingdon Press, 1993), 91. A more detailed description is provided in chapter 7.

2. Joseph N. Ashton, *Music in Worship: The Use of Music in the Church Service* (Boston: Pilgrim Press, 1943), 6.

3. Gustavus Vassa, *The Interesting Narrative of the Life of Olaudah Equiano,* or *Gustavus Vassa, the African* (London, 1794); and Venture Smith, *A Narrative of the Life and Adventures of Venture, a Native of Africa* (New London, 1798).

4. Although the giving of names is more related to the theological practice of Roman Catholics, the giving of names to slaves at their baptism is a reminder either that African names did not count as names, or that many slaveholders, regardless of religious traditions, presumed to "christen" new Christians.

5. Costen, *African American Christian Worship*, 38.

6. Edward D. Smith, *Climbing Jacob's Ladder: The Rise of Black Churches in Eastern American Cities, 1740–1877* (Washington, D.C.: Smithsonian Institution Press, 1988), 27. Reprinted from Thomas J. Holmes, *Cotton Mather: A Bibliography of His Works* (Cambridge, Mass.: Crofton Publishing Corp., 1974). See also Costen, *African American Christian Worship,* 142–43.

7. Costen, *African American Christian Worship,* 143.

8. *Boston Recorder and Telegraph*, January 13, 1826. Cited in Eileen Southern, *The Music of Black Americans: A History*, 3d ed. (New York: W. W. Norton, 1997), 70.

9. William Douglas, *Annals of the First African Church in the United States of America* (Philadelphia: Kerg & Baird, 1862), 54.

10. Edgar Pennington, *Thomas Brays' Associates and Their Work among the Negroes* (Worcester, Mass.: American Antiquarian Society, 1939), 82.

11. Dom Gregory Dix, *The Shape of the Liturgy* (reprint, London: Adams & Clark Black, 1978). In this classical work, Dix considers all of the stages and forms of the liturgy as a living expression of the worship of the living body of Christ upon the earth.

12. Irene V. Jackson, "Music among Blacks in the Episcopal Church: Some Preliminary Consideration," in *More Than Dancing: Essays on Afro-American Music and Musicians*, ed. Irene V. Jackson (Westport, Conn.: Greenwood Press, 1985), 112.

13. Ibid., 110.

14. Robert A. Bennett, "Black Episcopalians: A History from the Colonial Period to the Present Day," *Historical Magazine of the Protestant Episcopal Church* 43 (September, 1974): 239.

15. These and other appellations were also imposed upon blacks in Euro-American denominations.

16. Jackson, "Music among Blacks in the Episcopal Church," 111–12.

17. Douglas, *Annals of the First African Church*, 130.

18. George F. Bragg, *First Negro Priests on Southern Soil* (Baltimore: Church Advocate Press, 1909), 30.

19. Southern, *Music of Black Americans,* 127.

20. James M. Trotter, *Music and Some Highly Musical People* (1878; reprint, Chicago: Afro American Press, 1969), 132. This book is an excellent source of information about nineteenth-century African Americans, whose musicianship and professional training continue to be applauded.

21. Vivienne L. Anderson, preface to *Methodists a Singing People, AMEC Bicentennial Hymnal* (Nashville: African Methodist Episcopal Church, 1984), v.

22. Jimmie James, Jr., "African Methodist Episcopal Churches: Music," in *The Complete Library of Christian Worship,* vol. 4, *Music and the Arts in Christian Worship,* ed. Robert E. Webber (Nashville: Star Song, 1994), 5.

23. The Turner Seminary, a constituent member of the ITC, provides education for a large number of AME students, especially now that a seminary education is required of pastors.

24. C. Eric Lincoln and Lawrence H. Mamiya, *The Black Church in the African American Experience* (Durham, N.C.: Duke University Press, 1990), 25. Among the Baptist churches in this category are the Joy Street Baptist Church in Boston (originally the African Baptist Church [1805]), Abysinnian Baptist Church in New York (1808), and First African Baptist in Philadelphia (1809).

25. *African American Hymnal* (Chicago: GIA, 2001).

26. Carter G. Woodson, *The History of the Negro Church,* 3d ed. (Washington, D.C.: Associated Publishers, 1972), 195–96.

27. Ibid., 196.

28. The reference here is from a report in 1745 that a slave named Clark "raised a psalm" and 200 worshipers were moved to glorify their Maker with heart and voice. The most detailed accounts of the work of the Society for the Propagation of the Gospel in Foreign Parts are by Edgar Pennington, "Thomas Bray's Associates and Their Work among the Negroes," *American Antiquarian Society Proceedings* 48 (1938): 311–403.

29. Samuel Davies, "Letter to the Rev. Joseph Bellamy, of Bethlehem in New England" in *Letters from the Rev. Samuel Davies and Others: Shewing [sic] the State of Religion in Virginia, South Carolina, Particularly among the Negroes* (London: Printed by J. W. Oliver, 1761), 9.

30. Lorenzo Johnston Greene, *The Negro in Colonial New England, 1607–1783* (New York: Kennikat Press, 1966), 238.

31. Douglas, *Annals of the First African Church,* 54.

32. Daniel Payne, *History of the African Methodist Episcopal Church* (Nashville: Publishing House of the A.M.E. Sunday School Union, 1899), 452ff.

33. Daniel Payne, *Recollections of Seventy Years* (Nashville: Publishing House of the A.M.E. Sunday School Union, 1888) reprint of passages about music in Eileen Southern, ed., *Readings in Black American Music,* 2d ed. (New York: W. W. Norton, 1983), 65–70.

34. Payne, *Recollections of Seventy Years,* 70.

35. Southern, *Music of Black Americans,* 131.

36. Payne, *Recollections of Seventy Years,* 70. "Fuge" or "fuging" tunes are forms of hymn or psalm tunes freely improvised and popularized. This practice developed in New England during the eighteenth and early nineteenth centuries.

37. Dena J. Epstein, *Sinful Tunes and Spiritual Songs* (Chicago: University of Illinois Press, 1977), 194–95.

38. Charles C. Jones, *Association for the Religious Instruction of the Negroes in Liberty County,* Ninth Annual Report (Georgia, 1842), 12–13.

39. Charles C. Jones, *Suggestions on the Religious Instruction of the Negroes in the Southern States* (Philadelphia: Presbyterian Board of Publications, n.d.), 39–40.

40. Walter F. Pitts, *Old Ship of Zion: The Afro-Baptist Ritual in the African Diaspora* (New York: Oxford University Press, 1993), 8.

41. James Baldwin, *Go Tell It on the Mountain* (New York: Dell Publishing Co., Inc., 1953), 14–15.

42. Lincoln and Mamiya, *Black Church in the African American Experience,* 76.

43. Ibid., 79. Separate national organizational structures created other distinctions in leadership styles, including black Pentecostals' decision not to ordain women. Despite their status as founders of the movement, black Pentecostals have been excluded in national and international organizations of Pentecostalism.

44. Ibid., 81. The interracial period lasted until 1924.

45. George Ofori-Atta-Thomas, "The African Inheritance in the Black Church Worship," in *The Black Christian Worship Experience*, rev. and enlarged ed., ed. Melva W. Costen and Darius L. Swann (Atlanta: ITC Press, 1992), 55–56.

46. For an excellent explanation of kratophany, see William C. Turner, "The Musicality of Black Preaching: A Phenomenology," *Journal of Black Sacred Music* 2, no. 1 (Spring 1988): 21–34.

47. See David Douglas Daniels III, "The Cultural Renewal of Slave Religion: Charles Price Jones and the Emergence of the Holiness Movement in Mississippi" (Ph.D. diss., Union Theological Seminary, New York, 1992); Jon Michael Spencer, "Isochronisms of Antistructure in the Black Holiness-Pentecostal Testimony Service," *Journal of Black Sacred Music* 2, no. 2 (Fall 1988): 1–18; Paul McIntyre, *Black Pentecostal Music in Windsor* (Ottawa: National Museums of Canada, 1976); William C. Turner, Jr., "Singing in the Holy Convocation of the United Holy Church of America," *Journal of Black Sacred Music* 2, no. 2 (Fall 1988): 19–22; Donna McNeil Cox, "Contemporary Trends in the Music Ministry of the Church of God in Christ," *Journal of Black Sacred Music* 2, no. 2 (Fall 1988): 23–38; Cheryl J. Sanders, *Saints in Exile: The Holiness Pentecostal Experience in African American Religion and Culture* (New York: Oxford University Press, 1996).

48. McIntyre, *Black Pentecostal Music in Windsor*, 42.

49. Ibid.

50. See "General Conference of Seventh-Day Adventists," in *Directory of African American Religious Bodies*, ed. Wardell J. Payne (Washington, D.C.: Howard University Press, 1995), 195.

51. Ed Zackrison, "Worship Renewal among the Contemporary Churches: Adventist Churches," in *The Complete Library of Christian Worship*, vol. 3, *The Renewal of Sunday Worship,* ed. Robert E. Webber (Nashville: Star Song, 1993), 3.

52. See Roy E. Malcolm, ed., *The Aeolians: Directors Recall Precious Memories* (Huntsville, Ala.: Oakwood College Publishing Association, 1999). This book is a salute to the musical achievements of the Oakwood College Aeolians, in particular, and to the music program and other academic programs in general.

53. Alma Montgomery Blackmon, "Black Seventh-Day Adventists and Church Music," in *Perspectives: Black Seventh-Day Adventists Face the Twenty-First Century*, ed. Calvin B. Rock (Hagerstown, Md.: Review & Herald Publishing Association, 1996), 183.

CHAPTER 7: WESTERN ROOTS OF THEOLOGY AS REFLECTED IN AFRICAN AMERICAN MUSIC FOR WORSHIP

1. Johannes Quasten, *Music and Worship in Pagan and Christian Antiquity,* trans. Boniface Ramsey (Washington, D.C.: National Association of Pastoral Musicians, 1983), 75–87.

2. Richard Viladesau, *Theology and the Arts: Encountering God through Music, Art and Rhetoric* (New York: Paulist Press, 2000), 17.

3. Fortunately, Augustine recorded his concerns in his *Confessions*. See esp. books 9, 10, and 33.

4. Augustine, *Confessions 10 CSEL (Corpus scriptorum ecdes iasticorum latinorum)*, 33. Translated from the portion that begins *Nunc in sonis*.

5. Quasten, *Music and Worship in Pagan and Christian Antiquity,* 96.

6. *St. Augustine on the Psalms,* trans. Dame Scholastica Hebgin and Dame Felicitas Corrigan (New York: Newman Press, 1961), 2:111–13.

7. Donald Jay Grout and Claude V. Palisca, *A History of Western Music,* 6th ed. (New York: W. W. Norton & Co., 2000), 26.

8. Boethius, *Fundamentals of Music,* trans. and with introduction and notes by Calvin Bower, ed. Claude V. Palisca (New Haven, Conn.: Yale University Press, 1989), 51.

9. Grout and Palisca, *History of Western Music,* 26.

10. Willi Apel, *Harvard Dictionary of Music,* 2d ed., rev. and enlarged (Cambridge, Mass.: Belknap Press, 1975), 756. In the papal decree *Motu proprio* (1903), by Pope Pius X, new regulations for the music of the Roman Catholic service were provided that included: (a) absolution of the worldly style of church music; (b) return to Palestrina's music as the model for polyphonic music; (c) restoration of Gregorian chant according to specific principles; (d) suppression of instruments; (e) admission of "modern" vocal compositions as long as they are in agreement with the spirit of the liturgy.

11. Apel, *Harvard Dictionary of Music,* 147.

12. Quoted in Owen Chadwich, *The Reformation* (Harmondsworth: Penguin, 1972), 56.

13. Viladesau, *Theology and the Arts,* 25–26.

14. This resource is described in detail in chapter 3.

15. *This Far by Faith: An African American Resource for Worship* (Minneapolis: Augsburg Fortress, 1999), 11.

16. *With One Voice* (Minneapolis: Augsburg Fortress, 1995), 4.

17. John Calvin, *Institutes of the Christian Religion,* 3.20.31–32; Library of Christian Classics, ed. John T. McNeill, trans. Ford Lewis Battles (Philadelphia: Westminster Press, 1960).

18. See Charles Garside, Jr., "Calvin's Preface to the Psalter: A Re-Appraisal," *The Music Quarterly* 37, no. 4 (October 1951): 569.

19. Calvin, *Institutes* 3.20.32.

20. Wardell J. Payne, ed., *Directory of African American Religious Bodies: A Compendium by the Howard University School of Divinity* (Washington, D.C.: Howard University Press, 1995).

21. Emily R. Brink, ed., *Psalter Hymnal* (Grand Rapids: CRC Press, 1987).

22. Payne, ed., *Directory of African American Religious Bodies,* 206.

23. Gayraud Wilmore, *Black and Presbyterian: The Heritage and the Hope,* rev. and enlarged ed. (Louisville, Ky.: Witherspoon Press, 1998), 53.

24. *The Presbyterian Hymnal: Hymns, Psalms, and Spiritual Songs* (Louisville, Ky.: Westminster John Knox Press, 1990). Racial ethnic representation was evident in the membership of the Presbyterian Hymnal Committee, with an African American serving as chair.

25. Ibid., 7.

26. *Holy Is the Lord: Music for the Lord's Day* (Louisville, Ky.: Geneva Press, 2002).

27. Grout and Palisca, *History of Western Music,* 234.

28. Ibid.

29. Preface to *Lead Me, Guide Me: The African American Catholic Hymnal* (Chicago: GIA Publications, 1987).

30. See Clarence Joseph Rivers, "The Oral African Tradition versus the Ocular Western Tradition," in *This Far by Faith: American Black Worship and Its African Roots* (Washington, D.C.: National Office for Black Catholics and the Liturgical Conference, 1977), 38–49; *This Far by Faith: American Black Worship and Its African Roots* (ibid.) Essays delivered at a Conference on Worship and Spirituality in the Black Community, Clarence Joseph Rivers, *The*

Spirit in Worship (Cincinnati: Stimuli, Inc., 1978); Clarence Joseph Rivers, *Soulful Worship* (Washington, D.C.: National Office for Black Catholics, 1974).

31. For more information on this hymnal, see chapter 3.

32. Paul Westermeyer, *Te Deum: The Church and Music* (Minneapolis: Fortress Press, 1998), 166.

33. See Robin Leaver, "British Hymnody from the Sixteenth through the Eighteenth Centuries," in *The Hymnal 1982 Companion* (New York: The Church Hymnal Corporation, 1990), 1, 365–92. See especially p. 330.

34. Frank S. Mead, *Handbook of Denominations in the United States,* 9th ed., rev. Samuel S. Hill (Nashville: Abingdon Press, 1989), 102.

35. Irene V. Jackson, "Music among Blacks in the Episcopal Church," in *More Than Dancing: Essays on Afro American Music and Musicians,* ed. Irene V. Jackson (Westport, Conn.: Greenwood Press, 1985), 110.

36. For facsimile reprints, see *John Wesley's First Hymnbook: A Collection of Psalms and Hymns* (Nashville: United Methodist Publishing House, 1988).

37. Carlton R. Young, *Companion to the United Methodist Hymnal* (Nashville: Abingdon Press, 1993), 11.

38. Harry Eskew and Hugh T. McElrath, *Sing with Understanding: An Introduction to Christian Hymnology,* 2d ed. (Nashville: Church Street Press, 1995), 138.

39. *Doctrines and Discipline of the Methodist Church* (New York: Methodist Publishing House, 1939), 27–38. The five additional administrative jurisdictions were geographically located. This arrangement was apparently the church's concession to the southern church, which had approved the release of its black membership and helped found the Colored Methodist Episcopal (CME) Church, which later changed "Colored" to "Christian."

40. *The Book of Discipline of the United Methodist Church* (Nashville: United Methodist Publishing House, 1972), 87.

41. William B. McClain, preface to *Songs of Zion,* ed. J. Jefferson Cleveland and Verolga Nix (Nashville: Abingdon Press, 1981), ix. For more information on this resource, see chapter 3.

CHAPTER 8: MUSIC MINISTRY IN THEOLOGICAL PERSPECTIVE

1. Robert Hood, *Must God Remain Greek? Afro Cultures and God-Talk* (Minneapolis: Fortress Press, 1990).

2. Walter A. Elwell, ed., *Evangelical Dictionary of Theology* (Grand Rapids: Baker Book House, 1984), 721–22; W. E. Vine, *Vine's Dictionary of New Testament Words* (McLean, Va.: Macdonald Publishing Co., n.d.), 754–57.

3. Calvin M. Johansson, *Music and Ministry: A Biblical Counterpoint,* 2d ed. (Peabody, Mass.: Hendrickson Publishers, 1998), 7.

4. Walter Piston, *Counterpoint* (New York: W. W. Norton & Co., 1947), 9.

5. Johansson, *Music and Ministry,* 36; emphasis mine.

6. Andrew Wilson-Dickson, *The Story of Christian Music: From Gregorian Chant to Black Gospel: An Authoritative Illustrated Guide to All the Major Traditions of Music for Worship* (Minneapolis: Fortress Press, 1996), 11.

7. Ibid.

8. Robert Bruce McLaren, "The Threat of Aestheticism," *Christianity Today,* November 7, 1960, 16.

9. Francis Bebey, *African Music: A People's Art* (New York: Lawrence Hill & Co., 1975), 17.

10. Four resources that provide adequate discussions on this matter are Albert L. Blackwell, *The Sacred in Music* (Louisville, Ky.: Westminster John Knox Press, 1999); Frank Burch Brown, *Religious Aesthetics: A Theological Study of Making and Meaning* (Princeton, N.J.: Princeton University Press, 1989); idem, *Good Taste, Bad Taste, and Christian Life: Aesthetics in Religious Life* (New York: Oxford University Press, 2000); and Richard Viladesau, *Theology and the Arts: Encountering God through Music, Art, and Rhetoric* (New York: Paulist Press, 2000).

11. The academic curriculum at the Interdenominational Theological Center has incorporated courses in church music since 1973. A lecture series on Worship, Theology, and the Art was added in 1982, and the Master of Arts in Church music degree program was added as part of the curriculum revision process in 1985.

12. Jimmy Stewart, "Introduction to Black Aesthetics in Music" in *The Black Aesthetic,* ed. Addison Gayle, Jr. (New York: Anchor Books, 1971), 80.

13. Susanne K. Langer, *Feeling and Form: A Theory of Art* (New York: Charles Scribner's Sons, 1953), 27.

14. Rudolf Otto, *The Idea of the Holy* (London: Oxford University Press, 1969), 69.

15. Ibid.

16. Viladesau, *Theology and the Arts,* 40.

17. Ibid., 43.

18. S. Paul Schilling, *The Faith We Sing* (Philadelphia: Westminster Press, 1983), 35.

19. Benjamin E. Mays, *The Negro's God as Reflected in His Literature* (New York: Atheneum, 1973), 23.

20. Ibid., 30.

21. Ibid., 29.

22. Calvin M. Johannson, *Discipling Music Ministry: Twenty-first Century Directions* (Peabody, Mass.: Hendrickson Publishers, 1992), 1.

CHAPTER 9: AFRICAN AMERICAN MUSIC IN THE TWENTY-FIRST CENTURY

1. See Melva Wilson Costen, "African American Liturgical Music in a Global Context," *Journal of the Interdenominational Theological Center: African American Worship: Faith Looking Forward* 27, nos. 1–2 (Fall 1999–Spring 2000): 63–106.

2. Willi Apel, *Harvard Dictionary of Music,* 2d ed. (Cambridge, Mass.: Belknap Press, 1975), 298–99.

3. Harold M. Best, *Music through the Eyes of Faith* (New York: HarperCollins, 1993), 72.

4. The quickest way to keep abreast of copyright laws is via the Internet, where legal information can be obtained at www.nolo.com. Attorney Stephen Fishman, *The Copyright Handbook* (Berkeley, Calif.: Nolo, 2002).

5. *African Methodist Episcopal Bicentennial Hymnal* (Nashville: AME Publishing House, 1984); and the *African American Heritage Hymnal* (Chicago: GIA Publications, 2001).

6. Lester Ruth, "Praise-and-Worship Movement," in *The New Westminster Dictionary of Liturgy and Worship,* ed. Paul Bradshaw (Louisville, Ky.: Westminster John Knox Press, 2002), 379. Ruth refers to this pattern as an "order of worship."

7. Walter F. Pitts, Jr., *The Old Ship of Zion: The Afro-Baptist Ritual in the African Diaspora* (New York: Oxford University Press, 1993).